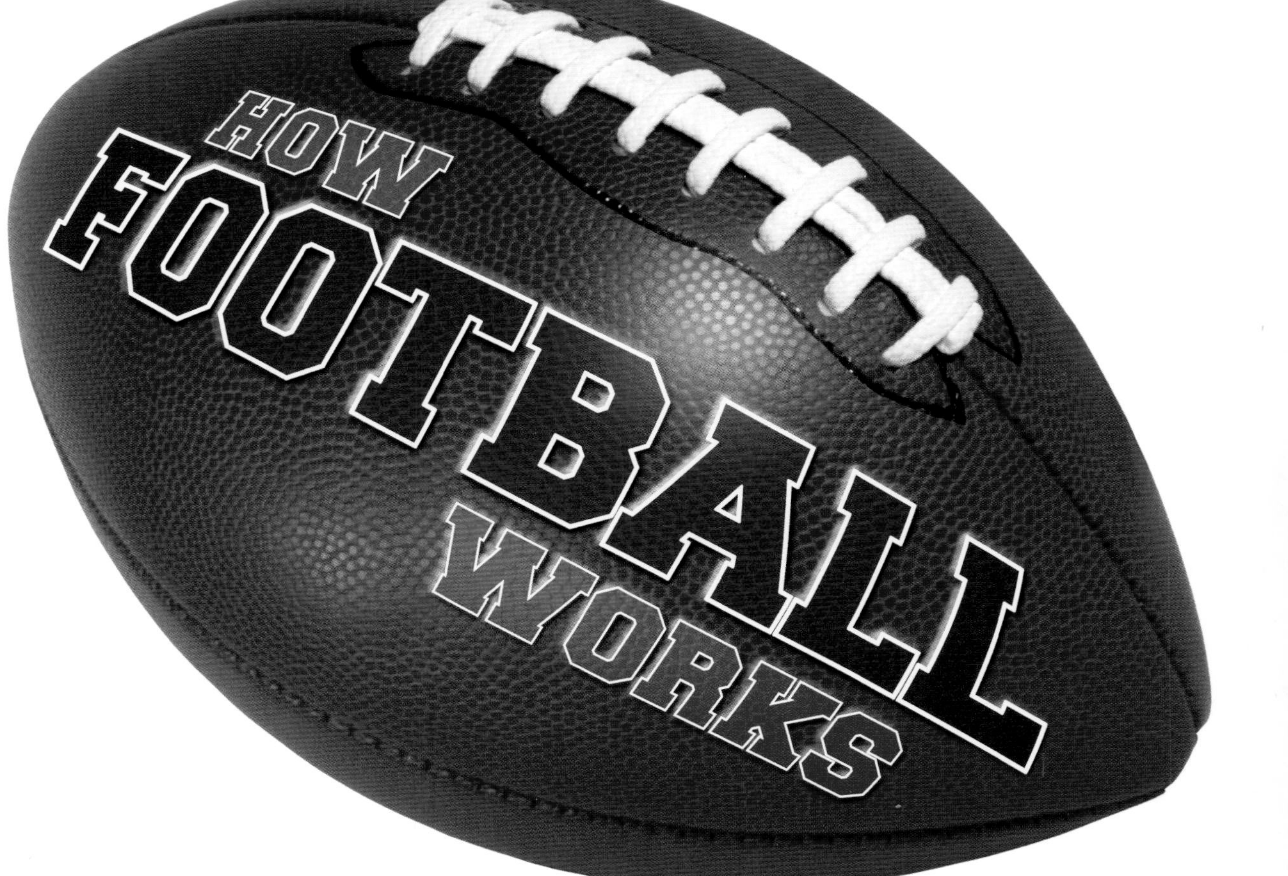

HOW FOOTBALL WORKS

Keltie Thomas

Illustrations by Stephen MacEachern

MAPLE
TREE
PRESS

Maple Tree books are published by Owlkids Books Inc.
10 Lower Spadina Avenue, Suite 400, Toronto, Ontario M5V 2Z2
www.owlkids.com

Distributed in Canada by Raincoast Books
9050 Shaughnessy Street, Vancouver, British Columbia V6P 6E5

Distributed in the United States by Publishers Group West
1700 Fourth Street, Berkeley, California 94710

Dedication
For football fans everywhere

Acknowledgments
Many thanks to all the wonderful people at Maple Tree and Owlkids,
especially Anne Shone, without whom this book could not have been written,
Stephen MacEachern, Ted Darling, Laura Stanley, Roger Yip, Ajax Pickering Dolphins
Football Club, Margaret Eskins, Holly Eskins, Taylor Eskins, Suzie Brown,
Delante Brown, Sarah Higgins, Katey Higgins, Robert Leduc, and Brian Findlay.

Library and Archives Canada Cataloguing in Publication
Thomas, Keltie
How football works / Keltie Thomas ; illustrated by Stephen MacEachern.

(How sports work)
Includes index.
ISBN 978-1-897349-87-8 (bound).--ISBN 978-1-897349-88-5 (pbk.)

1. Football--Juvenile literature. I. MacEachern, Stephen II. Title.
III. Series: How sports work

GV950.7.T56 2010   j796.332   C2010-900557-0

Library of Congress Control Number: 2010920481

Design and illustration: Stephen MacEachern   Photo Credits: see page 64

Canada Council   Conseil des Arts
for the Arts   du Canada

ONTARIO ARTS COUNCIL
CONSEIL DES ARTS DE L'ONTARIO

We acknowledge the financial support of the Canada Council for the Arts, the Ontario
Arts Council, the Government of Canada through the Canada Book Fund (CBF),
and the Government of Ontario through the Ontario Media Development
Corporation's Book Initiative for our publishing activities.

Manufactured by Print Plus Limited
Manufactured in Guangdong, China in July 2010
Job #S100700379

A   B   C   D   E   F

CONTENTS

HOW DOES FOOTBALL WORK?

Fans, players, and inquiring minds everywhere want to know!

What makes football the most strategic game on Earth? What makes the ball bounce and roll so unpredictably? Why do kickers get their very own ball? How do teams prepare for battle? How do ground crews get the field in tip-top shape? Why are helmets football players' most important piece of equipment? What makes a tackle such a big hit? How do the rules of the game differ between the NFL (National Football League) and the CFL (Canadian Football League)? And what's the score on touchdowns and field goals?

Well, just like everything else on Earth, it all comes down to science (plus a few things science hasn't managed to explain yet!). And if you think that makes football sound boring, you'd better check out what planet you're on. But, hey, why don't you turn the page and check out the world of football in action for yourself?

Whether you want answers to those burning questions, tips on becoming a better player, the scoop on inside information, or just to have a blast with the game, this book's for you.

Hey! You don't have to be a football maniac to read this book. The Rules and Regs and Football Talk are decoded on pages 60 and 62.

Harvard University
Football Club, 1875

Football: Born in the U.S.A.

Forget soccer! Forget rugby! Let's invent a new game. That's what a bunch of Boston schoolboys did in the 1860s. Bored out of their skulls with the two games, the boys combined kicking from soccer and running with the ball from rugby to create the "Boston Game."

As the boys grew up, some went to Harvard University and brought the Boston Game with them. But no other U.S. school played it. So Harvard looked to McGill University in Montreal, Canada, where students played

traditional rugby. The schools challenged each other to a couple of games: one played with Harvard's Boston rules and the other played with McGill's rugby rules.

The two games were very different and even used different balls. Harvard played with a round ball whereas McGill used a rugby ball that was twice as big and shaped like an egg. Harvard won the game played with their rules easily. But to everyone's surprise, Harvard held McGill to a scoreless tie in the game played with McGill's rugby rules.

Harvard took up the weird egg-shaped ball, and soon challenged Yale University to a rugby game. And even though Harvard trounced Yale, Yale fell in love with the sport and began playing it themselves.

The game spread to other U.S. schools and the schools began tinkering with the rules. Some elements of rugby were dropped, and some elements were invented on the spot, until a whole new game came to be. And so the sport of football bounced into the world on American soil.

Chapter 1

THAT'S THE WAY THE BALL BOUNCES

Whomp! Zoom! A kicker boots the ball toward the end zone as the clock counts down the game's final seconds. Fans hold their breath. Will the kick send the ball through the goal posts for a field goal? Or will it veer off target, dashing all hope of victory? *Boing!*

Pfffftt! A quarterback hurls the ball. Will the ball find an open receiver? Will the receiver carry the ball into the opponents' end zone for a touchdown? Or will the ball slip through his fingers?

Even though more than half of the players in a football game never touch the ball, the ball is always at the heart of the action. Players snap it, throw it, catch it, kick it, run with it, fight for it, and jump on opponents who have it. Find out what makes the ball bounce unpredictably and how it has put the *oomph* in the game through time.

Bounce this Way! ➤

BALL WITH PERSONALITY

What makes this oddball a tough character to throw and kick around?

IT WEARS A LEATHER JACKET.

The official NFL ball sports a brown leather jacket. The jacket is made of four panels of cowhide. Tons of tiny round bumps called pebbles cover the entire surface. These pebbles make the ball feel rough and grainy rather than smooth and slippery, which helps players grip the ball. According to the official rules of the game, the jacket must not have wrinkles or folds of any kind. After all, it's the rulemakers' job to iron out any kinks of the game.

IT'S A FUNNY SHAPE.

Baseballs, tennis balls, soccer balls, golf balls, volleyballs, beach balls, and even gumballs are all perfectly round. But not a football. Oh, no! A football is shaped like an egg. It's fat and round in the middle and thin and pointy at both ends. But unlike an egg, both ends of a football are exactly the same. This funny shape makes the ball difficult to handle and kick. It also makes the ball bounce and roll unpredictably. When the ball hits the ground, it might bounce forward, backward, or even roll over the ground before it bounces. Talk about a total oddball!

IT'S GOT LACES.

The ball has eight white laces across the center of its belly. Not only do these laces sew up the ball and hold it together, but they also help players get a grip. The laces stick out from the ball, giving players something to hold on to. In fact, quarterbacks wrap their pinky finger, fourth finger, and middle finger in between the laces for a good grip. Some college and high school teams have even used balls with pebbled laces that feel grainy, like the ball's jacket, to get a better grip on the ball.

IT STAYS IN SHAPE.

The size and weight of the ball affect how it flies through the air, so all NFL balls get measured and weighed to ensure they're fit to play. The official NFL rules say the ball must be 28 to 28.5 cm (11 to 11 ¼ in.) long, 53 to 54 cm (21 to 21 ¼ in.) around the belly, or middle, and weigh in at 400 to 425 g (14 to 15 oz.). What's more, the ball is filled with 5.7 to 6 kg (12 ½ to 13 ½ lbs.) of air pressure to help it hold its shape as players squeeze it, grab it, pound it, and kick it.

IT'S MARKED.

Pssst. The ball is marked for life or else it doesn't get into the game. Also, it must be handpicked and stamped with the signature of the NFL commissioner. Before every game, the referee unpacks twelve new balls specially marked with a "K" and sets them aside to be used only for kicking plays. That's not all: balls made especially for the Super Bowl get marked with a synthetic DNA. Just like DNA, which carries hereditary information, can identify people, the synthetic DNA identifies the official balls. The DNA marker glows under laser light. That way, people can tell real Super Bowl balls, which sell for big bucks, from fakes.

IT'S BROKEN IN.

Ever seen a shoe buffer machine? The NFL uses a machine like it to break in official game balls so that each one feels and handles the same way. It does the job faster and more effectively than rubbing the ball by hand, and more reliably than any team. The NFL began breaking in balls after the 1996 Super Bowl, when the Pittsburgh Steelers and Dallas Cowboys argued over how the job was done. Before that, some teams secretly doctored the ball to alter its performance. The sly teams cooked the ball, put it in a dryer, filled it with helium gas rather than air, and even rubbed it with oil.

TIP

Not quite the same size as the average pro? Play with a kid-sized football to complete your passes, kicks, and catches.

Get Under Its Skin

Here's how pro balls are put together inside and out. First, factory workers press and stamp cowhide with machines to create the pebble-grain finish of the ball's outer jacket. A worker then uses a cookie cutter-like tool to cut panels out of the cowhide. A vinyl-cotton lining is then sewn onto each panel to give the ball the strength to hold its shape even through kicking and pounding by 135-kg (300-lb.) linemen. Next, a sewing machine operator sews four panels together inside out. A worker then steams the panels and uses a machine to punch, or break, the ends. This softens the panels so they can be turned right-side out. Then a polyurethane bladder is inserted and filled with air. A worker then laces up the ball and puts it into a mold for final shaping. Once it pops out, the ball's ready to ship to the NFL.

Polyurethane bladder

Vinyl-cotton lining

Cowhide

SPIRALING THROUGH TIME

Quick Hit

A yard equals 3 ft. (.9144 m). That's just a bit longer than three footballs placed end to end. Even in Canada, where the metric system of measurement is used, football gains are talked about in yards.

Check out how the football got its funny shape and how it has shaped the game through time.

2000 BCE

The oldest-known balls roll into the world fashioned out of wood, leather, and papyrus by the ancient Egyptians.

2000–800 BCE

Ancient Greeks make a ball out of a pig's bladder, wrapped in pigskin. Men and women battle for the ball in a game called *Episkyros*. Greek scholar Julius Pollux describes players faking each other out by "showing the ball to one man and then throwing it to another."

146 BCE

The Romans conquer Greece and soon make the game their own. They add kicking, give the game a new name—*Harpastum*—and use a smaller ball made of leather and stuffed with sponges or animal fur. What's more, the Romans allow tackling.

1869

Rutgers and Princeton play what's called "the first college football game." But they play the game of soccer and use a round ball to boot.

1874

Harvard University picks up a love for rugby and the odd oval-shaped rugby ball in a series of games against McGill University (see page 6).

1876

Harvard combines soccer and rugby rules with the funny-shaped rugby ball and introduces them to Yale University. Several U.S. colleges take up the game—and football is born!

1880

When the ball goes out of bounds, opponents shove each other, fighting for it. Instead, rulemaker Walter Camp suggests an offensive player put the ball in play by snapping it back to his quarterback. This allows the team that had the ball to keep it. Since gaining possession of the ball is no longer left to chance, teams begin to plan maneuvers.

1882

With the snap rule (see above) comes trouble as it allows teams to keep the ball for an entire game. Camp solves the problem with a new rule that requires teams to gain 5 yards in three plays, or downs, or give up the ball.

1888

Carrying the ball becomes a tough job as a new rule allows players to tackle, or hit, opponents below the waist and above the knees.

1896

A ball that looks like a stretched-out pumpkin replaces the rugby ball. An official description of the ball mentions only its shape—a prolate spheroid—or imperfect sphere lengthened at the ends.

1905

Wham! Bam! Players collide and often pile up in a huge heavy heap. The bone-crushing collisions cause serious injuries and kill eighteen players. Many people demand the game be banned. So the next year, passing the ball forward becomes legal as rulemakers try to clean up the brutal violence. They also increase the distance teams must gain in three downs from 5 to 10 yards.

1930

The ball gets a makeover. It's made slimmer at the middle and more pointed at the ends to improve passing.

1999

Whomp! ...and another kickoff reaches the end zone. The NFL suspects that kickers are doctoring the ball to make it fly farther. Rumor has it they are doing everything from taking a power-sander to the ball to microwaving it, to wiping it down with milk. The NFL decides that kickers must use a new ball that gets only a brief rubdown by the team equipment handler. And so the K ball (see page 9) enters the game and the number of returns drops.

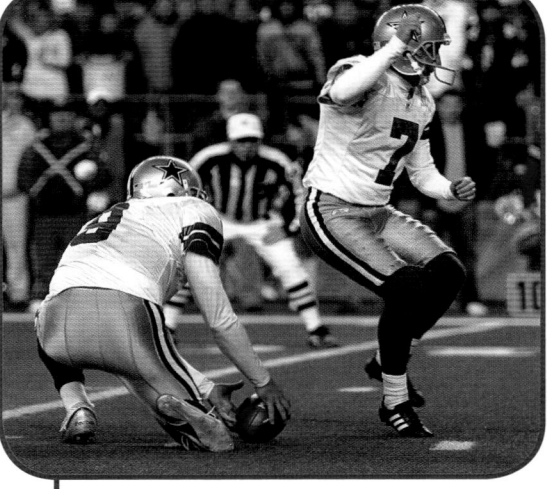

2007

With his team just a field goal away from victory, quarterback Tony Romo (above) holds the ball in place for the kicker and the ball slips out of his grasp. The fumble costs the Dallas Cowboys a playoff spot. Everyone blames the K ball for being slippery. And maybe the NFL bigwigs agree as they decide that equipment handlers can have more than twice as much time to rub down K balls before games.

Beyond

Making a ball that feels perfect in players' hands right out of the box, and stays that way, is the ultimate goal for ballmakers. Future balls may wear synthetic jackets that don't soak up as much rain or harden up as much in cold weather.

Quick Hit

NFL and CFL rules call for slightly different-sized balls. What's more, CFL balls sport a white stripe around each end while NFL balls have no stripes at all.

(see page 9)

Quick Answers to *Hard-Hitting* Questions

What's football?

You know it as a game played with a funny-shaped ball on a field shaped like a shoebox. But outside of North America, the name "football" almost always refers to the game of soccer. And in Australia, it refers to a game played with a rugby-like ball on an oval-shaped field.

What's "the pigskin"?

A nickname for the ball. Although the ball may feel like tough pigskin, it's actually made of cowhide (see page 9). However, some early soccer and rugby balls were made of inflated pigs' bladders.

Do officials keep tabs on the K ball?

You bet! The night before an NFL game, a sealed box of K balls is delivered to the officials' hotel. An official checks that the seal has not been broken and doesn't let the box out of his sight until he takes it to the stadium the next day. He even sleeps in the same room as the box!

LEGENDS OF THE GAME

Carlisle Indians

Totally Sick Hidden Ball Trick

Say your team is on defense. Your placekicker boots the ball downfield to your opponents and *poof*—the ball disappears completely. The Crimson of Harvard faced this situation against the Carlisle Indians in 1903. After receiving the kick, all the Carlisle players rushed toward the Crimson players, each one hugging his stomach as if *he* had the ball. The Crimson players looked around wildly. But the ball was nowhere in sight.

The Harvard fans burst into laughter in the stands once they figured out who had the ball, while the Crimson players remained clueless. Seconds later, the Indians' lineman, Charlie Dillon, zoomed over the Harvard end line. The Indians' quarterback, Jimmie Johnson, then grabbed the ball out of Dillon's jersey and slammed it on the turf. Touchdown! Harvard couldn't believe it. How had Dillon managed to sprint 103 yards with the ball right under their noses?

On the kickoff, Dillon and Johnson had dropped back behind a wall of their teammates. Johnson caught the ball and stuffed it into the back of Dillon's jersey, which had an elastic waistband specially sewn in for the trick. Then the Indians took off in all directions. Harvard protested, but there were no rules against the play, so the touchdown stood. This trick was eventually outlawed, but not before becoming one of the most spectacular plays in football history.

Chapter 2

THE PLAYERS

Sixty minutes or bust! In the early days of football, playing for the full hour was players' "code of conduct." The players didn't leave the field for the entire game unless they got injured. When their team lost possession of the ball, the players just switched from offense to defense and kept right on going—blocking, tackling, running, and hitting to their heart's desire. *Bam!*

But nowadays, pro teams have a different set of players for offense and defense and even special teams for kickoffs, kick returns, and other critical plays. So when teams change possession of the ball, they also change their onfield lineup. The offense or defense file off to the bench and their counterparts march on raring to go. Get the skinny on who's who on the field, what each position does, and how opponents line up in each other's faces to match wits.

Green Bay Packers'
Ryan Grant

Charge Ahead! ≫

WHO'S WHO?

Quick Hit

If it's "third and eight," that means it's third down with 8 yards needed to get a first down.

When two NFL teams duel on the gridiron, they each bring eleven players. That's twenty-two players, and each one has a different job. Check out this guide to who's who on the field, and match the numbers to the art to see who does what.

THE OFFENSE

The Offensive Line

Five big, agile players make up the offensive line: a center, flanked by two guards, and two tackles outside the guards.

1 The Center

The center snaps the ball between his legs to the quarterback, calls signals for the line, and coordinates the linemen to block—run interference for a running play or pass. A player blocks an opponent by making contact with the opponent and using his hands, arms, and shoulders to move the opponent aside.

2 The Guards

Powerful. That's what guards are. The guards push and shove defensive linemen to open up running lanes for their teammate carrying the ball. They also fend off defensive tackles, the biggest players on the field.

3 The Tackles

It sounds crazy but offensive tackles cannot tackle without getting a penalty. Their job is to stop defenders without wrapping their arms around the defenders or grabbing on.

TIP

The numbers on NFL jerseys can help you tell the positions players play:
- Quarterbacks and kickers wear 1 to 19.
- Running backs and defensive backs wear 20 to 49.
- Offensive linemen wear 50 to 79.
- Linebackers wear 50 to 59 or 90 to 99.
- Defensive linemen wear 60 to 79 or 90 to 99.
- Receivers and tight ends wear 80 to 89.

4 The Quarterback

He leads the team, calls plays, throws passes, runs with the ball, and reads the defense to figure out what they're up to. The quarterback has the biggest, most glamorous, and dangerous job on the field. But, hey, somebody's got to do it.

5 The Running Backs

These players take the ball from the quarterback and light out for the goal line. Often one running back, called a fullback, clears the way for another, called a halfback, who carries the ball.

6 The Tight End

This player lines up next to one of the offensive tackles. Not only does he receive passes, but he also blocks opponents. So he is usually bigger and stronger than other receivers and adds blocking power to the offensive line. What's more, the side of the line where the tight end sets up is called the strong side. And the defense often sets up to counter it.

7 The Wide Receivers

Clear it out! Wide receivers line up to the right or left away from the offensive line. They block on running plays. But their main job is to zoom down the field, get open to catch the football, and run with it to the opponent's end zone. Even if they don't get open, they lure defensive players on their tail, clearing out an area for a shorter pass or running play.

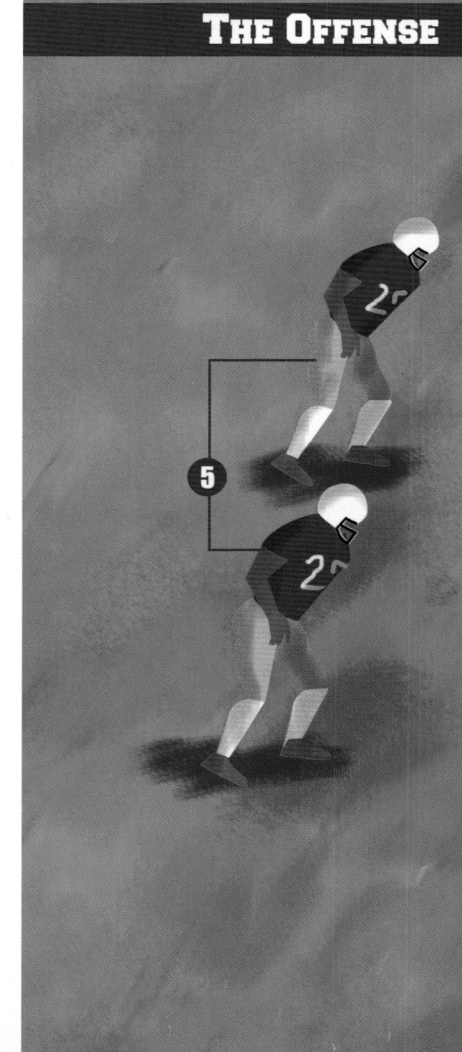

THE OFFENSE

THE DEFENSE

The Defensive Line

Four, or sometimes three, big, agile, and strong linemen called tackles and ends make up the defensive line.

8 The Tackles

One or two tackles set up in the middle of the defensive line. If it's one, this player is called a nose tackle because he lines up nose to nose with the center of the offensive line. Tackles are bigger linemen than the ends of the defensive line. Their job is to tie up opponents, and catch any and all ball carriers who come within reach.

9 The Ends

These defensive linemen are usually smaller and quicker than tackles. Their job is to break through the offensive line, creating holes for other defenders to come through to hit the ball carrier or the quarterback. And if they get a chance to make a hit themselves, they'll take it. *Bam!*

10 The Linebackers

Lining up a few yards behind the defensive line, linebackers are backup for the linemen. They stop running plays, rush and sack the quarterback, and help cover passing plays.

11 The Middle Linebacker

Say hello to the quarterback of the defense. In the huddle, the middle linebacker calls the plays for the defense. And once the huddle breaks, he scans the field and yells out what he sees. For example, he may yell "Strength right" to tell his teammates that the tight end is lined up on the right side of the offensive line.

The Secondary

As if backup from the linebackers wasn't enough, the defense also has a secondary of four defensive backs: two cornerbacks and two safeties.

12 The Cornerbacks

These players cover and tackle wide receivers. Their job is to stop receivers from catching the ball.

13 The Safeties

Meet the last line of defense. The safeties help out where needed. The "strong safety" plays on the same side as the tight end to cover any passes to the tight end. He also helps the linebackers and tries to stop running plays. The "free safety" lines up behind the middle linebacker and roams as deep or deeper than the deepest receiver. His job is to put the kibosh on big passing or running plays.

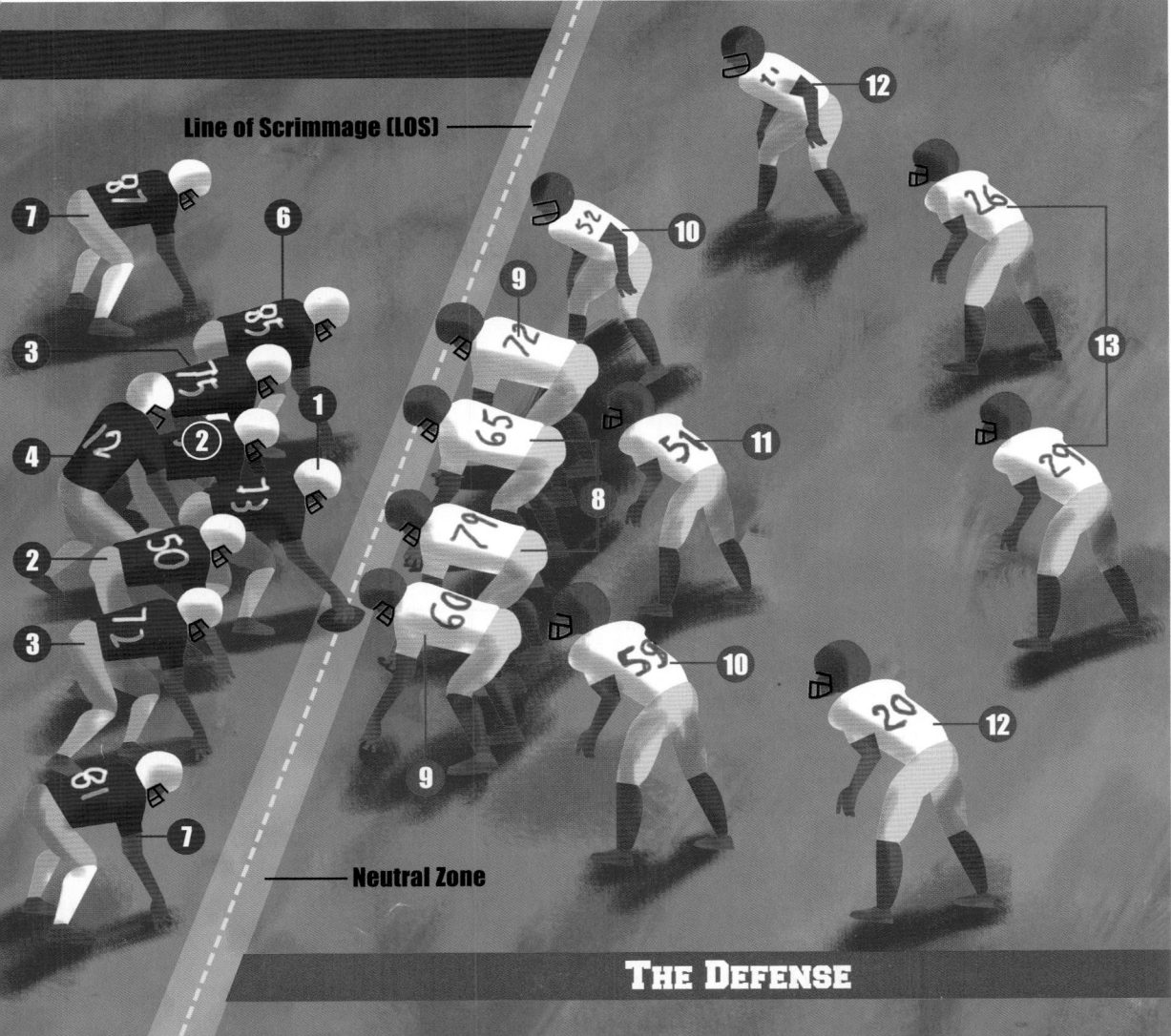

Line of Scrimmage (LOS)

Neutral Zone

THE DEFENSE

THE QUARTERBACK

When a team wins, the quarterback often gets all the fame and glory. But when it loses, the quarterback often gets all the blame and shame. And those aren't the only things that make the quarterback's job the toughest in pro sports.

LIGHTS, HUDDLE, ACTION!

In the old days, the quarterback used to call his own plays. But in the 1980s, head coaches took over to relieve quarterbacks of some of the mental pressure of the game. Nowadays, the head coach relays the play over a speaker inside the quarterback's helmet. Then the quarterback calls the play in the huddle just before leading the team to the line of scrimmage. But once they get there, if the quarterback sees that a different play would be better, he may call a play change, or "audible." When he does, he calls the play in a secret code of numbers, letters, and words that only his team knows. For example, the quarterback may yell "5–7–5 pump gut on two." And with that, each player knows exactly what to do. For example, the first three numbers may be routes for specific receivers to run, "pump gut" a pass route for a running back, and "two" the count on which to snap the ball.

ROCKET IN THE POCKET

Hut one! Hut two! Snap goes the football! Once the quarterback receives the snap, the ball is in his hands and it's up to him to make—or break—the play. Talk about pressure! Depending upon what play was called, the quarterback may turn and hand the ball to a running back, run with the ball himself, or drop back into the pocket to pass. The pocket is an area behind the line of scrimmage that the offensive line works hard to protect so the quarterback has time to set up a pass. In the pocket, the quarterback scans the field looking for holes in the defense, throwing lanes to pass the ball through, and receivers that are open for a pass. But he doesn't have long as the opposing team rushes and pushes into the pocket to get him—or at the very least to rattle his cage so that he hurries the pass and blows it. How's that for amping up the pressure?

So You Wanna Be a Quarterback...

Do you have what it takes to be a star quarterback? Go through this checklist and see.

√ Able to throw the ball accurately

A quarterback needs a strong arm, a quick release, and bull's-eye accuracy to throw passes to a target receiver faster than the defense can figure out what's hit them.

√ High IQ

Intelligence is a must. An NFL quarterback has to know more than fifty running plays and two hundred passing plays. What's more, the quarterback not only needs to know what he's to do, he also has to know what every other player has to do on each play. That's not all. A quarterback must be able to outwit the defense on the fly.

√ Born to lead

A quarterback must be able to command the troops on the field, inspire teammates by calling competitive plays, and rally players' fighting spirit.

√ Super size

Today, NFL quarterbacks must be big enough to withstand the pounding of punishing hits, and tall enough to see over the heads of huge linemen. According to the experts, that's at least 1.8 m (6 ft. 1 in.) and 95 kg (210 lbs.).

√ Head cool as a cucumber

Boiling over under pressure is a no-no. A quarterback must keep a cool head at all times so he can focus to direct teammates, make plays, find holes in the defense, and retaliate by throwing a long bomb, or pass, into the hands of an open receiver.

√ Nimble and quick

A quarterback must be able to move quickly to set up for a pass, dodge rushing defenders, and run with the ball when required.

Special Forces, er, Teams

Sure, quarterbacks are special. But just who are you going to call if you've got to kick, punt, or return the ball? Special teams for special plays—that's who! A team has several special teams:

- One for kickoffs and punts to pin the opposition close to their own end, and for punt returns to catch the ball, and run with it to gain yards

- One for field goals and extra point attempts (see page 47)

- One for kickoff returns to catch the ball and return it downfield as far as possible

- One for blocking field goals and extra point attempts

STAR ★ • • • • • • • • • • • •

Measuring 1.8 m (5 ft. 10 in.) and weighing just 81.6 kg (180 lbs.), Doug Flutie wasn't the size of a typical pro quarterback. But he held nothing back. In a college game, with his team trailing 45–41 at the 52-yard line with just 6 seconds left on the clock, Flutie threw a long bomb for a touchdown to clinch the game. Is it any wonder *Sports Illustrated* called him "the magic Flutie," or that he went on to quarterback teams in both the NFL and CFL?

Doug Flutie

IN BATTLE

Once players set up at the line of scrimmage, the battle is on. The offense tries to move the ball downfield to the end zone to score, and the defense tries to stop them. The offense has four chances (downs) to move the ball 10 yards. If they fail, they give up the ball and the other team goes on offense.

> ## Quick Hit
> If most of the offensive plays that a team makes in a game are runs, they are playing "smashmouth football." But if a team's ace quarterback makes about forty passes, they're playing "air-it-out football."

THE OFFENSE

Has the advantage.

At the line of scrimmage, the offense knows exactly what they're going to do and the defense doesn't. During the snap count, for example, the offensive players know when the center will hike the ball to the quarterback to start the play, so they can all explode off the line on the count.

Looks for clues.

If the linebackers set themselves up closer to the defensive line, the offense can tell a blitz—when several linebackers or defensive backs join the defensive linemen to rush the quarterback—may be on the way. Spotting a clue like this allows the offense to adjust. For example, the quarterback can quickly pass the ball to a receiver to avoid being tackled with the ball, and the receiver can run a shorter route to catch the ball.

Wants to run the ball.

If the offense can average 4 yards per running play, they'll get 12 yards every three downs—2 more than the 10 yards they need for a new set of downs. Successfully running the ball grinds down the defense, punishes them mentally, and eats time on the clock.

Wants to pass the ball.

Great teams can play both the running game and passing game. That keeps the defense guessing as to what's coming next. And this can open up the game for the offense to make big plays—long passes. Bombs away!

Fakes 'em out.

Sometimes a quarterback steps back as if to pass but instead hands the ball to a running back. This "draw play" may lure the defense to rush the quarterback, which creates holes in the defense for the running back. But sometimes, teams may fake a draw play and the quarterback does fire off a pass. If the ruse makes the defense hesitate, even for a split second, it gives the offense the advantage.

> ## Quick Hit
> The Canuck game just ain't the same. In the CFL, teams have only three chances to make a first down.

THE DEFENSE

Has the disadvantage.

The offense knows two things the defense doesn't: the count on which the ball will be snapped and what the play is. The defense can only react, so they surge off the line about a fifth of a second later than the offense. And football games can be won or lost in seconds.

Looks for clues.

Studying the offensive linemen can help the defense figure out whether they are going to run or pass. Say an offensive lineman crouches at the line of scrimmage in a three-point stance, both feet and one hand planted on the ground. If his knuckles and fingertips are white, he's probably about to move forward to block

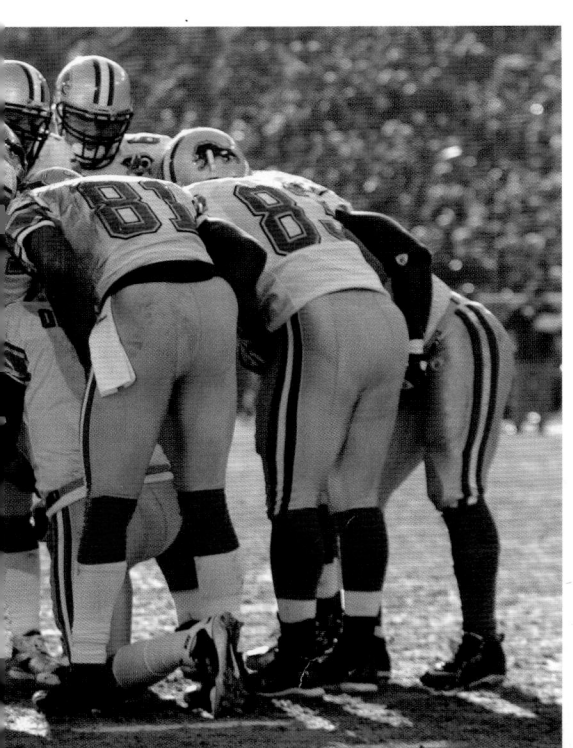

for a run. But on a pass he will move backward to block. The defense also looks in the offensive linemen's eyes: many look in the direction they're about to lunge.

Wants to stop the run.

The defense wants to hold running plays to an average of 3 yards or less, so the offense doesn't gain enough yards for a first down. If the defense stops the run consistently, they also force the offense to pass. Once a pass is airborne, three things can happen: a catch by a receiver, an incompletion, or an interception. And two out of the three ain't bad for the D!

Wants to stop the pass.

And how! The defense rushes the quarterback to sack him, or at least pressure him to make a bad pass. Then there's the bump and run. Even though the rules outlaw hitting receivers as they're running to catch passes, hits on receivers within 5 yards of the line of scrimmage are allowed. So cornerbacks bump receivers as they're coming off the line to disrupt the timing that's critical to catching a pass. Then the cornerbacks turn and run with the receiver.

Fakes 'em out.

Sometimes the defense pulls a stunt at the line of scrimmage. Before the ball is snapped, defensive linemen may jump to one side or switch positions with one another to throw off the offense. Their goal is to confuse the offensive linemen, so they won't know who to block.

Monsters in the Pit

Offensive and defensive linemen do the rough-and-dirty work of football—hitting, ramming, and blocking—in an area at the line of scrimmage called the pit. Check out some of the "monsters" that have ruled the pit.

Purple People Eaters

In the 1960s, the name Vikings wasn't tough enough for the defensive line of the Minnesota Vikings. Maybe that's because the four linemen devoured teams upfront. So people called them the Purple People Eaters, after the Vikings' purple jerseys.

The Hogs

They were large and heavy, and they liked to play mean, in-your-face football in the dirt. So one practice day in the 1980s, when the Washington Redskins' offensive coach said, "Come on you hogs, let's get down here," the name stuck to the offensive linemen like mud.

The Steel Curtain

Ever seen a curtain fall down in the blink of an eye? In the 1970s, the Pittsburgh Steelers' defense earned the nickname the Steel Curtain for bringing down opponents quickly and shutting out touchdowns. In fact, some people say the Steel Curtain is the best defense in NFL history.

William Perry

The Fridge Freezes the Opposition

He was so big that fans called him "The Refrigerator"—or simply "The Fridge." At his heaviest, 1.9 m (6 ft. 2 in.) defensive tackle William Perry rocked the scales at a whopping 173 kg (382 lbs.). What's more, Perry played for the Chicago Bears in the 1980s, when linemen who topped 136 kg (300 lbs.) were a rare item.

Perry's massive heft made him unstoppable. The defensive tackle plowed through opponents' offense and even did double duty as a fullback, carrying the ball or blocking, clearing the way for a running back with the ball. During Super Bowl XX, the Bears were on a third down at the 1-yard line in the third quarter when coach Mike Ditka sent in The Fridge to freeze the opposition.

The Fridge took a handoff from quarterback Jim McMahon and rammed through a stunned defensive line into the end zone for a touchdown. *Wahoo!* Chicago won the game and Perry got to chill out with a Super Bowl ring fit for a king, er, fridge. The Refrigerator's ring was a record-setting size 25—more than twice the ring size of the average guy. Now that's big bling!

Perfect, "turf-ect"! Not a mark or a bald spot to break up the "field of green." Not a lump or a bump to throw players off course. Not a hole or a mole to trip players up. Not a divot or a piece missing in action. Nothing less will do for the turf of pro football.

And here's the rub. When a football field is perfect, no one seems to notice. But when it is not up to snuff, it may make the national news as the coaches, the players, and even the fans complain.

Sounding off about the condition of the field is a good ol' football tradition. After all, the game is played mainly in open-air stadiums, whatever the weather. Check out how the turf has rolled out through time, how groundskeepers maintain the field, and how some teams have turned the turf into a home field advantage.

"Turf's Up!" ▶

How Turf Flies

Tufts of turf sure do fly as players run and dig their cleats into fields of natural grass. But that's not all. Turf also flies like time as trends take off around the league and natural grass and artificial turfs go in and out of style. Here's how the different surfaces have rolled out through time.

TIP

On a hot day, keep off the fake grass. When the air temperature is over 36°C (98°F), researchers have found that artificial turf can heat up to a scorching 93°C (199°F). In fact, former NFL quarterback Jim Plunkett remembers a game in which Astroturf burned the bottom of his feet!

1860s

Real grass is the battleground for the world's first football matches and the game is played on nothing but for the next 100 years.

1965

The first domed stadium, the Houston Astrodome, rises up. People call it the eighth wonder of the world. The only problem is the grass doesn't get enough sunlight to grow and it croaks.

1966

Got a field of dead grass and painted-green dirt? Roll out the green carpet! Fake grass made of plastic, which becomes known as Astroturf, replaces the natural grass at the Astrodome.

1968

The Astrodome becomes the home turf of the Houston Oilers and with that, Astroturf becomes all the rage in pro football. The big leagues like it because it looks great on TV. Owners like it because it doesn't need to be cut, watered, and fertilized like grass. Coaches and players like it because it's free of hazardous holes and divots players could twist their ankles in.

1970s

Astroturf becomes a sore spot for players. No kidding! As players run, jump, cut, tackle, and fall, they take a real beating. That's because Astroturf is a thin plastic covering on top of asphalt—a much harder surface than grass, with less give. What's more, when players slide on Astroturf, they get a "rug burn" on their skin. And to top it all off, sometimes players' feet can get caught in a seam between two pieces of the green "carpet."

1980s

Studies begin to show that playing on artificial turf is more likely to cause serious injuries than playing on real grass.

1990

More than half the NFL stadiums have artificial turf, and it's changed the game. Coaches and players say that the ball rolls faster and players run faster on artificial turf. The newfound speed allows quarterbacks, running backs, and wide receivers to take control of the game. The result? The search for speedy players becomes teams' number one priority.

1995

Natural grass starts to re-sprout on fields around the league as yet more studies show that playing on artificial turf is more likely to result in injuries.

2001

In the winter, as much as 1 m (2 ½ ft.) of snow often piles up on the Denver Broncos' playing field, which is 1.6 km (1 mi.) above sea level. To help the grass survive, the Broncos inject twenty million artificial grass fibers into their field. As the grass grows, it entwines with the artificial fibers and this strengthens and anchors the turf.

2002

The Seattle Seahawks install FieldTurf, a new artificial turf that looks and feels like real grass, at their new stadium. The turf gets rave reviews and NFL teams start ripping up their old artificial turf to "resod" with the new stuff.

Around 2009

A survey of NFL players reveals that almost three-quarters prefer playing on natural grass than artificial turf. In another survey, the players' most common comment is "make all fields grass to prevent injuries."

2010

In the NFL, natural grass playing fields outnumber artificial turf playing fields about two to one.

What Turf Will Fly Next?

Green blades and ham? No one knows for sure. But experts say new turf developments are happening all the time.

Quick Answers to Hard-Hitting Questions

What makes new artificial turf feel like real grass?

The new turf's blades of "grass" are made of softer fibers than those of Astroturf and they don't cause rug burn as players slide on them. The new turf also has a built-in cushion of sand and rubber granules made out of recycled tires. This cushion has more "give" than Astroturf, compressing to soften on impact as players' feet and bodies hit the turf.

Is the world, er, field flat?

Nope. A good football field is gently sloped in the center to encourage rainwater to run off and drain away.

THE TURF

How many college or pro players play the whole game?" Tennessee Titans' groundskeeper Terry Porch once asked. "None, right? But this field has to play every down... So you can imagine what happens out there in the middle with 300-pound guys in cleats." Once the game is over, the beat-up blades need some TLC from the ground crew to recover. Check out how teams keep natural grass in tip-top playing condition.

MEET MURPH THE TURF

It may sound crazy, but some teams treat the turf just like a person to keep the grass healthy.

The crew gives the turf regular "haircuts." They spend hours mowing the grass several times a week. This keeps the grass short and "burns in" the pattern of light and dark stripes you see on the field.

The ground crew feeds and waters the grass regularly. In fact, grass can "eat" as much as 350 kg (775 lbs.) of fertilizer a year.

After a game, the ground crew is ready with seed and new sod to clean up the grass and tend to its cuts and bruises—a.k.a. divots and cleat marks—which number in the hundreds. And if the grass turns brown or gets sick, they may call in the turf doc (see right).

PAINT BY NUMBER?

Well, not exactly. But the ground crew does use stencils and string to paint the numbers, hash marks, and yard lines on the field. The crew pulls a taut string down the length of the field to create a straight line. Then they place stencils of the numbers and hash marks along the string and spray white paint over the stencils. They go up and down both sides of the field. A hash mark is spray painted at every yard, a solid white line at every 5th yard, and a number at every 10th yard line. The crosshatch of white lines that they create is what gives the field its nickname: the gridiron. Since mowing the field cuts off the painted tips of the grass, crews may paint the field a few times a week!

Quick Hit

Lines didn't appear on the football field until 1882, when a new rule required teams to gain 5 yards on three downs to keep possession of the ball. They used chalk to draw a line at every 5th yard.

TURNING UP THE HEAT

How do you coax lush, green grass to grow in December? Turn up the heat! No joke. As the NFL season heads into winter, ground crews face the challenge of keeping the grass looking good in the stadium and on TV—not to mention soft and stable beneath players' feet. So some ground crews, like those of the Chicago Bears and the Green Bay Packers, fire up turf-conditioning systems installed in the ground underneath the field. The systems heat the roots of the grass by pumping hot water through the thousands of feet of underground plastic tubing. This warms the root zone of the grass and can even melt snow on the field when the air temperature hovers around the freezing mark. That way fans can still see the gridiron to follow the action and, more importantly, the field remains safe and relatively soft for the players during freezing conditions.

Turf Doc to the Rescue

Grass is a living thing, and if it doesn't get what it needs, football teams can't count on it to "play by the rules." Nobody knows that better than George Toma (below), an NFL groundskeeper who has earned a place in the Football Hall of Fame for excellent field maintenance, and has tended the field for the Super Bowl since 1965. In fact, when grass dies or doesn't take root, NFL teams often call in Toma to the rescue. Take the San Francisco 49ers, who found themselves playing on grass that had no roots. In the 1990s, after two weeks of record rainfall that triggered mud slides in California, the 49ers' field was a mess of sodden mud. Toma got to work on the field, growing a test plot of a grass called kukuya. The grass stood up well in a game played in the pouring rain. So he had the *kukuya* grass cut from another field nearby and sodded the 49ers' field with it. And the field held up beautifully in the next few games played in the rain. The fans even gave the ground crew a standing ovation.

"TURF OPS"

Ever heard the term "special ops" for special operations forces that carry out important military missions in the field? Sometimes football teams deploy special operations to try to gain a home field advantage. Check out some sneaky moves of "turf ops" in action.

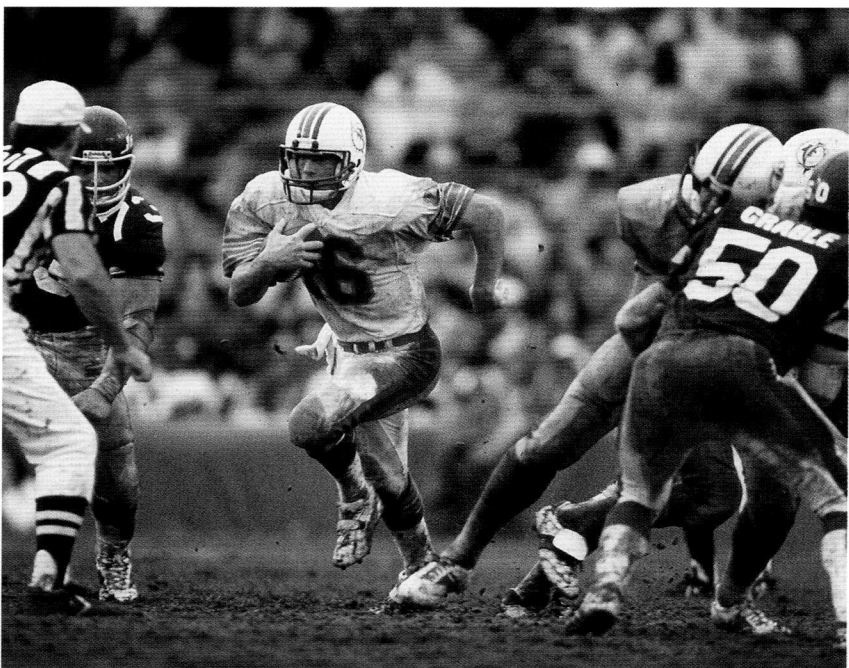

PATRIOTS PULL A SNOW JOB

On December 12, 1982, a heavy snowstorm raged over the New England Patriots' turf as the squad squared off against the Miami Dolphins. A blanket of snow covered the field so completely that none of the players could see the markings, yard lines, or sidelines. Both teams missed field goals as 23 cm (9 in.) of snow piled up on the field. With about five minutes left to go and the score 0–0, the Patriots found themselves within reach of a field goal and called a timeout. Suddenly, a makeshift snowplow—a tractor with a broom tacked onto the front— slid onto the field, clearing a 1.2 m (4 ft.) wide patch for Patriots' kicker John Smith. Dolphins' coach Don Shula protested fiercely. But to no avail. *Boom!* The kick was good and the Patriots won the game. The next spring though, the NFL outlawed the snowplow shenanigans with a rule that says groundskeepers cannot clear snow before a kick.

MUD BOWL IN MIAMI

According to NFL lore, it wasn't long before the Miami Dolphins' coach Don Shula ordered a sneaky "turf op" of his own. During the 1982–83 playoffs, the Dolphins were set to meet the New York Jets. Shula knew that the Jets' superior speed gave them an edge over the Dolphins. To slow the Jets down and take away their edge in speed, Shula told the ground crew to leave the field uncovered throughout a solid week of rain before the game in Miami. On game day, both teams struggled to play in the resultant "bowl of mud" and remained scoreless in the first half. Then Miami managed to light up the scoreboard and even shut out the Jets, earning a spot in the Super Bowl. Who knew the weather before a game—the rain on the plain—could be used as a secret weapon?

GRASS NOT GREENER IN PITTSBURGH

In 2007, NFL players rated Heinz Field, the home of the Pittsburgh Steelers, as the worst grass field in the league. When Heinz Field opened in 2001, the Steelers laid down natural grass. After that, they resurfaced the field several times, even adding artificial fibers to help hold the grass in place. But maybe having a reputation for the worst grass field in the league is exactly the way Pitttsburgh's club President Art Rooney likes it. "If people come in thinking these aren't ideal conditions and that's always in the back of their minds, who knows how it affects their performance?" Rooney once asked. "We tell our kickers, 'Make sure you tell the opposing kickers this is the worst field you've ever kicked off.'" How's that for playing mind games on the field?

BENCHES HEAT UP THE GAME

When the Cleveland Browns were set to meet the Oakland Raiders in the 1980 playoffs, the Browns thought they had home field advantage in more ways than one. That's because they didn't have heated benches on the sidelines, where frigid winter temperatures often froze opposing players, who just weren't used to the big chill. But Oakland Raiders' owner Al Davis was wise to that and borrowed heated benches for the match. And the benches turned up the heat on the game. In fact, the NFL ruled that Davis had to bring in heated benches for Cleveland as well. But it turned out to be worth the extra effort for Davis. The Raiders won the game 14–12.

STAR ✦ • • • • • • • • • • • • • • • •

Tom Brady has led the New England Patriots to not one but three Super Bowl victories. In 2002, during his first playoff game, even driving snow could not hold the star quarterback back. As the Patriots faced the Oakland Raiders, snow covered the field and made the ball slick to handle. Nevertheless, Brady completed a thrilling 32 passes for 312 yards and even ran the ball into the Raiders' end zone for a touchdown, spearheading the Patriots to a 16–13 win. You might say Brady threw snow in the face of the Raiders.

Tom Brady

LEGENDS OF THE GAME

Bart Starr

The Ice Bowl Rocks the Game

Slip, sliding, and shivering away! That's what the Green Bay Packers and the Dallas Cowboys were doing at the NFL Championship game in 1967. Not only did a solid sheet of ice cover the field, but high winds blasted it, and the wind chill made it feel like 40 below. The whistle even froze to the referee's lips!

During the off-season, the Packers had installed an electric heating grid under their field to keep the grass warm and dry during cold and snowy winter weather. So when Packers' groundskeepers heard frigid temperatures forecast for the big game, they turned on the electric grid and put a tarp over the field for extra protection. And that's what caused the most brutal field conditions pro football has ever seen.

Overnight, heat from the grid formed water droplets, or condensation, on the tarp. So when groundskeepers lifted off the tarp on game day, the droplets ran onto the grass and froze, instantly turning the field into a virtual skating rink. Players struggled to get a firm footing on the field. And though Green Bay grabbed an early scoring lead, the Cowboys came storming back and slid ahead 17–14. With less than five minutes left in the fourth quarter, Green Bay quarterback Bart Starr led a scoring drive that moved the Packers all the way from their 32-yard line to the Cowboy's 1-foot yardline. After a few fumbles and slips, Starr managed to fake a handoff to a running back, hang onto the ball, and dive headfirst into the end zone. Touchdown on ice!

Is it any wonder the Super Bowl is rarely played in places with cool winter climates anymore?

Chapter 4

THE COMPLETE ATHLETE

Grunt! Squat! Lift those dumbbells! You can do it. Now, hit the deck for forty pushups. Lunge, turn, lunge. Do ten high-knees, driving your knees into your chest, ten buttkicks, ten jumping jacks, and the list goes on and on.... The daily workouts of pro players are action-packed all right, as some perform seventy or more moves and exercises. Is it any wonder that some modern football pros can bench-press, or lift, 250 kg (550 lbs.) and run 40 yards in just 4.2 seconds flat?

Long gone is the era when pro football players could play baseball in the off-season and use training camp to shape up for the season. Nowadays, pro football players grind it out in the gym all year round. Get the scoop on how the pros train their bodies and minds to meet the punishing demands of the battle on the gridiron.

Get Fit!

THE BODY

Getting into first-rate playing shape is a big job. Since 1985, the average NFL player's weight has ballooned ten percent to a whopping 112 kg (248 lbs). But this super-size doesn't mean a thing unless they have the strength, speed, and endurance to back it up.

SHAPING UP FOR FOOTBALL

Hit and run. That's what football players do most on the gridiron. In fact, some players describe the game as a series of traffic accidents. After all, opposing players set up on the line of scrimmage and run and smash into each other on each and every play. *Slam, bam, wham!* And their bodies often pile up on top of each other in a big heap on the field. Oh sure, players also throw, catch, and kick the ball, and they need to practice these skills to perfect them. But physical conditioning for football focuses on building strength and speed. Players need the strength to hit and take hits from opponents, no matter what their size. They also need the speed to boot it down the 100-yard field in seconds flat carrying the ball or to catch an opponent with the ball and take him down.

TRAIN TO GAIN

Whether you're playing for your school team or in the big leagues, the secret of success for all athletes is the same: train, train, train. To build the strength and speed they need, pro players work out with the team each week during the season, pumping iron and running sprints. Many also work with a personal trainer, especially in the off-season. Their personal trainers design workouts to challenge individual weaknesses and build on strengths. And some players will do whatever it takes to gain an edge on opponents. For example, part of defensive end Dwight Freeney's fitness routine is to do pushups with 40 kg (90 lbs.) of thick chains on top of his back. Freeney also pulls a giant tire along the ground like a bull pulls a plow. No joke! Other players are cagey about their workouts. For example, when rocket-footed running back LaDainian Tomlinson, a.k.a. L.T., was interviewed by the TV show *60 Minutes*, he wouldn't let them see part of his routine designed by his personal trainer. How's that for a top-secret trade secret? He also works with a massage therapist and doctor to help repair muscle damage from injuries. Talk about total body conditioning!

THE FUEL

Everybody knows you can't run and jump without any fuel in your tank. But that doesn't mean eating everything in sight to "bulk up." Lugging around extra weight will slow you down and make you less agile. To make sure NFL players get the proper nutrients and energy they need, teams have a cafeteria where they eat together during the practice week and chow down a pre-game meal on game day.

NFL teams serve up rice or pasta with every meal, so players can load up on complex carbohydrates. Team meals also include a mound of vegetables, fruit, and a small piece of meat on the side.

The team eats the pre-game meal about three to four hours before the game, so they have ample time to digest it. But it's the meal that players eat the night before the game that gives them the fuel to go all out during the game—as long as it's balanced in the following "pro-portions:"

60% carbohydrates. Rice, pasta, cereals, breads, vegetables, and fruit are players' main source of energy. Carbohydrates provide fuel for intense exercise and help keep players going during a game's last thirty minutes, when many wins and losses are decided.

20% proteins. Proteins from lean meats and fish, as well as peanut butter, eggs, grains, nuts, and seeds, help players build and repair their muscles.

20% "good" fats. Fats from red meat, cheese, eggs, milk, butter, salad dressing, nuts, and seeds get stored in the body as potential energy. Once carbohydrate energy gets low, fats begin to supply energy. They also help muscles develop and provide a protective cushion for players' inner organs.

WHAT'S UP DOC?

Smack! Two players collide full on. *Bam!* A player tackles an opponent and slams him on the ground. *Whack!* A player's head smashes into an opponent's knee. *Ouch!* Football is a collision sport all right, and injuries are part of the game.

TIP

What's the best way to prevent injuries in football? Warm up and stretch your muscles before you play or practice. Stretching your muscles regularly will develop flexibility. And research shows that the more flexible players are, the less prone they are to injuries.

PLAYING THROUGH PAIN

Before Super Bowl XLIV, all eyes were on Dwight Freeney (below). Would the Indianapolis Colts' big defensive end, known for explosive speed, recover from a sprained ankle in time to play? The scuttlebutt was that Freeney had a third-degree sprain with a torn ligament, or connective tissue. But nobody was more determined than Freeney. He put in seventeen hours of rehab a day. He iced the swollen ankle over and over. He lay in a hyperbaric chamber, a sealed tube that combines high air pressure with pure oxygen to pump lots of oxygen to the injury to help it heal faster. He also used a device to pump extra blood to the injury. And when the big game started, Freeney took the field and gave everything he had. He busted out into his signature speedy spin and even dropped opposing quarterback Drew Brees into the dirt. However, by halftime, Freeney's ankle stiffened up and didn't come back to life enough for Freeney to be his usual force to reckon with. Nevertheless, Freeney gave his all for all four quarters of the game.

CONKED IN THE HEAD!

What do quarterback Kurt Warner and running back Clinton Portis have in common besides playing pro football? They've both been knocked out of the lineup by a concussion—a chemical imbalance in the brain caused by a blow to the head. The human brain sits inside the skull like a person sitting in a car without a seatbelt. If your head gets hit, your skull stops or twists suddenly. Since the brain has nothing holding it in place, it crashes inside of the skull. *Wham!* This sets off a chain of chemical reactions that can cause dizziness, memory loss, headaches, balance problems—even personality changes or brain damage. Symptoms can be very subtle, which makes concussions hard to diagnose. However, recent research shows that suffering several concussions can lead to brain damage, so now the NFL encourages players to come forward with head injuries. And a neurologist—a doctor who specializes in the nervous system, which contains the brain—must test the players to make sure they are free of symptoms before they can return to the action.

Quick Hit

Playing football can be really draining! Offensive linemen and defensive backs can lose as much as 7 kg (15 lbs.) of water weight during a single game.

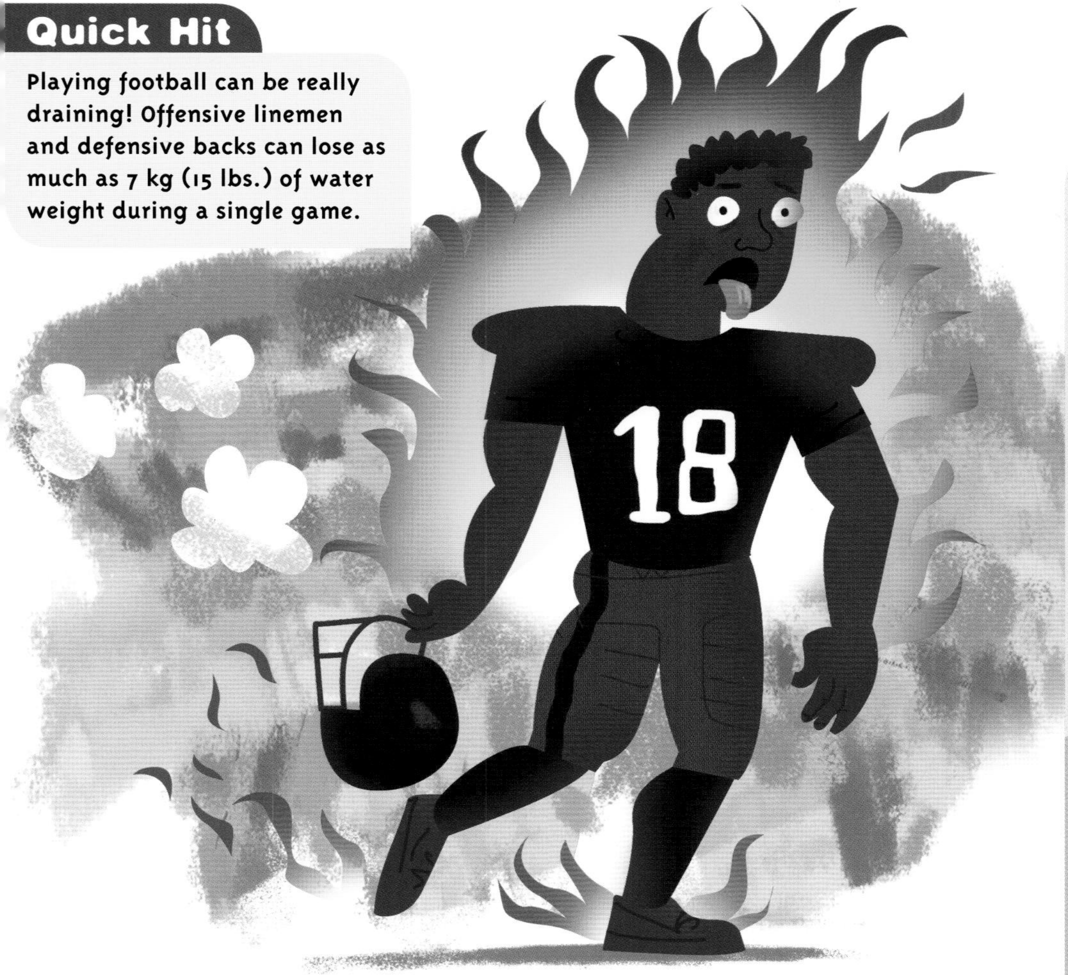

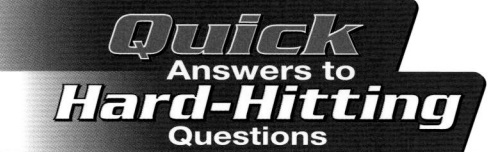

DRIP, DRIP, AND LET IT RIP

It's not easy keeping cool on the gridiron, especially in the southern states where temperatures of 54°C (130°F) or more may practically bake the field. After all, football players lug around 9 kg (20 lbs.) of equipment with every step they take. And their equipment and uniforms cover all their skin except for their face, neck, and part of their forearms. What's more, their helmets put their body's natural cooling system on the fritz by trapping heat that normally escapes through the head. Players can overheat and lose body fluids easily through sweating, so trainers constantly remind them to drink water and sports drinks on the sidelines and even to increase the amount they drink the week before the game. Nevertheless, some players get heat stroke or severe bouts of dehydration in which all their muscles cramp up. During halftime or after the game, the team doctor hooks up these players to an intravenous (IV) drip bag to quickly replace lost fluids, sugar, salt, potassium, and electrolytes. *Drip, drip, drip....*

Quick Answers to Hard-Hitting Questions

What's the injury report?

To prevent "inside information" from giving gamblers betting on the game or teams an edge, NFL teams must file weekly reports on injured players. The report lists injured players, the injured body parts, whether players took part in practice, and if they are likely to play in the next game. But filling out the report is a game itself. For example, to disclose as little meaningful information as possible to opponents, some teams list almost every player as having an injury. Others list almost none. And some will even list the wrong injuries on purpose.

Are pro players pumped up on steroids?

Steroids are drugs that can help people build larger muscles than we can build naturally. In an anonymous survey in 2009, about one in ten retired NFL players admitted they had used steroids while playing. Today, NFL rules ban the use of steroids. Not only can steroids give players an unfair advantage over competitors, but studies show the drugs can lead to more injuries as players' bodies don't adapt fast enough or well enough to the bigger muscles they develop. These drugs have many other side effects, which can lead to serious long-term health problems. So it doesn't pay to use drugs to play.

THE MIND

Some players rehearse plays through the technique of *visualization*. They watch mental movies of themselves successfully making a play over and over, so these pictures take root in their minds and they can make the play instinctively in games. Does it work? Studies show that athletes who do visualization and physical practice outperform those who do not. Check out how else players train their minds.

IMAGINE THIS...

You are a defensive back covering a shifty wide receiver who has a knack for making seemingly impossible catches. The opposing quarterback throws a long pass, and the ball hangs in the air above both of your heads for what seems like forever. Can you knock the ball away before the receiver gets his hands on it? Or maybe even intercept it? But what if you blow it? What if you don't jump in time...?

MONKEY THINK, MONKEY DO

Gotcha! Before you know it, the receiver has leapt up and made the catch, and you and your feet are on the ground. Your thoughts distracted you and you blew it. "I'm such a loser," you say to yourself. Stop right there. Don't get down on yourself. According to sports psychologists, your thoughts rule your actions. If you think you won't jump in time, for example, your body will follow. What's more, research studies show that athletes' thoughts and self-talk—things they say to themselves as they perform—influence their success. Researchers believe that negative thoughts can lead to poor play, while positive thoughts can give players the chance to play well. So instead of focusing on what went wrong, focus on what went right—like the fact that you stuck with the receiver all the way downfield and now you've got a chance to tackle him and shake the ball loose.

FOOTBALL IS SO MENTAL

Experts say that talent and physical skills are pretty much even among top football players and that what separates the best from the rest is mental toughness. The fact is, when players begin to lose confidence in their abilities through negative thoughts or self-talk, their muscles tense up and they can no longer perform to the best of their abilities. So pro players train their minds to develop mental toughness and use positive thoughts to remain focused even in pressure-filled situations. First, players identify the negative thoughts and self-talk that run through their minds during games. Then players replace these with positive thoughts and statements and practice saying the statements over and over. Players may also write them out, post them in their locker, tape them on their mirror, and even record them on their MP3 player to listen to them over and over. That way, when players make a mistake in a game, they don't fall apart. The positive thoughts and self-talk refocus them, so they can keep their heads in the game. Talk about being mental!

Quick Hit

Does the way you think stink? Players and team psychologists often call negative thoughts that go through players' minds in game situations "stinking thinking."

Gotta Have Heart

Sure, you need size, strength, speed, tip-top physical conditioning, and a good mental attitude to excel on the gridiron. But don't underestimate the power of heart. Experts say that desire is a key ingredient of athletic success. A strong desire to play can motivate athletes with less talent to outperform those with exceptional talent. Take running back DeAngelo Williams. People have always told him that he's not big enough for football, and going into the NFL 2006 draft it was no different. "A lot of teams looked at me and thought 'He's a third-string back at best,'" Williams once said. But in 2008, Williams cracked the starting lineup for the Carolina Panthers and set the field ablaze. The determined running back rushed for 1515 yards and eighteen touchdowns on 273 carries. "It's just a testament that they can measure your height, they can measure your weight, and they can somewhat measure your skill," said Williams. "But they can never measure the size of a man's heart."

TRY THIS!

How can you remain cool, calm, and collected on the outside when you have butterflies in your stomach on the inside? Try this experiment and see.

YOU WILL NEED
- a high-pressure situation where you feel nervous

1 When you feel under pressure, take a deep breath.

2 Act as if you feel perfectly fine and smile.

3 Notice how smiling makes you feel inside.

Why does smiling help you "fake it until you make it"?

Answer on page 64.

Quick Answers to Hard-Hitting Questions

What does it mean for players to "give 110 percent"?

Experts say that there is only one way to play football: to go all out. Not only must players play with their minds and bodies, they must play with their hearts. Emotional energy, will, and desire can drive a player to achieve incredible physical feats, like rushing through a maze of opponents for a touchdown with an opponent clinging to his back.

STAR

Who's the greatest receiver of all time? Chances are any coach, TV announcer, or journalist will say Jerry Rice. From 1985 to 2004, the star wide receiver set NFL records for the most receptions, receiving yards, touchdown receptions, and touchdowns. What set Rice apart from other players was his desire. He never let up. He kept coming at the defense with the same level of intensity throughout the entire game. This wore down defenders and they wavered, opening up the field an inch or two for Rice to make big plays.

Jerry Rice

Drew Brees

Brees and the Saints Go Marching In

When Drew Brees signed with the New Orleans Saints in 2006, the city was still reeling from Hurricane Katrina. More than three-quarters of New Orleans lay in ruins underwater in the wake of one of the deadliest hurricanes to ever hit the U.S. And maybe Brees fit right in. The quarterback was recovering from a devastating shoulder injury. In fact, some people thought he would never play again.

But people had always underestimated Brees. In high school, he didn't lose a single football game he played. Nevertheless, a college scholarship was hard to come by. In college, Brees led his team to their first Rose Bowl in thirty-four years, setting a record for career passing yards along the way. Yet doubts about his abilities still dogged him. People said he was too short for a quarterback—a mere 1.8 m (6 ft.). They said he didn't have a strong arm, and "yadda, yadda, yadda."

What they failed to see was that Brees is an amazing athlete who is quick on his feet and mentally tough, with great hand-eye coordination. When the TV show *Sports Science* measured Brees's accuracy in throwing footballs at a target, Brees was more accurate than top archers. He hit the bull's-eye ten out of ten times.

What's more, Brees has a work ethic and motivation like no other. Brees put in four solid months of grueling seven-hour days of rehab to recover against all odds and play again. As he rebuilt himself as a player, he helped rebuild New Orleans and give the city something to cheer about. Within four years, he led the Saints to their first Super Bowl victory. Is it any wonder people started to call him "the miracle man"?

Chapter 5

PREPARING FOR BATTLE

Snap, buckle, pop! Smear on the grease, er, glop! Football players gear up from head to toe much like ancient gladiators once clad themselves in armor to step into the ring with lions. But it wasn't always so.

In the early days of football, players went head to head without helmets or pads of any kind. No joke! In the 1870s, the standard football uniform was a canvas smock worn over a team jersey, pants made of padded canvas or thick cotton, wool stockings, and high-top shoes with leather spikes. However, it wasn't long before players began stuffing leather shin guards down their stockings for protection from kicks and blows. Discover how helmets evolved to protect players' heads, how modern players gear up to take to the battlefield, and how NFL teams bone up on their enemies—a.k.a. their opponent of the week.

Michael Robinson,
San Francisco 49ers

Let the Battle Begin!

MODERN GLADIATORS GEAR UP

**W**hen you gear up for a battle on the gridiron, you'd better cover your body from head to toe. Check out the "armor" players wear to protect nearly every body part.

A Real Head Case

You don't have to be a head case to play football, but pros don't leave the locker room without one. Huh? It is an NFL rule to wear a helmet on the field at all times. Helmets have a hard plastic shell, and they are fitted to an individual player's head to provide maximum protection from the kicks and blows of the game.

A Skintight Jersey

Players' jerseys are made of nylon, with spandex on the sides for a skintight fit. So there's not much for an opponent to grab onto. In fact, some jerseys worn by offensive and defensive linemen are so tight that the players need help to get them on and off. Some linemen even spray their jerseys with non-stick cooking spray to help them slip through opponents' fingers.

Pants that Rule

Football pants are made of nylon and spandex. They are designed to hug players' lower bodies and to hold the hip, thigh, and knee pads underneath the pants. According to NFL rules, the jersey must be tucked into the pants at all times. So players' pants have a wide strip of Velcro inside the waistband that sticks to Velcro at the back of the jersey. The pants also house an extension of the bottom of the jersey that wraps from front to back for extra "tucked-in" insurance. That's not all the "ants" in football pants. Some players have even worn nylons under their pants for warmth on cold days.

Smudges 'n' Stickers

As players gear up for battle, many apply a smudge of grease or a sticker beneath each eye. Is it all just for show? Recent studies show that the grease does improve visibility by absorbing light and cutting down glare. But the stickers don't. Nevertheless, no one knows whether eye black actually gives players a leg up, er, eye up in games.

Socks to Rock

Players wear one-piece socks or stockings. According to NFL rules, socks must cover the entire leg from the bottom of the pants to the shoe. What's more, the sock must be white from the top of the shoe to the middle of the calf. How's that for a strict sock code?

A Shoulder to Hit On

Underneath their jerseys, players wear shoulder pads made of a hard plastic shell and foam padding. The pads protect the shoulders, chest, and ribs. Some players, like quarterbacks, running backs, and wide receivers add a flak jacket that looks like a vest for extra rib protection. Other players, like linemen, add attachments that make their pads difficult for opponents to use as handholds. Players can add foam padding for extra protection. The pads absorb the shock of hits by deforming on impact. They also spread out the shock over a larger area, which reduces the pressure at the point of impact.

If the Glove Fits...

Different players with different jobs choose different gloves. Linemen wear gloves thick with padding to protect their hands and fingers, which can get stuck in other players' face masks or stepped on by a pile of feet. Receivers wear tact gloves with a sticky rubber palm, or gloves covered with a sticky substance like rosin or a spray, to help them catch the ball. Nevertheless, NFL rules forbid players from applying any type of sticky gel or "stick 'em" to their gloves or their bodies. Go figure!

Shoes for All Fields

On natural grass, pros wear shoes with cleats, or plastic screw-in spikes, that allow them to dig into the field. And the wetter the grass, the longer the cleats they wear. In fact, equipment managers use electric screwdrivers to change players' cleats to match changing field conditions during games. On artificial turf, players wear shoes with rubber cleats to match the field conditions, or shoes without cleats. Who knew football could be so choosy about its "shoesies"?

Suiting up in Armor

Hip pads, thigh pads, knee pads, elbow pads, and a tailbone pad are all part of a football player's armor, along with a jockstrap. The pads come in a variety of styles, depending on players' position, personal preferences, and injuries.

Tape It and Take It, Dude!

Did you know it's a league rule for players to have their ankles taped before playing a game? Taping their ankles gives players extra support and protection. So players tape their ankles for practices and many tape other body parts as well. In fact, the average NFL team uses up more than 480 km (300 mi.) of tape in a single season. And get this: in the 1960s and 1970s, some defensive linemen taped hockey pucks and ashtrays to their hands to sock it to their opponents on the field of battle.

THE HELMET

No piece of protective football equipment is as important as the helmet. Without one, a hit to the head can result in a concussion that knocks players out of the game, and may even scramble their brains.

A HELMET THAT FITS JUST RIGHT

A football helmet is not your average lid, dude. It has several parts—a hard plastic shell, jaw pads, inflatable air bladders, a face mask, a chin strap, and a mouth guard—that come in different styles and sizes so players can mix and match to fit their noodle best. An equipment manager helps each player choose a shell by measuring the player's head with a pair of calipers. Then they add foam pads and inflatable air pads inside the top and sides to make sure the helmet fits snugly. The player puts on the helmet and the equipment manager pumps up the air pads through holes in the shell.

This fills up any gaps so the helmet stays fixed in place. Then it's time to add the face mask, chin strap, and mouth guard. Quarterbacks like face masks with few protective metal bars to block their view of the action, and linemen like face masks with a "cage" of several bars for maximum protection in pileups and collisions. The mouthguard attaches to the face mask with a strap and is made of plastic shaped like a half moon. Quarterbacks and one defensive player per team also get their helmets outfitted with a speaker, so the coach can talk to them during games.

HEADS 'N' HELMETS ROLL THROUGH TIME

Check out how helmets have evolved to protect players' heads through time.

1890s
Ads appear for football skullcaps made of silk to protect players' hair and ears.

1891
Players' ears are easy targets for boxing and pulling by opponents. James Naismith, the inventor of basketball, designs ear muffs to protect players' ears, when he plays center for his school's football team in Springfield, Massachusetts.

1893
A doctor tells football player Admiral Joseph Mason Reeves that another kick to the head might kill him or turn him into a vegetable. So Reeves has a shoemaker make a leather helmet and wears it to play.

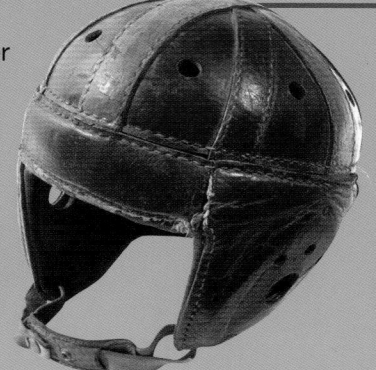

1896
Halfback George Barclay lives in fear of getting a "cauliflower ear" from a blow to the head. So a harness maker makes him a leather hat that covers his ears. And so Barclay wears the first head harness into the game. And early helmets that trickle onto the field become known as head harnesses.

Gear to Cheer

Check out some of the whackiest head gear around that not one but thousands of fans wear in the stands.

The Cheeseheads Are Here

The fans of the Green Bay Packers don head gear like no other—foam hats that look like giant wedges of Swiss cheese. Before the hats existed, people called the Packers' fans "cheeseheads" as an insult because the team's home state,  Wisconsin, produces more than 9 million tonnes (2 billion lbs.) of cheese a year. In the late 1980s, a man made a cheese hat out of an old couch cushion, and soon cheesehead hats began bobbing up and down in the Green Bay stands. And so the Packers' fans turned the cheesy insult on its head!

Invasion of the Melon Snatchers

When fans of the Saskatchewan Rough Riders arrived in Calgary for the 2009 Grey Cup championship game, there was a run on watermelons in grocery stores throughout the city. Some stores even ordered in special shipments so fans could gear up for the game. What was up with that? Rough Riders' fans like to scoop out a watermelon, cut the rind into a helmet, and stick it on their heads to wear at the game. How's that for cool headgear?

Emmitt Smith had an uncanny nose for holes in his opponent's defense. In 1995, the star running back slipped past defenders for a record-setting twenty-five rushing touchdowns in one season. Once over the goal line, Smith would rip off his helmet to celebrate. And though the NFL quashed his helmet dance in 1997 with the "Emmitt Smith rule," which calls for a 15-yard penalty if a player removes his helmet on the field, nobody could stop Smith from scoring.

Emmitt Smith

Around 1917

Helmets: some players wear one and some players don't. But helmets offer better protection as a suspension system to absorb shocks is added.

1920s

Hinkey Haines dons a leather helmet for full face protection.

1940s

Helmet makers begin making football helmets out of plastic and add the first face masks.

1970s

Pump it up! The first inflatable liners appear in football helmets.

Beyond

Will helmets with a sensor, or thermistor, to measure players' skin temperature become required gear?

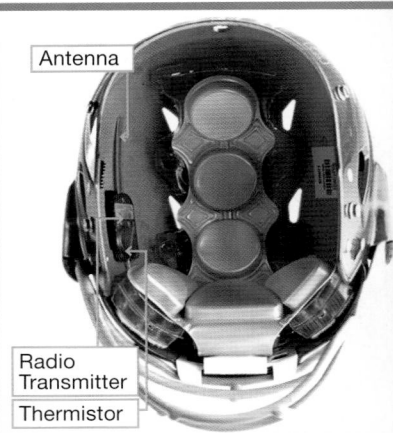

Antenna

Radio Transmitter

Thermistor

THE WEEKLY GRIND

Short and oh-so-sweet. That's what the football season is. Unlike the grueling eighty-two-game schedule of pro hockey and basketball, NFL players play only sixteen times. And often only once a week, usually on Sunday. But that doesn't make football any less of a grind. Players spend an entire week planning and practicing to beat their opponents. Check out a week in the life of a pro team.

Quick Hit

The scribbles and diagrams of x's and o's found in a team's playbook look like ancient Egyptian hieroglyphics to the average Joe or Jane. Nevertheless, by the end of the season, other teams have most of it figured out from watching films of the team play.

VICTORY MONDAY?

If the team won last Sunday's game, the coach may give them the day off—a.k.a. Victory Monday. But if not, the players have to show up for work.

8:00 a.m. All players must attend a team breakfast.

8:30 a.m. The coaching staff meet to begin writing the playbook for their next opponent (see Players Hit the Books, right).

9:00 a.m. Victory Monday or not, any injured players report to the team doc for examination, re-evaluation, and treatment of yesterday's injuries.

9:30 a.m. Healthy players work out: stretch sore muscles, run cross-country, and lift weights.

11:00 a.m. Lunchtime! Players refuel in the team cafeteria.

11:30 a.m. Meetings begin. Teams may have a Special Teams meeting so the entire team sees what each player contributes to the team in his role as a punter, kick returner, or the like.

12:00 p.m. The head coach guides the team through all the things in yesterday's game that helped them win or lose.

12:30 p.m. The team breaks up into offensive and defensive teams and each has its own meeting. Players hunker down to watch and analyze footage of the mistakes they made in yesterday's game.

2:00 p.m. Players hit the field to do "on-field corrections"—a walk-through practice without any gear—to fix the plays they botched in yesterday's game.

3:00 p.m. Call it quits for the day.

TUESDAY—A DAY OFF

Whew! Players kick back and rest their sore and football-weary bones.

WEDNESDAY—HUMP DAY

This middle-of-the-week day may be the toughest and longest day of practice but, once it's over, game day is a lot closer.

6:30 a.m. Players report for treatment of injuries. And if they're not on time, some teams may make them pay fines.

7:45 a.m. Players have a Special Teams meeting like the one on Monday. But the team quarterbacks have their own meeting.

8:30 a.m. The coach gives everyone the lowdown on the strengths and weaknesses of their next opponent. Players watch footage of the opposing team in action, get reports on individual players, and get the playbook for the week. Then the offensive and defensive players have their own meetings to study the playbook.

10:45 a.m. Players hit the field to walk through the plays they've just studied. Coaches show the upcoming opponent's plays on cue cards. Team scouts then line up in the opposing team's formations that players have just seen on film and in the playbook, so players can learn to recognize them on the field.

Players Hit the Books

At training camp, players receive a playbook of their team's secret plays and strategies. It may be as long as 800 pages, and players must know it inside out. What's more, every week the coaching staff writes a new 250 plus—page playbook for the upcoming game, with zillions of their opponent's plays, reports on players, and plays to counter the opponent's plays. That way, players will recognize the opponent's plays and know what to do in the heat of the action without having to stop and think. Who knew playing football required so much study?

11:10 a.m. Lunchtime! Players grab a bite and a break. The head coach, the quarterback, and star players may talk to news reporters.

12:00 p.m. It's back to the meeting rooms to review the plays.

12:30 p.m. Players go out to the practice field and do drills for running, handling the ball, and making hits. The team's video department films the whole practice.

2:30 p.m. Coaches and players watch footage of the day's two-hour practice to see what went right and wrong. That way, they can smooth out problems tomorrow.

4:30 p.m. The team packs it in for the day. But before they do, players will have squeezed in a workout lifting weights and running sprints. Whew!

THURSDAY—NOT AGAIN!

No, it's not a dream. Players pretty much repeat the same schedule as Wednesday. The only difference is that they study and practice different plays and parts of the game.

FRIDAY—DÉJÀ VU, TAKE TWO

Yup, Friday is another repeat of Wednesday. Coaches usually cut the practice short but not necessarily the meetings.

7:00 p.m. On a "short" day like this, the defensive players may get together for dinner at a teammate's or go out to eat. The offensive players do the same. It's a chance to hang out with their gang.

SATURDAY—COUNTDOWN TO GAME DAY

A.M. Players get treatment for injuries, go to meetings, and walk through plays again.

P.M. The team may meet again at the team hotel for a final review of the opponent. Players get psyched for Game Day tomorrow!

SUNDAY—GAME DAY

Players arrive at the stadium pumped and ready to rock. They get dressed to kill, er, play:

12:00 p.m. Teams head out to the field to warm up as fans stream into the stands. Then they return to the locker room briefly.

1:00 p.m. Teams take the field. The referee tosses a coin. The team that wins the coin toss chooses to kick or receive the ball. Then teams go head to head on the gridiron, trying to outwit, outsmart, outthink, outmuscle, outplay, and outdo each other in each and every way.

4:30 p.m. The final buzzer of the game sounds and it's all over. Whether they've won or lost, many players are banged up, cut, and bruised. If it's an away game, they board a plane and fly home.

In-flight Treatment of any obvious injuries begins on the plane. Trainers bandage up cuts and sprains and break out ice packs to reduce swelling of any lumps and bumps players took for the team.

Midnight Chances are some of the coaching staff are already preparing a battle plan for the next game, watching footage of the upcoming opponent's games to spot their strengths and weaknesses. And so the weekly grind begins again on the gridiron.

LEGENDS OF THE GAME

Bronko Nagurski
(with ball)

How the Giants Outsmarted the Bears

The Chicago Bears were on top of the world as they headed into the 1934 NFL championship game. The Bears had charged through the regular season with a perfect record—all wins and no losses. Whereas their opponents, the New York Giants, had fumbled through the season with eight wins and five losses.

The night before the big game, freezing rain fell on Polo Grounds, New York. The field froze, patches of ice formed, and neither team could get a firm footing the next day.

Even though the Giants had home field advantage, the Bears bounced ahead 10–3 by halftime. But the Giants weren't about to pack it in! When one of their players thought that basketball shoes would give them better grip, the coach dispatched equipment manager Abe Cohen to buy the shoes.

The only problem was that no stores were open. But Cohen was a man on a mission! According to NFL lore, Cohen broke into the lockers of Manhattan College with a hammer and "borrowed" their basketball shoes.

Whatever happened, Cohen returned with nine pairs of sneakers and the Giants laced them up for the second half. The soft-soled shoes gave the Giants better traction than the Bears. "We were slipping and sliding around and they were running all over us," former Bear Bronko Nagurski said years later.

The Giants leaped ahead 30–13. The sneakers seemed to give the Giants the winning edge, and the game became known as the "sneakers game." Later Nagurski declared, "They just outsmarted us."

Chapter 6

THE SCIENCE OF EXPLOSIVE MOVES

Whoosh! A quarterback lets a pass rip, a receiver leaps up to make the catch, and bolts over the goal line for a touchdown. *Boom!* A tackle hits a ball carrier and takes him down and out of the action. *Hut!* A center snaps the ball to a punter, opponents rush over the line of scrimmage to try to block the punt. *Whomp!* The punter boots the ball up, up, and away!

What makes passes, hits, and kicks so exciting and explosive beyond the effort players put into them? Find out exactly how these moves electrify the game and make fans jump out of their seats with a roar. *Woo hoo!*

Blast into Action!

PUNTING THE BALL

O kay, maybe punting the ball doesn't seem like an explosive move. After all, teams usually punt on a fourth down, giving up the ball when they're struggling to make the 10 yards needed for a new set of downs. But nothing changes the field position of the game like a punt. Check it out.

Ready, Set, Punt!

A punter sets up about 15 yards behind the line of scrimmage (LOS). A teammate lines up halfway between the punter and the LOS to block anyone who might break through to block the punt. The center snaps the ball and feeds it to the punter in less than a second flat. The punter catches it, takes one or two steps, and drops the ball to kick it. *Boom!*

No Easy Job

A punter has two goals. One: to kick the ball as far away from his end zone as possible so his opponents are less likely to score on the return. Two: to make the ball hang in the air as long as possible so his teammates have time to hotfoot it downfield and tackle the kick returner, who's trying to catch the ball and run it back.

Playing, er, Punting the Angles

The angle of the kick helps determine the hang time and how far the ball travels over the field. A steep angle (60°) sends the ball high up for a long hang time and a relatively short distance away from the LOS. A shallow angle (30°) results in less hang time but makes the ball travel a longer distance away from the LOS.

Getting Hang Time

The greater the vertical distance the ball travels, the longer it hangs in the air. NFL punters aim for a hang time of 4.5 seconds. A kick that sends the ball spinning in a spiral can make the ball hang in the air longer and fly faster and farther than a kick that sends the ball tumbling end over end.

Arcing Over the Field

Whenever a football sails through the air, it cuts a curved path due to the force of gravity. As the force of a kick or pass sends the ball up, the force of gravity pulls it down to Earth.

60°

30°

Veritcal Distance

Getting Distance

The greater the horizontal distance the ball travels, the farther the ball moves away from the punter's end zone. NFL punters try to boot the ball at least 45 yards beyond the LOS.

Horizontal Distance

Kicking vs. Punting

Just in case you were wondering, kicking is not the same as punting. In fact, teams usually have different players for each and some even have another player for kickoffs. Here's the scoop:

Play	Who	When	Where	Tee Used?	Destination
Kickoff	Placekicker or kickoff specialist	Opening of game, beginning of second half, after every score	Team's 30-yard line	Yes	Downfield away from end zone
Field goal attempts	Placekicker	Up to coach's discretion when team has possession	7 yards behind LOS	No, a player holds the ball in place	Over the crossbar between the goal-post's uprights
Extra point attempts	Placekicker	After scoring a touchdown	7 yards behind LOS	No, a player holds the ball in place	Over the crossbar between the goal-post's uprights
Punt	Punter	On a fourth down	15 yards behind LOS	No, the punter receives the snap and drops the ball to kick it	Downfield away from end zone

STAR •

Tom Dempsey was an exceptional kicker like no other. Dempsey was born with the toes of his right foot missing, and his unusual foot proved to be perfect for kicking. In 1970, Dempsey hammered the ball with it for a record-setting 63-yard field goal.

Tom Dempsey

Quick Answers to Hard-Hitting Questions

Why punt on a fourth down instead of going for the yards?

It comes down to field position. Unless a team is behind their opponent's 40-yard line, they don't want to risk not gaining the yards and giving up the ball to their opponents within easy scoring reach of their own end zone. They'd rather boot the ball to send their opponents as far away from their end zone as possible.

Can a punt returner get a touchdown?

Yes, and how! Sometimes a punt returner can rip and zip down the field through an opponent's entire lineup all the way to the end zone, rocking the ball for a touchdown.

What if a punt returner "muffs a kick"?

When a punt returner fails to get the ball, the punting team may pounce on it but they cannot advance it on the play. But if the returner touches the ball and fumbles it, the ball is up for grabs.

TACKLING THE BIG HIT

Wham! Bam! Gotcha, Sam! A linebacker tackles a ball carrier, knocks the ball out of his hands, and slams him to the turf. When players tackle, they use their hands and arms to bring down the player who has the ball. What packs the punch of these big hits? Check out the forces at work in a tackle and see.

MAY THE FORCE BE EQUAL

When any two players collide—whether each is big or small, or fast or slow—the forces they exert on each other are equal and opposite in direction. Those are the laws of motion. So why does a smaller player often go flying through the air? A smaller player has less mass than a bigger one. Therefore, he also weighs less. So the force of gravity that attracts him, and all objects, to the Earth is smaller.

CENTER OF WHAT?

All objects are made of matter. A player's mass is the amount of matter in his body. His center of mass is the point where his mass is greatest. (In guys, this is above the belly button. In gals, it is below the belly button.) When a force like a hit strikes the player on either side of his center of mass, the player will rotate around this center. So if he's upright, he may go down. *Slam!*

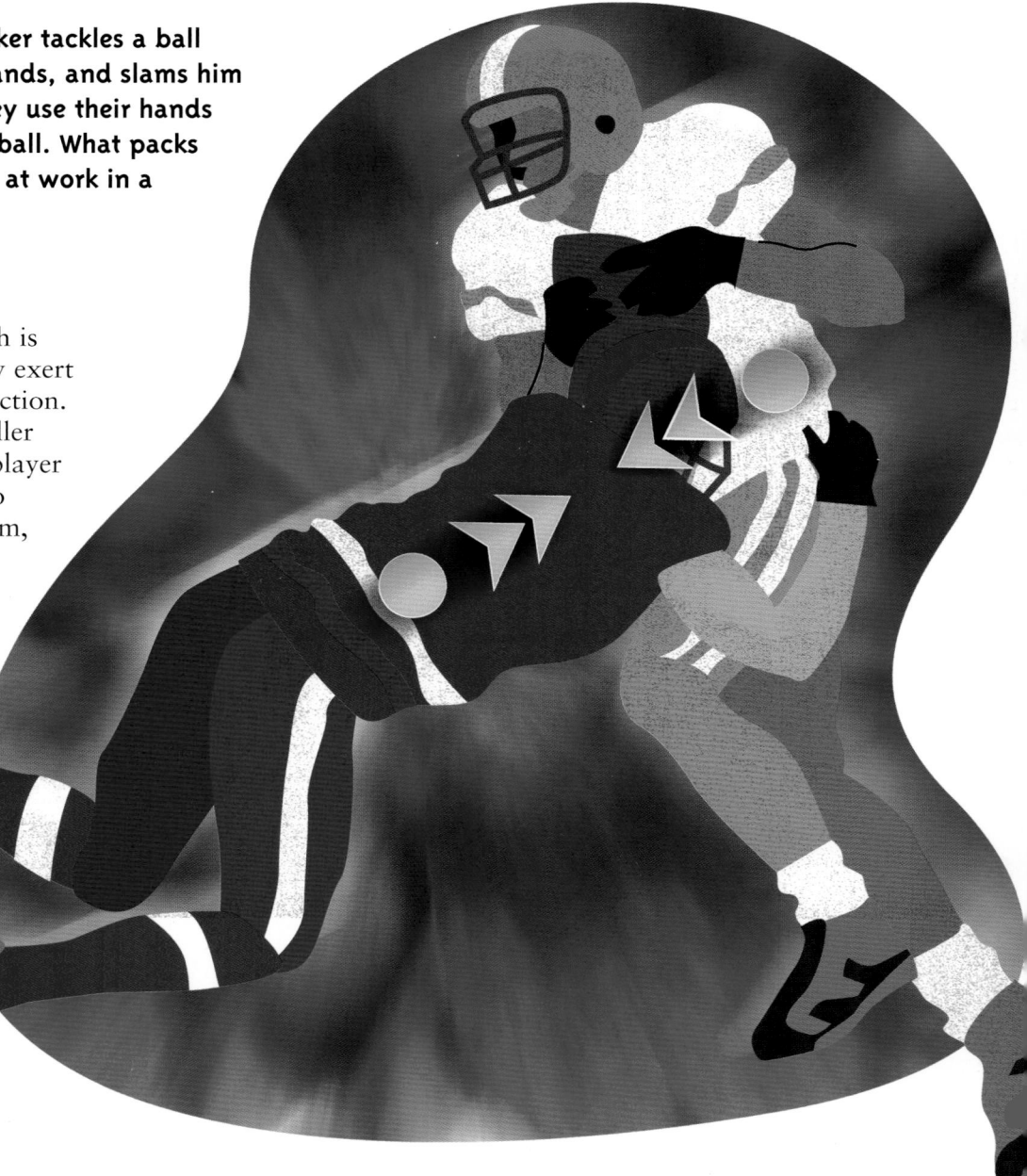

THE TRUTH BEHIND THE INCREDIBLE BULK

No doubt about it. Some players, like offensive tackle Willie Anderson (see right), are massive. In fact, at the beginning of training camp for the 2006 NFL season, more than five hundred players weighed in over 135 kg (300 lbs.). Offensive tackles like Anderson are the biggest players in the game, because their job is to protect the quarterback by staying between him and the defensive linemen who are gunning for him. The more a player weighs, the bigger his mass. And mass matters. According to the laws of motion that govern our universe, the more massive a player (or any object), the more his body will want to continue doing whatever it's doing—moving or staying still. So the less likely he is to be stopped, shoved aside, slowed down, or knocked down by an outside force—a.k.a. a hit from another player. Is it any wonder that so many players are so massive in the hard-hitting game of football?

HIT LOW TO DELIVER A BLOW

Effective linemen know to tackle ball carriers down low. When a lineman hits a ball carrier low (above, left) rather than high (above, right), he strikes the carrier farther away from the carrier's center of mass. And the farther he strikes from the center of mass, the less force he needs to make the carrier rotate around the center of mass and go down. Of course, linemen don't study physics to know this. They learn it on the gridiron's "school of hard hits."

STAR ★

T.O. is no easy foe to tackle. The star wide receiver, a.k.a. Terrell Owens, has the size, strength, and speed to dance his way through the clutches of a team's entire lineup of defenders. When T.O. gets the ball, you better "getcha popcorn ready." In three seasons, he averaged a touchdown per game. What's more, T.O. danced all over the opponents' end zones to celebrate and rub it in.

Terrell Owens

THE BULLET PASS

Players and TV announcers don't call an awesome pass a "bullet pass" for nothing. A well-thrown short pass really does fly through the air like a bullet. Check it out and see it spin.

TIP

If a quarterback stands a few yards behind the center and receives the ball in-flight—a.k.a. a shotgun snap—watch for the next play to be a pass rather than a run. Getting the ball in the shotgun position means the quarterback doesn't have to drop back. He can scan the field and target his receivers better.

Firing a Pass

A football has an oblong shape like a bullet. To throw a pass, a quarterback raises the ball in his hand slightly above and behind his head. Then he brings his arm forward rapidly and releases the ball. As he lets the ball go, he snaps his wrist down and out to give the ball spin.

Spinning Like a Bullet

The spin the quarterback gives the ball makes the ball turn in a tight spiral just like a speeding bullet. (When a rifle fires, spiral grooves inside the barrel give a bullet spin.) This spiral spin keeps the ball flying straight through the air nose-first without tumbling or wobbling. That way it can meet its target—the hands of a receiver.

A Nose for Speed

Whizzing through the air nose-first like a bullet rather than belly-first also cuts down on air drag, or resistance, met by the ball as it bumps into air molecules, the microscopic clumps of atoms that make up air. That's because a smaller area of the ball strikes the air molecules. The result? A nose-first pass travels faster than a belly-first pass.

STAR

In the 1970s, quarterback Terry Bradshaw led the Pittsburgh Steelers to four Super Bowl wins. The strong-armed quarterback had an unusual way of throwing passes. As Bradshaw gripped the ball, he placed his index finger on the back tip.

This added more force to his throws, increasing the speed of his passes, and gave the ball more spin, increasing its steadiness in the air. How's that for having a finger on the pulse?

Terry Bradshaw

TRY THIS!

How does spin affect the flight of the ball? Try this experiment and see.

YOU WiLL NEED

- a football

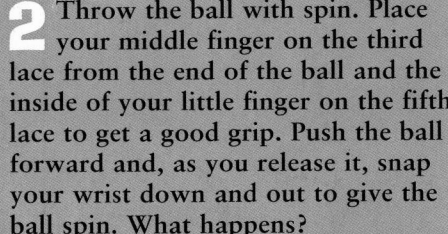

Quick Hit

A strong-armed quarterback can hurl the ball as far as 80 yards. *Whoosh!*

1 Throw the football without any spin. Hold the ball in your hand. Then just push the ball forward and release it. What happens?

2 Throw the ball with spin. Place your middle finger on the third lace from the end of the ball and the inside of your little finger on the fifth lace to get a good grip. Push the ball forward and, as you release it, snap your wrist down and out to give the ball spin. What happens?

Answer on page 64.

What's the bomb?

When the bomb goes off, look out. Not only is it one of football's most exciting plays but it's also one of the most bungled. The bomb is a long pass that fires the ball 40 yards or more into the ready and waiting hands of a receiver.

What makes a pass complete?

Catching the ball. No joke! In football speak, a forward pass caught by a receiver inbounds is called a completion.

How fast is a pass?

Star quarterbacks like Peyton Manning (below) throw some of the fastest passes in the NFL, which clock in at speeds of more than 65 km (40 mi.) per hour.

LEGENDS OF THE GAME

Bradbury Robinson

The Ball Takes Flight

Coach Eddie Cochems was fed up. His team, St. Louis University, was getting nowhere trying to run the ball in a game against Carroll College. So the coach ordered his players to break out the "air attack."

That was the situation in Waukesha, Wisconsin, in September 1906. Back then, teams didn't throw the ball much because the forward pass had just become legal. But the rule change had prompted Coach Cochems to study the ball.

Once Cochems discovered that the ball's laces give players' fingers something to grip onto to throw it, he focused the entire training camp on passing. Cochems told his players to put their fingers between the laces of the ball and throw it with a "twist of the wrist" to make it spiral through the air.

The result thrilled Bradbury Robinson: "Coach, I can throw the dang thing 40 yards!" After that the team secretly practiced forward passes but had yet to try one in a game. So Robinson launched the air attack

with a pass to Jack Schneider. The bold move caught the Carroll defense off guard, but the pass was incomplete and St. Louis had to give up the ball.

That didn't stop the air attack, though. When St. Louis got the ball back, Robinson fired to Schneider again. Schneider caught the ball this time and zoomed over the Caroll goal line for a touchdown. St. Louis trounced Carroll 22–0. What's more, the team went on to use the air attack to win each and every game that year.

Chapter 7

GAME TIME

We're here to fight! We'll win this game tonight! We're here to move. Get in the groove!" That's what some cheerleaders chant to set the tone for victory. But no matter what cheerleaders, fans, and players chant and cheer, excitement crackles in the air as soon as the players burst out of the tunnel from the locker room to the field.

The team captains meet the referee at center field. The referee tosses a coin and the visiting captain gets to call heads or tails. The winner of the coin toss then decides whether to receive the ball or to defend a particular end zone. If the winner chooses the ball, the other captain gets the pick of end zones. And with that, one team kicks the ball to the other—*whomp!*—and the battle is underway. Get the skinny on game time action and how teams vie for a winning edge.

Louisiana State University (LSU) Tigers

Get Your Front Row Seat ➤

BATTLE STATIONS

As players take their places on the field, the coaching staff hunker down at their battle stations—the bench and the booth. They use surveillance and communication equipment to collect "enemy intelligence" and feed it to the players. Check it out!

UP, UP, IN THE BOOTH

The defensive coordinator and assistant coaches usually stake out the booth in the press box at the top of the stadium. This gives them a bird's eye view of the game action unfolding below, allowing them to recognize the opponents' formations and identify offensive and defensive strategies. They look for little things that can give the team an edge. For example, they might notice that an opposing linebacker takes a certain stance when the defense is about to blitz. They communicate all this information through headsets to the head coach and other coaching staff at the bench, who then pass on the nitty-gritty to the players at large. Sometimes, they also talk to specific players one-on-one over the phone. *Brrrring! Brrrring!* Coach calling, booth to bench.

THE BENCH

Looking for the head coach and offensive coordinator on the sidelines? They're the dudes yammering away on headsets, talking to the coaching staff in the booth and the quarterback. Since all video equipment is off limits during the game, one of them has a printout of the game plan, which details the team's opening plays and formations, along with options for different field positions and situations. As the coaches in the booth feed them "enemy intelligence" and what's working and what isn't, the head coach communicates with the troops on the field. What's more, fax machines at the bench spit out photos taken by cameras perched around the stadium. The photos reveal the opponents' formations, player stances, and where each opponent moves on his first step. The coaches share this intelligence with the players, making any adjustments to win.

Spying Coach Busted!

It's no secret that coaches spend hours watching videotapes of opponents, trying to crack their codes by matching their signals to the actions that unfold. In fact, one coach routinely sent a scout out to watch opponents' signals firsthand. And some always cover their mouths as they call plays from the sidelines just in case their opponents are trying to read their lips. But that doesn't mean anything goes. In 2007, the NFL busted Bill Belichick, head coach of the New England Patriots, for spying on the New York Jets' defensive signals, when the team's video assistant was caught with a video camera on the Jets' sideline. The league fined Belichick and fined the team, and took away some of the team's draft picks. The fact is, NFL rules forbid teams from using video recording devices of any kind during games. And videotaping an opponent's signals is strictly forbidden. Case closed.

Game Changers

Meet some players who can change a game in seconds flat with one big play. In fact, opponents often design game plans to hold these guys at bay.

Quick Hit

In 1958, the New York Giants had the best defense in the NFL. Fans knew it and whenever the defense took the field in tight games, they chanted: DEE-FENSE! DEE-FENSE! DEE-FENSE!

Running Back

LaDainian Tomlinson
No running back can change the game like L.T.—a.k.a. LaDainian Tomlinson (above right). L.T. moves through holes in the defense that no one else can even see, making extraordinary plays that can turn a game in an instant. In 2006, L.T. scored a record-setting thirty-one touchdowns.

Wide Receiver

Randy Moss
You just got "Mossed"! That's the saying around the NFL when wide receiver Randy Moss (above left) gets by a tackler and boots it with the ball all the way to the house. Moss's ability to elude opponents and spectacular one-handed catches make him a threat to change the game every time.

Return Specialist

Devin Hester
Left, right, left, right. *Zoom*—and he's gone! Devin Hester cuts his way around defenders, leaving them to eat his dust. The return specialist can turn a game around in a flash, returning a kick or a punt for a touchdown. Hester set a record for the most kick returns in a single season. Some fans call him "Anytime."

Free Safety

Ed Reed
Free safety Ed Reed likes to get his hands on the ball and has a knack for making interceptions that turn games around. Reed once returned an interception for a record-setting 108 yards! He is also an expert at tackling and forcing fumbles. He's ready to rumble anytime, anywhere.

ONLY IN FOOTBALL

Quick Hit

In 2010, six countries, including the U.S. and Canada, participated in the first women's world championship of football.

Where else could a running back and rookie foil an assassin? A two-minute drill change the outcome of an entire game? Or a player use "not-so-secret intelligence" to outwit opponents? Check out some sizzling action that has stunned football fans, players, and coaches alike.

FRENCHY, THE ASSASSIN, AND THE ROOKIE

In 1972, the Pittsburgh Steelers were down 7–6 to the Oakland Raiders on a fourth down, with only 26 seconds on the clock. Steelers' quarterback Terry Bradshaw sent up a pass to teammate John "Frenchy" Fuqua at the 35-yard line. But Frenchy wasn't alone. The Assassin— Raiders' safety Jack Tatum—homed in on the incoming ball, too. And he rammed into Frenchy as the pass arrived. Frenchy and the ball went flying. Mission accomplished! The only thing was that Pittsburgh rookie running back Franco Harris scooped up the ball and ran it all the way to the end zone for a touchdown. "Tell them you touched it, Frenchy!" The Assassin demanded. According to the rules back then, once an offensive player touched the ball, no other offensive player could touch it unless a defensive player touched it first. So if the ball had touched Frenchy without touching The Assassin, the rookie's touchdown was illegal. The officials scratched their heads, but finally let the touchdown stand. And to this day, Frenchy has never confessed whether he touched the ball.

JOHNNY U'S TWO-MINUTE DRILL

At the 1958 NFL Championship Game, the New York Giants led the Baltimore Colts 17–14 with just two minutes to go, when Colts' quarterback Johnny Unitas fired up the field with a "two-minute drill." Calling plays with the briskness of a drill sergeant, Unitas spearheaded a drive of short, quick passes to receiver Raymond Berry. Johnny U's drill marched the Colts downfield within range of a field goal and, with just seven seconds left, the Colts' kicker tied the game. *Bzzzzzt.* The final buzzer went and the Colts and the Giants found themselves in sudden-death overtime. The first team to score would win. Johnny U took charge again, driving the Colts 80 yards downfield. Unitas hit Berry with a pass at the 1-yard line. Then just when the Giants were convinced that he was going to pass again, Unitas handed the ball to fullback Alan "The Horse" Ameche, who galloped into the end zone. Touchdown, Colts! Fans cheered and Johnny U's two-minute drill became a standard mode of attack in close games.

WIN AT ANY COST

10, 9, 8… The last seconds of the game were ticking down, and quarterback Ken "The Snake" Stabler (above) was running out of options at the 14-yard line. His team, the 1978 Oakland Raiders, was behind, 20–14, to the San Diego Chargers. The Snake wound up to pass, but saw he was about to get sacked. So he deliberately fumbled the ball forward. The ball rolled to the 12-yard line, where running back Pete Banaszak managed to bat it forward. Tight end Dave Casper got to it next, kicked it into the end zone, and then fell on the ball to tie the game. *Oof!* The Chargers protested, but the ref ruled that the touchdown was legal. Then kicker Errol Mann put the Chargers away by getting an extra point. The next season, the NFL made it illegal to advance the ball downfield by swatting or kicking it. Nevertheless, the Raiders stood by the play. "The play is in our playbook," Oakland guard Gene Upshaw once said. "It's called 'Win at Any Cost.'"

CORNERBACK JUMPS A RUNNING ROUTE

Sometimes, defensive players can turn the tables on their opponents and score big. Take Super Bowl XLIV in 2010: late in the fourth quarter, New Orleans Saints' cornerback Tracy Porter (far right) spotted Indianapolis Colts' wide receiver Austin Collie (near right) going into motion at the line of scrimmage and recognized the Colts' formation. Then, thanks to all the footage of the Colts he had studied to prepare for the big game, Porter knew that Colts quarterback Peyton Manning would try to hit receiver Reggie Wayne with a pass long enough to get a first down. Porter used this not-so-secret intelligence and jumped onto Wayne's running route, intercepting the pass. Once he had the ball, Porter sprinted 74 yards for a touchdown. The play sealed the game, and the Saints marched on to victory, 31–17.

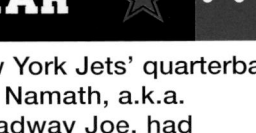

STAR

New York Jets' quarterback Joe Namath, a.k.a. Broadway Joe, had a natural showmanship that attracted the spotlight. In 1968, when the Jets were about to meet the heavily favored Baltimore Colts in the Super Bowl, Namath made a personal guarantee his team would win. People thought it was just big talk. But Namath backed it up with a rock-solid performance, passing for 206 yards and fueling the Jets to upset the Colts, 16–7.

Joe Namath

LINE UP IN FORMATION

Offensive Positions

C = Center	E = End	FL = Flanker
FB = Fullback	G = Guard	HB = Halfback
QB = Quarterback	SE = Split End	T = Tackle
TE = Tight End	TB = Tailback	

Football is a bit like a supersize game of chess. Teams line up their players on the gridiron in formations, or arrangements, for particular plays. Get the skinny on the offensive and defensive formations you're likely to see in the football nation.

For a refresher on who's who and what these positions do, see page 14.

OFFENSIVE FORMATIONS

The "T" Formation

If you play football, chances are you've seen your opponents line up in this T-shaped formation. Or maybe your own team uses it on plays to run the ball. Notice how it has three running backs lined up in a row behind the quarterback. This is the oldest formation in the football nation. As teams began to pass the ball more, it fell out of use among the pros.

The Pro "T" or Split "T" Formation

As pro teams bumped up the passing game, splitting the "T" formation gave them an extra wide receiver, the flanker, along with the split end and tight end for three receivers in all. With two running backs split, or positioned on opposite sides of the quarterback, this formation allows teams to run or pass the ball to either side of the field. So the defense has a tough time telling what the offense is going to do. Maybe that's why this is one of the pros' most popular offensive formations today.

The "I" Formation

Teams can run or pass from this formation in which a fullback and a tailback line up behind the quarterback in the shape of the letter "I." The fullback usually blocks for the tailback who carries the ball. The formation allows the tailback to hit full stride by the time he reaches the line of scrimmage. It also allows the tailback to see where his blockers are, see how the defense responds to the play, and spot holes in the defense to skedaddle through. Maybe it should be called "I Spy"!

Chess on the Gridiron

- A team chooses offensive formations that help their players do whatever they do best—run or pass the ball.

- When an offense takes a particular formation, they watch and wait to see how the defense lines up. Then if the defense lines up the same way the next time they take that formation, they have discovered a "characteristic" of the defense that they can try to use to their advantage.

- For example, once the offense knows what the defense is likely to do, they can adjust their play to break through any "soft spots" they see in the defense.

- The T formation has three running backs. Other formations have fewer running backs and more receivers. The fewer the running backs, the lesser the threat of the team's running attack and the greater the threat of its passing attack. Defenses know this and can adjust their coverage accordingly.

- What teams learn about their opponents in the first quarter helps them choose what formations and plays to run in the rest of the game.

Quick Answers to Hard-Hitting Questions

What's a "quarterback sneak"?

It's one of the oldest tricks in the playbook. The quarterback runs, carrying the ball, behind a guard who acts as a blocker, clearing the way. Teams go for the quarterback sneak when they need less than a yard, even just a few inches, to make a first down.

What's a "scramble"?

A play when the quarterback runs with the ball because all his receivers are covered.

DEFENSIVE FORMATIONS

The 4–3 Front

Today, most NFL teams use this defensive formation named for the number of linemen and linebackers, 4 and 3, in it. The 4–3 front can stop both the pass and the run. It also allows defenders to use man-to-man coverage (each player is responsible for covering a specific opponent), or zone coverage (each player is responsible for covering a specific zone or area of the field).

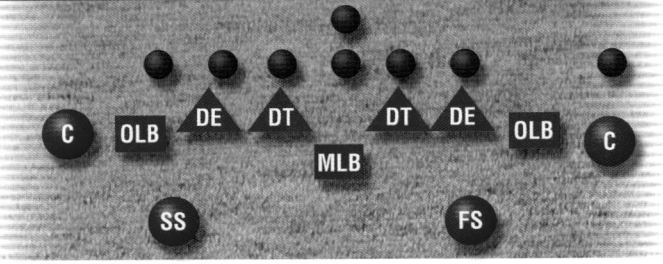

The 3–4 Front

No one defensive formation can cover all situations. So teams switch up as needed. The 3–4 front has three linemen and 4 linebackers up front and is more effective at stopping the pass than the 4–3 front. The extra linebacker can drop back to help cover passes and also run at the quarterback.

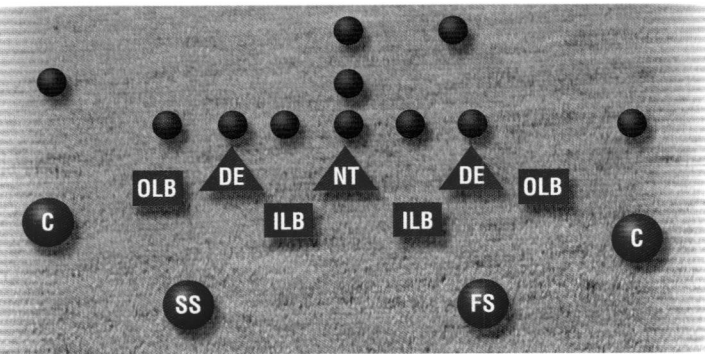

Defensive Positions

C	=	Cornerback
DE	=	Defensive End
DT	=	Defensive Tackle
FS	=	Free Safety
ILB	=	Inside Linebacker
MLB	=	Middle Linebacker
NT	=	Nose Tackle
OLB	=	Outside Linebacker
SS	=	Strong Safety

RULES & REGS

THE FIELD

Football is played on a field shaped like a rectangle so play can flow between two end zones.

Sideline When the ball and/or a player go beyond the sideline, they are out of bounds.

50-yard line This line runs down the middle of the field, dividing the field in half.

End line The line at each end of the field.

End zone The scoring zone—an area 10 yards long between the goal line and end line.

Goal post The post that stands at the center of the end line.

Goal line The goal line represents an imaginary wall, or plane, on the field. To score, a player has only to break the plane of the goal line with the ball.

Field numbers and yard lines On an NFL field, yard lines appear every 5 yards and field numbers every 10 yards to help players and fans tell how far a team has to move the ball for a first down.

Arrows A white arrow pointing toward the nearest end zone appears at every number except that for the 50-yard line.

Team bench Each team has its own bench about 12 feet behind the sideline. Players, coaches, team doctors, and trainers hang out in this area during games.

Hash marks White marks appear one yard apart to help officials spot the ball. All plays begin in the area between the two center sets of hash marks.

Chain crew or gang A group of three people: two rodmen who use a 10-yard-long chain attached to two rods to measure distances critical for first downs when called for by officials; and a boxman who holds a marker that shows where the ball is and which down it is.

Officials In the NFL, a group of seven officials oversees and enforces the rules of the game.

Goal post To score a field goal or an extra point after a touchdown, teams must kick the ball over the crossbar and between the two uprights of the goal post.

Uprights

Crossbar

NFL vs. CFL

Football is football, right? Nope. The rules of the game just aren't the same in the NFL and CFL. Check out the key differences:

- NFL teams have four downs, or chances, to make 10 yards whereas CFL teams have only three.

- NFL fields are 10 yards shorter and about 12 yards narrower than CFL fields.

- In the NFL, the goalposts stand on the end line but, in the CFL, they stand on the goal line.

- NFL teams play with eleven players apiece on the field while CFL teams play with twelve. This extra player takes a backfield position and results in different formations.

- NFL teams have a tight end, a player who lines up with the offensive linemen at the line of scrimmage. CFL teams often have a slotback, a player who is a large receiver like a tight end but can also do the job of a running back. The slotback lines up in the slot—the area between the offensive line and wide receiver (see right).

- In the NFL, offensive and defensive linemen set up "eyeball to eyeball" at the line of scrimmage—with only the length of the ball to separate them. In the CFL, defensive linemen set up one full yard away from the line of scrimmage.

- In the NFL, once players set up at the line of scrimmage, only one offensive player can move before the snap. However, in the CFL, every offensive player in the backfield is free to move except the quarterback.

- In the NFL, receivers need to have both feet in bounds for a catch to count as a reception but, in the CFL, receivers need only one foot in bounds.

- NFL punt returners can wave an arm in the air to signal a fair catch. This means opponents must let the returner catch the ball without interference and he cannot try to advance the ball downfield. No such fair catch rule exists in the CFL.

- In the CFL, a team can score a single point, called a rouge, on a kick or a punt if the ball goes into the end zone and the opponent doesn't return it out of the end zone, or if the ball sails through the end zone. In the NFL, no such scoring opportunities exist.

- Even the ball is different (see page 11).

The slotback (SB) lines up in the slot between the wide receiver (WR) and offensive linemen.

HOW TO PLAY

- The object of the game is to score points by moving the ball into the opponent's end zone.

- The team who scores the most points wins.

- In the NFL, each team may have no more than eleven players on the field at once. The team with the ball is on offense and the team without the ball is on defense.

- In the NFL, the team on offense has four downs—plays or chances—to move the ball 10 yards downfield. If they do not gain 10 yards, they must give up the ball.

HOW TO SCORE

There are five different ways to score points in football. Teams can score:

- 6 points for a touchdown by getting the ball into the other team's end zone.

- 1 point for an extra point after a touchdown by kicking the ball over the crossbar and between the uprights of the goal post.

- 2 points for a two-point conversion after a touchdown by getting the ball into the other team's end zone again.

- 3 points for a field goal by kicking the ball over the crossbar and between the uprights of the goal post.

- 2 points for a safety by tackling an opponent who has the ball in his own end zone or getting an opponent to take a penalty in his end zone. This allows teams to score points while on defense. Not only do they get the points, but they also get the ball!

FOOTBALL TALK

Air-it-out football — passing the ball on most plays.

Audible — codes called by the quarterback, at the line of scrimmage, to change the play.

Blitz — when more than five defensive players rush or run at the quarterback.

Block — making contact with an opponent using your hands, arms, and shoulders to move the opponent aside.

Bomb — a long pass.

Breaking the plane — when the ball breaks an imaginary wall, or plane, at the goal line to score.

Bullet pass — a well-thrown short pass.

Center — an offensive linemen who snaps the ball between his legs to the quarterback and calls signals for the line.

CFL — Canadian Football League.

Clear it out — when a wide receiver runs downfield luring defensive players on his tail to clear out an area for a shorter pass or running play.

Cleats — plastic, screw-in spikes or studs on the soles of players' shoes; also a term for shoes with cleats.

Completion — a forward pass caught inbounds by a receiver.

Conditioning — physical training.

Cornerback — a defensive player who lines up at a "corner" of a formation, usually opposite a wide receiver.

Defensive line — three or four defensive linemen who line up at the line of scrimmage.

Down — a period of play in which the offense tries to advance the ball.

End zone — the area at each end of the field where teams score by crossing the goal line with the ball.

Extra point — when a team scores a point after a touchdown by kicking the ball from the 2-yard line over the crossbar of the goal post between the uprights.

Fair catch — when a punt returner signals a catch by raising an arm in the air and waving it; then he can't run with the ball and players trying to tackle him can't touch him.

Field goal — when a team scores three points by kicking the ball from anywhere on the field over the crossbar of the goal post between the uprights.

First down — every time a team gets possession of the ball, it begins a first down; to get another first down, it must advance the ball at least 10 yards in four downs, or plays.

Formation — the way a team lines up for a particular play.

Free safety — a defensive player who lines up deep behind the middle linebacker to prevent big passing and running plays.

Fullback — a running back who often blocks or clears the way for a halfback who is carrying the ball.

Fumble — when an offensive player loses the ball by dropping it or by the force of a tackle.

Grey Cup — championship game of the CFL.

Guard — an offensive lineman who lines up next to the center.

Hail Mary — a pass thrown in desperation far away from the end zone.

Halfback — a running back who carries the ball, often following a fullback who clears the way.

Handoff — giving the ball to another player.

Hang time — length of time a ball is in the air during a punt or pass.

Huddle — when a team's players crowd together on the field to discuss the next play.

Incompletion — a forward pass that falls to the ground, is dropped by a receiver, or caught out of bounds.

Interception — a pass caught by an opponent.

Kickoff — kick that puts the ball into play at the start of the game and the third quarter as well as after every touchdown and field goal.

Line of scrimmage — where the ball sits on the field at the start of a play.

Linebacker — a defensive player who lines up behind the linemen.

Linemen — offensive and defensive players who line up at the line of scrimmage at the start of a play.

Man-to-man coverage — a style of defense in which each defender covers a specific offensive player.

Mental toughness — ability to deliver your best performance regardless of the competitive circumstances.

Middle linebacker — the "quarterback of the defense" who lines up behind the linemen and calls plays for the defense.

Neutral zone — the area between the offensive and defensive linemen at the line of scrimmage.

NFL — National Football League.

Nose tackle — a defensive player who lines up nose to nose with the center of the offensive line.

Offensive line — Five offensive linemen—a center flanked by two guards and two tackles outside the guards—who line up at the line of scrimmage.

Pass — when a player, usually the quarterback, throws the ball.

Pocket — an area the offensive line protects so the quarterback can pass the ball; the pocket extends 2 yards out from either offensive tackle and extends behind the offensive line to the team's end line and includes the tight end if he drops back to pass protect.

Point after touchdown (PAT) — see extra point.

Punt — when a player drops the ball and kicks it, usually on a fourth down.

Punter — a player who receives the ball from the snapper to drop it and kick it.

Quarterback — the player who leads the team's offense, receiving the ball from the center at the start of each play and then passing, handing off, or running with the ball.

Running back — an offensive player who runs with the ball, such as a halfback, fullback, or tailback.

Sack — tackling the quarterback behind the line of scrimmage before he can pass.

Safety — when the defense scores 2 points by tackling an opponent who has the ball in his own end zone or getting an opponent to take a penalty in his end zone.

Secondary — four defensive backs, two cornerbacks and two safeties, who line up behind the linebackers.

Special teams — players who take the field for kickoffs, punts, kickoff and punt returns, field goals and extra point attempts, and blocking field goals and extra point attempts.

Split end — a wide receiver who lines up on the line of scrimmage on the opposite side from the tight end.

Smashmouth football — running the ball on most plays to grind down a defense.

Snap — when the center throws the ball to the quarterback, punter, or ball holder for a kick attempt.

Strong safety — a defensive player who lines up behind the linebackers on the same side as the tight end.

Strong side — the side of the offensive line where the tight end lines up.

Super Bowl — championship game of the NFL.

Tackle — using your hands and arms to bring down an offensive player who has the ball; also a position on the offensive and defensive lines.

Tight end — a big wide receiver who lines up next to one of the offensive tackles and adds blocking power to the offensive line.

Two-point conversion — scoring 2 points after a touchdown with a pass or run into the other team's end zone rather than an extra point attempt.

Touchdown — scoring 6 points by getting the ball in the other team's end zone.

Visualization — mentally rehearsing moves so you can do them instinctively and successfully in games.

Weak side — the side of the offensive line without the tight end.

Wide receiver — an offensive player who uses speed and quickness to elude the defense and catch the ball.

Zone coverage — a style of defense in which each defender covers a specific zone or area of the field.

INDEX

Photo Credits

Roger Yip: Front cover, 3, 5 (girl), 17, 29, 30, 38, 39, 45, 50, 63;
Brian Snyder/Reuters: 4, 30 (Colts), 59 (Porter); Jeff Haynes/Reuters: 5
(Bears), 36; Bettmann/CORBIS: 6, 44, 47, 51 (Bradshaw), 58; Wilson
Sporting Goods: 9, 11 (Wilson Ball); World-rugby-museum.com:
10 (Ball); Robert Sorbo/Reuters: 11; Cumberland County Historical
Society: 12; Jason Cohn/Reuters: 13; Str Old/Reuters: 17; Allen
Fredrickson/Reuters: 18, 19; Berstein Associates/Getty Images: 20;
Reuters Photographer/Reuters: 23; Stephen Dunn/Getty Images: 25; AP
Photo/Mike Kullen: 26 (Snow Job); Andy Hayt /Sports Illustrated/Getty
Images: 26 (Dolphins); Michael Fabus/Getty Images: 27 (Heinz Field);
Gary Wiepert/Reuters: 27 (Brady); Vernon Biever/Getty Images: 28;
Mike Segar/Reuters: 32 (Freeney); Reuter Photographer/Reuters: 32;
Pierre Ducharme/Reuters: 35; Lucas Jackson/Reuters: 37; Jayne Oncea/
Icon SMI: 39 (Hayes); Mark Wonderlin, courtesy of Schutt Sports:
40 (orange helmet), 41 (inside helmet); Ray Stubblebine/Reuters: 41
(Smith); Hulton-Deutsch Collection/CORBIS: 41 (full-face helmet);
Jeff Haynes/Reuters: 43; Scott Boehm/Getty Images: 49 (Anderson);
Mike Stone/Reuters: 49 (Owens); Matt Sullivan/Reuters: 51 (Manning);
Jessica Rinaldi/Reuters: 53; Mike Blake/Reuters: 57 (Tomlinson);
Adam Hunger/Reuters: 57 (Moss); Rebecca Cook/Reuters: 57 (Hester);
Scott Audette/Reuters: 57 (Reed); Michael Zagaris/Getty Images:
59 (Stabler); Walter Iooss Jr./Sports Illustrated/Getty Images: 59
(Namath); All other images: Royalty-free (iStockphoto, Dreamstime)

Answers

Try This, page 35: Smiling on the outside when you feel nervous or
scared on the inside is part of what's called "outside-in training." You
do something on the outside—in the way you present yourself, act, or
behave—that your brain and body interpret as feeling good and this
makes you feel good inside. Smiling, for example, releases chemicals
in your brain that trigger relaxation and feelings of happiness. In fact,
smiling is one of the best "outside-in" things any player can do.

Try This, page 51: Throws without spin tend to send the ball tumbling
through the air end over end on a crooked path. Whereas, throws with
spin can send the ball nose-first through the air and keep it stable as
it flies. This helps the ball travel on a straight path horizontally, and
travel farther and faster than a throw without spin. What's more, this
gives your throw more accuracy and makes it easier to catch.

sippewissett

sippewissett

Or, Life on a Salt Marsh

Tim Traver

Illustrations by Bobbi Angell

CHELSEA GREEN PUBLISHING
WHITE RIVER JUNCTION, VERMONT

Editor: John Barstow
Managing Editor: Marcy Brant
Project Editor: Collette Leonard
Copy Editor: Kate Mueller
Proofreader: Eliza Thomas
Designer: Peter Holm, Sterling Hill Productions
Design Assistant: Daria Hoak, Sterling Hill Productions
Map by Molly O'Halloran

Printed in the United States
First printing, August 2006
10 9 8 7 6 5 4 3 2 1

Our Commitment to Green Publishing

Chelsea Green sees publishing as a tool for cultural change and ecological stewardship. We strive to align our book manufacturing practices with our editorial mission, and to reduce the impact of our business enterprise on the environment. We print our books and catalogs on chlorine-free recycled paper, using soy-based inks, whenever possible. This book may cost slightly more because we use recycled paper, and we hope you'll agree that it's worth it. Chelsea Green is a member of the Green Press Initiative (www. greenpressinitiative.org), a nonprofit coalition of publishers, manufacturers, and authors working to protect the world's endangered forests and conserve natural resources. *Sippewissett* was printed on Rolland Enviro Edition 100, a 100 percent post–consumer waste recycled paper supplied by R.R. Donnelley.

Library of Congress Cataloging-in-Publication Data

Traver, Tim, 1954-
Sippewissett, or, Life on a salt marsh / Tim Traver.
  p. cm.
ISBN-13: 978-1-933392-14-1 (hardcover)
ISBN-10: 1-933392-14-2 (hardcover)
 1. Natural history—Massachusetts—Great Sippewissett Marsh. 2. Natural history—Massachusetts—Little Sippewissett Marsh. I. Title. II. Title: Sippewissett. III. Title: Life on a salt marsh.
QH105.M4T73 2006
508.744'92--dc22
                    2006013664

Chelsea Green Publishing Company
Post Office Box 428
White River Junction, Vermont 05001
(802) 295-6300
www.chelseagreen.com

TO MY PARENTS
with love and gratitude

contents

list of illustrations

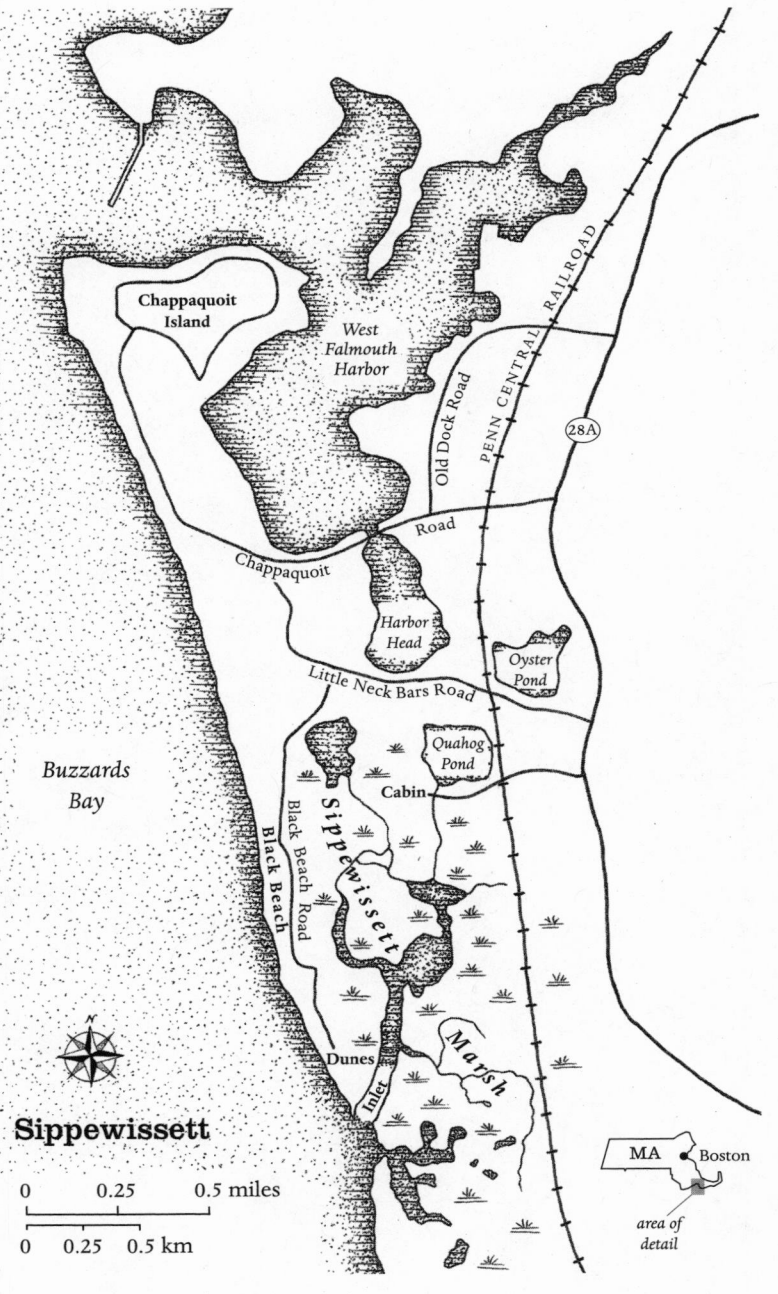

Chappaquoit Island

West Falmouth Harbor

Old Dock Road

PENN CENTRAL RAILROAD

28A

Chappaquoit Road

Harbor Head

Oyster Pond

Little Neck Bars Road

Quahog Pond

Buzzards Bay

Cabin

Sippewissett

Black Beach Road

Black Beach

N

Marsh

Dunes

Inlet

Sippewissett

| 0 | 0.25 | 0.5 miles |

| 0 | 0.25 | 0.5 km |

MA • Boston

area of detail

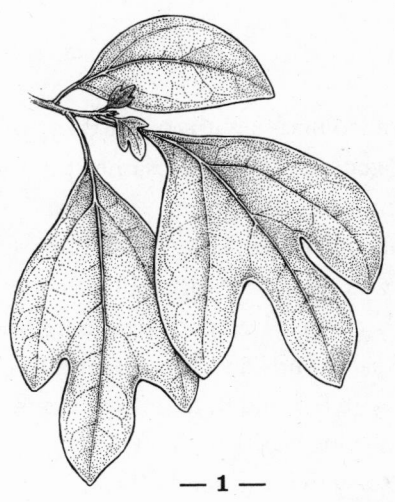

— 1 —

home

For love all love of other sights controls,
And makes one little room an everywhere.
　　—JOHN DONNE, from "The Good Morrow"

There is always something for which there is no
accounting. Take, for example, the whole world.
　　—LEONARD MICHAELS

IN THE EARLIEST days of May with the crab apples and the sassafras trees in flower, a marvelous event occurs on the salt ponds of Sippewissett. The striped bass return. They come up from the Chesapeake into Buzzards Bay and through the inlet into the marsh, then up Agassiz's creek by the oyster lady's house and through the culvert into a small pond called Quahog Pond. Or they swim into West Falmouth Harbor and up into its far reaches to the Head of the Harbor past our house and up a short creek full of glacial boulders encrusted with seaweeds and through a culvert under the railroad tracks to a slightly larger pond called Oyster Pond bordering on Route 28-A.

The bass's arrival coincides with the hatching of clam worms. These are of the genera *Nereis*, the same type of marine segmented worm nineteenth-century scientists collected and brought to the lab in Woods Hole for embryological studies. Reddish in color, with two rows of undulating flagella running laterally the length of their bodies, they emerge out of the bottom sediments of salt ponds and harbors and freely swim close to the surface. They're fast and frenetic swimmers. Wiggling this way and that and darting swiftly up and down, they move with a sort of nervous ecstasy that can send shimmering dimples across the entire surface of salt ponds and shallow bays—looking for sex, of course. Unrequited in love, alas, they are also eaten in abundance. The bass, ravenous from their long migration up the coast, swirl about and slash up the surface of the ponds and, at first, take whatever looks like a worm.

We fly fishermen, with fair worm imitations and average casting ability, can cast either from shore or kayak and catch big fish. But by the third day of the hatch, the fish have grown bellies full of worms and become reticent to take anything but a live, inch-and-a-half-long, red, flagella-rimmed undulating worm, rejecting most artificial baits. Feeding slows and becomes more selective. If you miss the first few days, you might cast for three hours with pink or red sparkle flies, poppers, deceivers, spooks, duns, muddlers, trout flies, or even kitchen spoons, red shoestrings, bark mulch—and catch nothing. It's maddening. But welcome to paradise. It's the madness fishermen live for.

Paradise is on Cape Cod. It contains our home and these ponds. It's a labyrinthine country of dune grass–covered horizons, stony dirt roads, scrub too thick to walk through unless you know the paths, old trees, rickety docks, boats, low-tide mud, and sunlight that dapples the cove. It's a postage-stamp nation, with a center of salt marsh—a wet, horizontally branching saltwater tree whose trunks and burls are creeks and potholes teeming with a universe of creatures that breathe together by virtue of tides. Named Sippewissett, which in the Mashpee Wampanoag language means "little cove" or "little river," our name for it was simply "the inlet." And it was truly the gate by which we entered a magic world—an atavistic land of clamming, crabbing, swimming, and wandering—far down at the end of Black Beach, but accessible to us through the woods behind the house. It was our own little Eden, where the world is still being made.

Salt marshes, scientists tell us, are microcosms of the world, held together by invisible strings of inscrutable complexity. By chemistries, geomorphologies, and biocontingencies that make the world one. Sippewissett, I can tell you, is a fine place in which to thrash around at the beginning of a life. I can tell you that dirt roads and dunes are good for barefoot souls. An inlet may not be LA's mean streets, but it has love, death, and fiddler crab gangs. It has clam and quahog money. Sippewissett Marsh, science's microcosm and a cultural landscape, transforms things. It both endures in the heart and fills the stomach. Here, a day can have a month of salt water and sun in it, and life, in spite of the great social distances that separate us from nature, can approach the nearly indigenous again. I say that with a straight face. In my youth, bankers built bonfires on the beach and sang lusty sailor songs with old friends. Corporate executives, clergy, and other members of the ruling class took off their cuff links and collars, put on their cutoffs, and went a-clamming in the mud. We children, free from doing time in schools, disappeared in a scruffy, barely clad pack and came back only when we got hungry. We plied the waters in small aluminum boats and wandered the dunes at night. We hit tennis balls on the backboards of a sandy tennis court until it got too dark to see. Tried cigarettes. Discovered first beer and first kiss. First love. First illicit drugs. Mostly, we survived.

There is something close to the aboriginal in all this, in spite of our one-hundred-year transformation to hydrocarbon man, to plastic clothing, gas engines, autos for legs, prisonlike schools, and industrial farms. There in those cricket nights, redolent of honeysuckle, we were reborn for a few brief weeks and experienced a fundamental joy in being alive, in being part of a place and part of a clan. Sippewissett contained everything essential. In it, we kids were surrounded by that potent combination of influences: summer in New England, family love, friends, salt water, earth, and our own beings. "One little room, an everywhere." Of course, the poet Donne was writing of romantic love. But is it a different species of love that extends to home? And can it prevail? Paradise with a small *p*, home, romantic love? Can the whole of it, and can we, endure?

I would like to know the answer to that question of endurance. Durability. Not immortality. My five brothers and sisters are grown. Between us we have seventeen children. Our parents are old, and aging with a kind of grace and humor most pray for. By the end of the coming summer, they will entrust ownership of the house and our little piece of world to us—the third generation. I hope we can do as well by it. What kind of stewards of our place and the community will we baby boomers make? How long can something good and important like a home in paradise with a salt marsh at its heart remain strong, healthy? How long can it go on providing? How long can it be passed on intact? Into how many parts can a small ownership be subdivided? If small places like our Sippiwissett—which isn't really ours—are microcosms of the big planet home, then these questions are important. What threatens our durability? Sea level rise and global warming? Yes.

Poisoned clams? Yes. Too much privacy? Complacency, greed, and a loss of heart? Probably. Something deeper? Vital connections to the people, birds, fish, night around us? Some loss of sacred bonds? Something beyond that?

Our house is ordinary. It's no historical gem or architectural oddity. Plainly attractive, it isn't special in any way. It doesn't sit boldly on a promontory. It doesn't have much history. It's the second home of Everyman if every man could have one. It isn't grand enough to be a mariner's landmark like the houses of Chappaquoit at the mouth of the harbor, not a kind of beautiful monstrosity like the big house at Wings Neck. Our house is small, in scale with the place, and full of Yankee wit and practicality. It was built by the same people who once farmed the land. They subdivided it as a sort of final harvest, and now live off the residue: the building trades, lawn care, real estate, and lawyering.

Great Sippewissett Marsh behind us is, in most respects, ordinary as well. While it does contain some noteworthy biodiversity, it is not one of the Nature Conservancy's Last Great Places. It is not a wilderness—"A Last Terrifying Place" where one encounters one's utter insignificance—where "the hand of man has not yet trod [sic]." It has been trod by many hands. Ten thousand years before European settlement, ancestors to the Mashpee Wampanoag Tribe lived here. They left shell middens on some of the small upland island hammocks on the marsh. Since European settlement, farmers have cut timber off the uplands for houses and boat building, and they have grazed cattle and sheep on the lower ground and cut salt hay for feed and mulch. The marsh has been host to fish traps and salt vats. Salt was produced by pumping salt water with windmills through hollowed logs to evaporators. Thoreau, on his first trip to the Cape, delighted in these windmills and "turtle shell" tubs. Between 1776 and 1870, there were more than 440 individual saltworks operating on the shores of Cape Cod Bay and Buzzards Bay.

The marsh has been well used and not so well used. It is not the empty desert of the New Testament or Old, though it has its temptations. It palls in size and importance next to the great marshes north of Boston. It's so small and so easy to violate—barely five hundred acres if you count every inch of its fringe of uplands and dunes—that it hardly gets the attention of the local shellfish warden. Its clam flats are closed thanks to high coliform counts and have been for years. It has little economic worth today, not counting the dollar value of its ecological and recreational functions, which can be tallied up, though I question the wisdom of doing so. When it comes to enduring, I suppose knowing the economic value of nature's beauty and ecological functions is important, but economy is a poor measure for most of what is truly valuable. Pricelessness is a better, more encompassing, measure. What is pricelessness worth to us? What are our children worth to us? Our cedar trees? Our stony beaches? And what is, say, four hundred years of not only enduring but thriving, of endlessly arriving into our places, worth? Say four thousand years? This is like a Jeopardy answer to the question, What is legacy? A salt marsh is legacy ground, even a small and ordinary one like Sippewissett. But what is ordinary? Is any piece of ground on the planet ordinary? Aside from the metaphysical aspect to the question of ordinariness, Sippewissett does have its claim to extraordinary fame. There is a scientific legacy that sets it apart, and no dollar value can come close to expressing what that legacy is worth.

I knew, but only vaguely, at the age of fifteen, that our little marsh with its mummichogs, glass shrimp, and penny-sized flounder had long served as an outdoor laboratory where scientists put on their rubber boots, rolled up their sleeves, and went to work. I knew nothing of their work, only that it happened over a period of many years. They started coming in the mid-1970s, alone, in pairs, and in small groups, from nearby Woods Hole. Sometimes they had on white lab coats and carried clipboards, but more often than not they wore cutoffs and old tennis sneakers like us of the banker tribe. They carried test tubes, nets, probes, pumps, scopes, and buckets. They entered the marsh on the far side along paths I didn't know and conducted their mysterious studies generally away from our corners, though sometimes we'd see them seining fish or taking samples of plankton or bottom sediments in the main and side channels of the inlet. The scientists and their graduate students came from research institutions in Woods Hole, such as Woods Hole Oceanographic Institute, and beyond, including the Marine Biological Lab (MBL), the MBL's Ecosystem Center, and the Boston University Marine Program (BUMP). Over the years, biologists from Harvard, Yale, Tufts, the Universitiy of Massachusetts, and from across the globe found their way to Sippewissett.

Woods Hole, the oldest center of marine science in the United States and containing the largest independent oceanographic institute, is the Rome of ocean studies. All watery scientific roads at one time or another lead there, bringing the best minds, the newest ideas, and emergent scientific technologies to this town sitting at the water lane between Buzzards Bay and Vineyard Sound— the meeting place of southern and northern Atlantic waters. The first scientific enterprise in Woods Hole arrived in 1870 with the establishment of the U.S. Fish Commission—progenitor of today's National Oceanic and Atmospheric Administration's U.S. Marine Fisheries. And so began a different kind of questioning. What is the world? And how do we save it? Woods Hole became home to the emerging science of ecology. And it has been that for over a hundred and thirty years. Other institutions moved in or sprouted up anew—like minds attract like minds and from these sprang new institutions—so that today some six hundred scientists, including marine chemists, molecular biologists, ecologists, physicists, soil scientists, shoreline engineers, microbiologists, and shipwreck pirates, live and work in and around Woods Hole at a dozen or so institutions. Earth Station, Woods Hole. Scientists regularly sail from Woods Hole to travel the oceans and return home with cargoes of numbers. The twenty-first century's version of whaling expeditions harpoon new data on the workings of the biogeochemical interactions of ocean, air, and land. Earth as one body appears to be the universally central and important reality to our lives, and Earth's splendid phenotype and genotype are unfolding in Woods Hole. It is a place where, to borrow from W. H. Auden, who was writing about Woods Hole, "shabby curates" like myself can walk among scientists, the "dukes . . . the true men of action of our time." It's a place where science has been enthroned. Onto its hallowed stage come Nobel laureates, world-renowned biologists, authors including Rachel Carson and Lewis Thomas, and the Teals. Sippewissett has played more than a bit part in this story of science and place. It's been collecting ground and hunting ground, favorite haunt of scientists on a stroll and outdoor laboratory—first Marine Biological Lab director Charles Otis Whitman's "biological farm."

With its history of significant research supporting them, two young professors from Woods Hole arrived at Sippewissett in 1975 to begin a new kind of scientific undertaking. Dr. John Teal from Woods Hole Oceanographic Institute and Dr. Ivan Valiela from Boston University teamed up to create a study of pollution impacts on marshes and estuarine ecosystems. To do so, they had to establish long-term study plots that could be monitored over many years. Sippewissett was a convenient proving ground: small, contained, and close by. Onto these they began methodically applying nitrate fertilizers, some laced with faint traces of heavy metals. Initial funding from the National Science Foundation was directed at one seemingly simple question in applied science: Was it conceivable that salt marshes could serve as fourth stage treatment plants for sewage sludge waste? Back in the late 1960s and early 1970s, the federal government and its newly minted Environmental Protection Agency (EPA) had begun in earnest to address water pollution problems. Sewage treatment plants were sprouting up in cities and towns everywhere, and they were working. In my own town here in Woodstock, Vermont, the Ottauquechee River was so polluted with dyes from tanning factories and woolen mills active in the 1950s that it ran red and sometimes green. It smelled so putrid that it drove Little Theatre goers back inside early during intermission in spite of sweltering summer temperatures. The town selectmen, in a fit of Yankee obstinance, refused to spend any local money to match federal funds for sewage treatment until a court order and the threat of arrest forced them to do so. Now, our river runs much cleaner.

What to do, though, with highly enriched nutrient sludge wastes generated by sewage treatment plants—the remains of the treatment process? An explosive question, literally, when you consider the potential uses of nitrates and their ammoniated cousins in weapons manufacturing. The goal of Sippiwisset research in the early 1970s was to map the effects of excess nutrients and metal pollutants on the system. How much carbon were they producing from sunlight and where was the excess, if any, going? To answer these questions required a depth of understanding about the chemical functioning of salt marshes that didn't exist. It required an understanding of the chemical transformations that occur inside anaerobic and aerobic bottom sediments. It required knowing, if not the names of hitherto unknown thousands of bacteria types, at least the functions of some of these organisms, since a salt marsh is, from an engineering point of view, a vast chemical factory—microbes transforming organic compounds faster than you can say "stick."

To science, Sippewissett was a nested set of black boxes that boggled the mind. It required a complexity in ecological systems modeling unknown at the time the studies began. Though one of the principal researchers, John Teal, had already put in years of work on salt marshes at Sapelo Island, Georgia, and with his first wife Mildred, written the highly acclaimed *Life and Death of the Salt Marsh*, so little was known about the intricacies of salt marsh ecosystem functions that the whole system had to be broken down to be reassembled again and understood. Teal's and Valiela's studies morphed into hundreds of side investigations. Though the end in mind was to apply science to solve some of our most pressing environmental problems, it was basic science that ruled the day.

For a dozen years or so beginning in the early 1970s, Sippewissett was the most intensively studied salt marsh in the world. The Salt Marsh Project at Boston University, with Valiela in charge, employed more than thirty faculty and graduate students. They worked at the marsh for years, considered the various components of function, then began to piece together a picture of the functions of the whole. Sippewissett became the alpha marsh, and the lessons learned there about nutrient transformations and energy flow became textbook models for ecological patterns and processes found in salt marshes everywhere. What were we kids doing all this time? Eating clams and growing up.

In my mind it is an easy jump from Sippewissett, microcosm, womb of science and childhood, to Earth as home. Marsh and

Earth as holy grail—sunlight and water pour in and green plants, clams, blue crabs, fish, and birds spill out, like grapes transformed to wine overflowing a silver cup. But things are going wrong at home and in the world. In spite of all that we have learned about how the world works and our role and place in things, ecosystems are declining. Losses outstrip knowledge. Before we knew how wetlands functioned in this country, we'd filled nearly half of them in. Once we learned about the critical nature of wetlands, we got busy filling in the other half. It's as if the sciences that focused for years on understanding how the world works now enable destruction. Worse, no one seems to care. Have we enriched ourselves to the point where our ears are deaf with the clang of the forge? We know how to do and make things. But have we lost the knowledge of how to be in the world?

What does it mean to save home, the place where we live? To be right with the world? A physical place, it turns out, can be preserved, its biodiversity mostly intact, even as its biogeochemical functions, its capacity to regenerate abundance in perpetuity, and its cultural nuances and meanings fade. Is it scientific knowledge or is it some mandate from the heart that matters most when it comes to stewardship? Dr. Sylvia Earle, distinguished scientist and pioneer in deep ocean exploration, laid out the promise and missed opportunity of science when she noted that we've learned more through scientific inquiry in the past twenty-five years than in all the preceding years of human history, yet we've also lost more in the last fifty years and more has been fundamentally changed than in all of human history. How can this be? Dr. George Woodwell, first director of the Marine Biological Laboratory's Ecosystem Center in Woods Hole, made virtually the same observation. "The world is laying itself out before us in a very lucid way," he said to a room full of scientists at the twenty-fifth anniversary of the Ecosystem Center. And in nearly the same breath he added, "The systems that serve to support life on Earth are on the verge of failing." We are on the brink of botching it on the Cape. We have overenriched ourselves to the point where the eelgrass is dying and the scallop beds are disappearing. The fish declines continue, and we squabble over property boundaries and rights of way. But somehow, at the very most local of local levels, a line must be drawn. And there, within those arbitrary lines around home, our hope resides.

How can it be that we've learned so much about how the world works and during the same time lost so much? Theologian Thomas Berry refers to this disconnection as a "mind-tormenting ambivalence." He writes, "We have such a vast understanding of the universe and how it functions, and yet we manifest such an inability to use this knowledge beneficially either for ourselves or for any other mode of Earthly being." This discontinuity appears to be a streak of latent self-destructionism, or even the belief that a self-wrought deluge is necessary or inevitable. Rapidly, it seems, we are all becoming homeless.

Our future, it appears, is one of being bound up together, reds and blues, believers and nonbelievers, practicing the best of what ecology, harnessed to the transcendent and to home places we know and care about, is capable of delivering. Ecology, from *oikos*, the Greek word for "household," and *logos*, "knowledge," is our science of home. Home science's prospects and its predictions are, by and large, hopeful. It has, after all, given us a vision of one world utterly interconnected, and mysteriously so. We will endure, in part, by learning its measures and acting by what it proscribes for clean water and air, and, in part, by loving what is immeasurable—the sound of wings at night and all that is undeniably magic in every ordinary day.

Earle stepped outside the framework of her scientific mind to suggest that saving home requires something bordering on giving self up to spiritual mystery. Science isn't enough, she said. It will take a giving up, a getting beyond ourselves to fully realize the power of science to sustain us. We need to identify with a greater Self, she suggested, to save ourselves. We need to leave ourselves behind and embrace something bigger. Of course, Earle would be such a "thought diver." She held records for the longest and deepest dives into the ocean by a woman. The idea that caring for the world requires a deep dive into reflective self-understanding and, paradoxically, to surrendering the self isn't new. It may be one of the oldest civilized ideas around, this enlargement of the notion of local community to global village. Of dying to live. Of accepting death—both the good old-fashioned compost kind and the metaphorical kind. A salt marsh, with all its prismatic and moving watery surfaces, is a fine place for reflecting—a mirror to the soul of the universe.

How can our different ways of knowing places—through science, through memory and history, and through self-discovery and spirit—become synthesized into stewardship, which is the work of sustaining the world? How do we save both the soul of a place like Sippewissett and our own souls?

This suite of connected stories is the product of several years of traveling home: of reading; of sneaking around and listening; of remembering and reflecting; of spending time in the marsh fishing with a religious fundamentalist brother-in-law scientist; of digging sand castles with children; of spending time listening to scientists and citizen soldier activists; of diving into eelgrass beds; of hiding out in a small cabin on the last ten acres of woodland at Sippewissett; of listening to wind and birds at night; of running into old girlfriends; of remembering just how charmed, happy, and hexed my childhood was. These are stories of binding together scientific understanding with family fidelity and love of place. Undoing the excesses of the twentieth century may require a lot of undoing bad things and of renewing our native sense of being bound up together at home. Home is the place in the world where everything arrives over time. Home is where we are going.

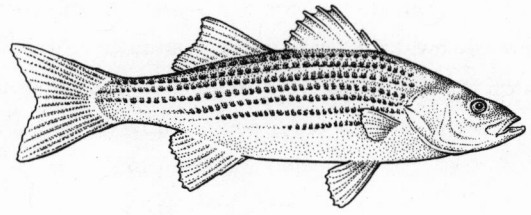

fish

Dear Baird,

. . . I have been collecting the small fish [of the Bosphorus Strait in Turkey] for several weeks and now have about 20 species . . . the larger fish are interesting but I don't know what to do with them . . . some of the specimens have lost the back fin, the fisherman, ignorant wretch, cut it out because it was poisonous. . . . The lizards are almost impossible to catch besides the people are afraid of them.

GEORGE PERKINS MARSH in a letter to
Spencer Fullerton Baird, 1850

My dear Mr. Marsh:

Do not measure my affection by the length of the epistles I write, but inversely—if I had a dozen hands, I would keep one going all the time in writing news to you, but I haven't and so I must be content with one every month…don't be distressed about the last keg.

The things came well . . . the pockelung was quite sufficient . . . when are you coming home? I am tired of having you away longer. If I were a politician, I would petition for your recall. I am praying for the election of a Low, that he may order you home.

SPENCER FULLERTON BAIRD in a letter to
George Perkins Marsh, 1851

In the loveliest town of all, where the houses were white and high and the elm trees were green and higher than the houses, where the front yards were wide and pleasant and the back yards were bushy and worth finding out about, where the streets sloped down to the stream and the stream flowed quietly under the bridge, where the lawns ended in orchards and the orchards ended in fields and the fields ended in pastures and the pastures climbed the hill and disappeared over the top toward the wonderful wide sky, in this loveliest of all towns Stuart stopped to get a drink of sarsaparilla.

E. B. WHITE, from *Stuart Little*

MY WIFE SUSPECTS that fishing is the whole reason I started spending so much time at Great Sippewissett Marsh. We live with our three children in Vermont. I think she believes that I've thrown away a decent career in land conservation to fish my way into divorce and probably oblivion—not necessarily in that order, for she knows I depend on her, and she on me. And I tell her, "Dearest, your fear is totally unfounded." I've always loved fishing, and fishing has always been a small bone of contention in our otherwise worthy marriage—long before my turning fifty, my shift in jobs, my shopping at thrift stores, my love affair with an accordion and an old Gibson mandolin, and my desire to spend more time with a salt marsh. "But I love you more." And divorce is not a good option, certainly not before oblivion. From my perspective, anyway.

"Sure," she said obstinately. "You're doing research. Is that why you've packed three fishing rods?" "Well, there is a fish story or two to be told," I offered.

"Uh-huh," she said.

"Look," I said, backing slowly down the driveway. "I have grant money and I'm going now. See you and the kids in June." She was walking beside the car on its downward slippery slope.

"Fine," she said. Always beware when your wife says "fine." Does she mean *everything is fine,* or is she ticketing you?

"And don't forget to send in your invoices," I said. My wife is a consultant, since her recent job change. I count on her income, which she has managed to boost while I've managed to finagle a major cut in mine.

"You forgot a kiss," she said.

"Fine," I said and rolled down my window. Then, one thing led to another, and I wasn't going anywhere.

I did get off a few days later. Actually, it is very hard to leave family and Vermont in May. Finally, after interminable winter, the ground is thawing. I'm the kind of person who hates leaving anywhere. My family and friends, the quasi-religious Unitarian Universalist community, the garden, the town, the occasional journalistic gig, and music hold me. It's close to perfection here in May in Vermont in the hills. We live on a tributary brook that flows into the Ottauquechee River a quarter of a mile away. Our village brings to mind E. B. White's perfect place in *Stuart Little* called Ames Crossing, and his perfect sentence that begins that chapter. But we do Ames Crossing one better because our river is filled with trout. We've got cows, bushes, fields, orchards, sheep, and forests and pastures that climb up over the tops of hills. We've got horses grazing on the hills. In a kind of class reversal, the rich among us keep sheep and the poor have horses. My neighbors cannot seem to trap the flying squirrels in their attics without calling me up four times a day. The neighborhood children sled down the middle of the town road after a snowstorm before the sand truck arrives. We even have a general store where you can get your mail and buy beer on account. There's a bit of the eighteenth and nineteenth centuries still here. This was the home of George Perkins Marsh, fountainhead of the American conservation movement. Frederick Billings and Lawrence Rockefeller, devotees of Marsh, followed him and further advanced the natural resource stewardship cause. Together, the three are enshrined in our own national park. And there is plenty of make-believe here. Stuart Little could pull up in his tiny red sports coupe, sit on the concrete steps of our redbrick general store, with its own tiny post office, sip a root beer, and feel the morning sun golden on his whiskers. No one would bat an eye. Our three children have explored the stream with toy boats not unlike Stuart's trinket canoe. Why would anyone want to leave?

But there *are* fish stories on the marsh. And fish to catch in May. Salt marshes are important sanctuaries, breeding grounds, and nurseries for pelagic fish—fish matrimonial places. Without salt marsh habitat, many fish species would disappear. Fishermen know this intuitively and through observation to be true. Scientists strive to know it by the numbers, by calculation, determined to understand the numerical causes of abundance and decline. And that means seeking to understand how nutrient cycling within estuarine systems works—how land and water link.

But it's difficult to put boundaries on these aqua-terra systems. Everything connects to a marsh. Oceans are large; fish are small and migratory. The air is big. Marine food webs are vastly more complicated than land webs, and in salt marshes, which are land-marine interfaces affected by changes to the land and the daily influx of salt water, relationships are more complex still.

Many Woods Hole researchers have conducted research on fish populations at Sippewissett over the years. Ecosystem Center researchers Bruce Peterson, John Hobbie, and particularly Linda Deegan have looked at ecosystem structure, the effects of marsh fertilization, population dynamics and nutrient cycling and energy exports in the form of fish. Deegan, who earned her PhD at Louisiana State University with an ecological study of menhaden in the Gulf of Mexico, spends more time studying rivers in Alaska now, but she still comes back home to publish at Sippewissett where her work over the years has been more about minnows and less about lunkers. Understanding mummichogs, killifish, and their miniscule kin's relationship to food sources in the marsh and to the predatory fish that eat little fish helped solve the puzzle of a salt marsh's nutrient export system and helped quantify a salt marshes' value to global fish production. Deegan is connected to a long line of esteemed fish people doing science out of Woods Hole. Fisheries conservation began there.

Plenty has been written by science historians about the earliest years of scientific development at Woods Hole. It all started with Spencer Baird and his family's arrival in June 1863 for a summer of collecting and observing the nature of the region's fisheries. In June 1870 he set up again, this time intent on establishing a formal study of fish declines. Baird was officially appointed as the first (unpaid) director of the U.S. Commission of Fish and Fisheries in 1871. The commission evolved over the years into the Bureau of Marine Fisheries and then into National Marine Fisheries, a branch of the National Oceanic and Atmospheric Administration. Their small marine aquarium—free to the general public—is a highlight to any trip to Woods Hole. Other institutions followed, to the point where the Woods Hole waterfront became so crowded with their piers and ships, labs, offices, libraries, and classrooms that science development had to occur elsewhere, far from the waterfront. Louis Agassiz's Anderson School of Natural History came and went, from 1873 to 1874, on nearby Penikese Island. The Marine Biological Lab, partly inspired by Anton Dohrn's marine lab in Naples, Italy, was established in 1888. Woods Hole Oceanographic Institute, perhaps the best-known marine institution in Woods Hole, came onto the scene in 1930. In 1975, the MBL established the Ecosystem Center. Now you can find the National Academy of Sciences in Woods Hole, the Woods Hole Research Center, the Boston University's Marine Program, SEA Semester, and the U.S. Geological Survey. I'm sure I haven't included them all. Why the interest in Woods Hole? Partly because it's just a very fine place to live, and partly because the need for information changed over time. The job was always too big for any one of them. They specialize and then collaborate, we trust, to get the picture of the whole and to make their basic scientific enterprise an effectively applied one. Spencer Baird led the way.

I could spend all my time in the libraries at Woods Hole researching the history of fisheries conservation, but as I reasoned with my wife, Earth stewardship is as much about connecting to the spirit of the place as it is about understanding the science of it. It's about catching. We need both to endure. Large fish are big flashy objects of desire fashioned by millions of years of natural selection. Trying to catch one at night is like hunting for a star.

And it's through desire—star hunting—that we catch the spirit of things. Sometimes even minnows will do. Netted in large numbers, especially the dartlike Atlantic silversides, carefully washed free of all sand, and fried whole in hot oil, minnows, or "white bait," with a little white wine, are delicious. Fisherman, especially the unreasonably dedicated ones and those that make their living at it, know something about their quarry, as much or more sometimes than the scientist working the numbers off a flame spectrometer.

I arrived at the empty house in the afternoon. There is something so visceral about coming home, even to a closed-up house, musty from winter dormancy and unnaturally quiet. Once over the green bridge and down the road through the dunes, my senses begin to anticipate their pleasure—smell things before they arrive, see things that aren't there yet. The perfume of low-tide mud, even if it's high tide, the sound of gravel under the car wheels before the car arrives, the creak of the garden gate, though the gate is long since gone. Inside, it's all vertical pine boards. A small desk and daybed stand at the west end of the large front room. The fireplace in the middle with its mantle clock and last October's tide chart. I wound the clock on the mantle, turned on the propane heater, pulled on my old black rubber boots, and wandered down the lane to the ponds by the tracks.

Our house sits facing a small cove fringed by cordgrass. Across the cove is a stand of dark green juniper. The roads are narrow and dirt. There are only two of them. To get anywhere, you follow them to the beach or dunes or marsh, or to woods between marsh and salt pond where a cabin sits. One road leads to the beach, dunes, and the west side of the marsh. The other skirts the cove then dead-ends at the railroad tracks. A right on the tracks takes you out to the east side of the marsh, a left takes you to one of two salt ponds.

There was nothing going on at Oyster Pond. But up the tracks a quarter mile, walking in the direction of Woods Hole—careful to avoid the poison ivy that had begun unfurling—I found the fish rising and splashing on Quahog Pond. Roger, an elfin man and local fishing guide, was already there floating in his red inflatable boat on the far side of the pond. Roger lives on the edge of the pond in a pretty shingled house hidden by willows. Scattered over his lawn is an assortment of small boats. Rods of many vintages lean against the rails of his porch, and waders are drying there. His red guide boat rests on its trailer in the drive. My kayak was snoozing in amongst his clutter of small boats. I hauled it to the pond.

Roger is no slouch when it comes to knowing the fish. He studies their whereabouts and habits with scientific zeal. It's his business through spring, summer, and fall, through winds, tides, and water temperature fluctuations to know fish and their changing quarry. Fish move with generalized regularity and particular unpredictability. They follow a changing procession of baits, from clam worms to herring, mackerel, sand eels, American eels, silversides, and mummichogs, up into the marsh and out into the bay. Bass and bluefish are here all summer chasing silversides, but the prized false albacore and the swift bonita don't arrive until August. Huge schools of menhaden arrive in fall, too, and the large blues and stripers chase them up and down the bay. It matters to Roger to know them all; catching fish is how he catches his living. And he knows how to fish the marsh as well as I do, though he's a newer arrival, preferring a low tide at night when the marsh becomes a slow-moving creek to my preference for high tide when you can float through it all. Every dark corner of it can hold fish. That's where we catch our pleasure.

I watched Roger casting toward the circles of rising fish along the rocks of the far shore of the pond. His presentation was fine.

The loops moved fluidly. He didn't waste much effort in false casting. The fly pulled out to the full length of the leader and settled near the latest small eruption of fish. Nothing. Then he'd look around, spin the boat slowly, and begin casting to the next rise, and the next. When he did false cast, it was to wait for the rise so as to put the fly just so. Shadows crept out from that west shore near the crumbling bridge and bright creek, but the sun was still high enough to illuminate most of the pond, and the worms were active—thousands of them, leaving wiggling tracers on the surface. There were dozens of circles widening on the pond surface around Roger, but he wasn't catching fish. Hmmm, I thought, this must be the fourth day. Catching choosey fish now would require a minor miracle—say, a cast that landed inside a fish's mouth. It could happen.

I rigged my rod and put in and with a stroke or two was gliding toward fish. Soon I was false casting too, aiming to land a cast on a fish's lip. Not hopeful. Fishermen hope, but with hopeful resignation. One has to be detached from the goal of catching to catch anything really worthwhile. That we were here fishing for bass at all, in the dawning years of the decline of Western civilization, is a kind of miracle of science. A fisheries success story. Striper numbers were in a steep fall by the mid-1970s. There were very few small fish coming out of Chesapeake Bay. There were gaps in year classes. In other words, bass were not producing sufficiently, and no regulations limited the taking of large fish capable of replenishing stocks. As large fish disappeared, the young-of-year were not coming up to replace them. You could keep everything you caught. Commercial trap fishermen, gill netters, and sport fishermen were all in on the kill. Science knew why the striper declines were occurring and what had to be done to stop them. But making and implementing new regulatory laws that will hurt someone's livelihood in the short run—even if they're designed to save it in the long run—is famously difficult, especially when you're dealing with fishermen, each a self-professed expert. The tension between fishermen and scientists fascinates me. It's a feud as old as the first scientist who subversively predicted, no more. What immediately came burping out of the fisherman's mouth was, bullshit. Why the fighting when both need the same end to be successful—healthy fisheries that can sustain yields in perpetuity? The truth is that in spite of excellent science, the oceans are going to hell in a handbasket, and it's the journey from good science to good management and policy—a minefield of unexploded stakeholder ordinance and political razor wire—that gets us every time.

That the United States has an excellent science of fisheries and oceans at all is thanks in large measure to a modest, hardworking bureaucratic genius, a collector of birds, named Spencer Baird who arrived in Woods Hole with his wife Mary and their baby Lucy in 1870. Before the U.S. Geological Survey even knew the marsh existed, Baird came to Sippewissett to collect fish.

Spencer Baird was foremost a collector of birds—a roving naturalist. By the time he was hired on at the Smithsonian Institute in 1850 to work as the assistant to the institute's first secretary, Joseph Henry, his personal bird skin collection had reached three thousand and it took several railroad cars to move it to the Smithsonian. Baird was twenty-seven years old. At the Smithsonian, Baird's job of curating natural history collections and publishing scientific reports and journals put him in touch with every eccentric birdman working in the field, including John LeConte (Leconte's sparrow), Thomas Brewer (Brewer's blackbird), John Cassin (Cassin's finch), John James Audubon (Audubon's warbler,

Audubon Society), and Robert Ridgeway (Ridgeway, Brewer, and Baird published *The History of North American Birds* in 1874). Through his contacts with field biologists, ethnographers, bone people, cowboy pot hunters, geographers, mappers, and Victorian explorers of every type, maintained mostly through written correspondence, his collections flourished. In 1860 Baird notes that he had written 3,050 letters of which 200 were drafts for Joseph Henry. He became a walking database. He'd logged thousands of miles on foot all over the Midwest, Southwest, and Canada, exploring and collecting, not only birds but the "quadripeds," every one of which he and others of the natural philosopher ilk were determined to taste. Bobcat seemed to be a favorite wild food, and opossum. Collecting was his passion. On the evening of the day he attended his daughter Lucy's birth (which he noted with great joy in his journal, along with a thumbnail sketch of his wife and himself dancing a baby aloft), he prepared a fish skeleton. Baird was good with children. He was shy. He worked harder than most people. He loved to whistle. Once he tried to mesmerize a lizard on a fence post by whistling to it. "You recollect what Swainson says about the faculty possessed by lizards of being charmed, so upon seeing this one on a fence, I commenced to whistling a beautiful tune. When it stopped, it opened its mouth, cocked its head to one side, and drank in the divine melody as if it never could get enough. I could not succeed in killing it however." Love and death intertwined. Everyone who met him seemed to like him, including a majority of Congress.

It was Baird who convinced Congress in 1870 to authorize the establishment of the first U.S. Fish Commission. Baird himself, while still maintaining his position at the Smithsonian, was put in charge, but without a budget and no salary. Baird had influential friends, among them Vermonter George Perkins Marsh, a

Smithsonian regent, statesman, polymath speaker of twenty-five Nordic dialects, historian of Goths, and famed author, who in 1864 published *Man and Nature*, which synthesized the first popular, grand conceptualization of man shaping, changing, controlling, and degrading nature. It was a work as large in scope and as important as Darwin's *On the Origin of Species* (1859). He is considered the founder of today's conservation movement— the pragmatic and utilitarian face of it, anyway. Baird met Marsh on a collecting trip to Vermont in 1847 through his wife Mary, who'd gone to a private girls' school in Burlington, Vermont, run by George Perkins Marsh's brother. The wives became close friends and visited each other in Vermont and later in Washington. During those trips the friendship between the elder scholar and statesman and the young scientist grew. The record of their correspondence suggests almost a father-and-son fondness between the two.

Marsh had a deep, but what he considered amateur, enthusiasm for the natural world. He was a faithful collector of fish, reptiles, mammals, and insects for Baird's new museum, sending specimens preserved in arsenic powder and alcohol to Washington in large wooden kegs. Baird seems to have been strongly influenced by Marsh's ideas long before the publication of *Man and Nature*. Baird had been impressed by a study and report on the state of Vermont's fisheries Marsh had completed for the Vermont legislature in 1832. In his 1832 study, Marsh had asked why the number of fishes in Vermont's rivers and streams had declined. In his findings he mentions the "improvidence" of fishermen taking too many fish during the spawning season and sawmills, dams, factories, and other obstructions and pollutants as having negative impacts. But it is to interpreting other "obscure causes" that have "a very important influence" that Marsh devotes nearly half of his report. Marsh made a link between forest clearing and cultivation and in-stream flows. It may seem like an obvious connection to us today, especially considering that 90 percent of the precolonial forest was gone by 1832. But it was not obvious then: Marsh's ecological theories were revolutionary in his time, and Baird picked up on them and applied them to his situation in Woods Hole.

The fish commission's charge was to investigate the decline of fish catches on southern New England coasts. It was given two years to do so, and then report findings to Congress in 1872. Baird wasn't the first scientist to set up shop in Woods Hole. Louis Agassiz, famed Swiss-born scientific lecturer, founder of Harvard's museum of comparative zoology, friend and self-perceived rival to Baird, had led the way to Woods Hole and Penikese Island several years earlier.

Why did Agassiz and Baird choose Woods Hole as the place to launch studies of the ocean? And why studies of the ocean and ocean creatures in the first place? Morphology and embryology were the foremost biological pursuits of their day. Morphology is the study of relationships between forms. It's an ordering of life and the linking between form and function. The ultimate questions in morphology sought human origins. Where do we come from? Who are we? Embryologists looked at the stages of the developing embryo for answers to these questions. Darwin postulated that life started in the sea, so there was a great interest among morphologists and embryologists in the simple and ancestral life-forms found in the ocean. Thoreau, walking the outer beach of Cape Cod near Truro in 1849, reflected that "Agassiz and Gould [the botanist] tell us that the sea teems with animals of all classes, far beyond the extreme point of flowering plants . . . that modern investigations, to quote the words of Desor, merely go to confirm the great idea which was vaguely anticipated by the ancient poets and philosophers, that the Ocean is the origin of all things." Woods Hole was the chosen location for investigating the origin of all things because it lay at the confluence of cold northern New England waters and the warmer southern coastal waters influenced by the Gulf Stream. Northern and southern species intermingle in these waters to create rich biological diversity. We saw evidence of this seasonal northern expansion of tropical and subtropical species as children wandering Black Beach in late August. Under the August sun we might have occasionally seen an expiring emerald flying fish flip-flopping about in the shallows, or pulled up strange-looking fish from the bathtub-warm bay waters around the Barn Rock. Hanging out under the raft were little schools of tropical-looking striped fish we called zebra perch. Today every serious fisherman anticipates the runs of false albacore and weakfish (*cynoscion regalis*) that arrive out of the north-wandering Gulf Stream in August. Warming global temperatures have been pushing the ranges of southern species, marine and terrestrial, even farther northward.

Why is Baird so important to the history of fish conservation? Not, I think, because of what he did for fisheries management in 1870. He didn't find the cause of fish declines. It's what he did for ecological science—the science of home—a hundred years later. After George Perkins Marsh, it was Baird who brought a refined conservationist's view to fish and oceans and who foresaw the kind of science that would be needed for good stewardship in the future.

Baird was the ideal person to head the U.S. Fish Commission, though he had none of Agassiz's charismatic presence. Instead, his biographer notes that Baird had a humble, down-to-earth nature that put him in good stead with the fishermen he needed to work with in the region. In his letters to Baird, Marsh liked to scold him about being overworked and deskbound—too focused on administration. But Baird thrived in his demanding position at the Smithsonian, tackling all manner of duties in a characteristically self-effacing, quiet way but never losing touch with work in the field, much of which he delegated to his assistant, a local fisherman named Vinal R. Edwards, who began his remarkable collecting career for Baird in 1870.

Edwards kept meticulous journal entries of his forays, noting in small thin notebooks the day of the year; the weather, wind, and water temperature; and type, number, and locations of all the fish he caught. Rarities were written larger and often circled. Edwards regularly visited half a dozen fish traps in the area, including the commission's own after 1887 and the trap of Captain Isaiah Spindle not far from Sippewissett marsh. He seined with a two-hundred-foot tow off the back of a steamboat called the *Fishhawk* and sometimes employed a small drag for bottom dredging. He used fyke nets for surface hauls for small fish and invertebrates. While Edwards did much of the physical work of collecting, work on board was overseen by Yale professor Addison Emery Verrill.

Verrill was Yale's first professor of zoology and became the first curator of zoology at the university's new Peabody Natural History Museum. Verrill was the first to collect and describe the giant squid. It was an incestuous time among natural philosophers. Verrill had been Agassiz's assistant at Harvard from 1860 to 1864. That Baird gave equal weight to collecting as he did to ecological and conservational musings is witnessed by the fact that Verrill's five-hundred-page report on marine invertebrates is attached as an addendum to Baird's first report on fish declines to Congress from the U.S. Fish Commission in 1872. It was a hedge, perhaps, for continued congressional support. Verrill, with Edwards' help, had captured over one thousand invertebrate species new to science, and one hundred new species of fish. Even if the report couldn't answer definitively the reasons for fish decline, who could argue that the discovery of so much new life wasn't important?

Edwards traveled all over Vineyard Sound, the Elizabeth Islands, Buzzards Bay, and Narragansett Bay. It wasn't always fish and invertebrate marine life he was after. On June 6, 1878, he visited the Weepecketts, several small islands in the Elizabeth chain, where he collected twelve tern eggs, two barn swallow eggs, six kingfisher eggs, and "golden-crowned thrush eggs, blue-yellow buck warbler eggs, vireo eggs (four), found purple finch nest with four eggs plus three barrel of scup." On the fifteenth he collected four hundred tern eggs at Penikese Island. The eighteenth of June found him "blowing gull eggs." On the fifth of July he "went to Nantucket in steamboat heard that they had a small whale." On the sixth: "bought the mottled grampus [pilot whale] for $10 and brought it to Woods Hole in steamboat."

On the twenty-eighth of June, 1887 Edwards went by steamboat to Sippewissett marsh and seined at the mouth of the creek, where he caught "tautog, seabass, squeteauge, cunners, alwifes, striped minnows, sticklebacks, menhaden, flat fish, spotted flat fish, silverside, sea robin, butter fish."

Each month of the off-season, when Baird was back in Washington, Edwards sent him a fish report, and he kept it all going long after Baird's death in 1887. Edwards' rare fish report in 1894 includes records of "trunkfish, Chaetodons, leather jackets, Pensacola snappers, sailor's choice, pampano, red bass, trigger fish, big-eyed herring, tarpon, spanish sardine, half-beaks, gloss-eyed snapper." On one occasion he caught two two-inch dorado (*Coryphaena hippurus*) from the commercial wharf in Woods Hole and sent these, along with several rare file fish, to Washington. Baird's fish commission study contained the testimonials of fishermen up and down the coast along with the reports of fishes collected by Edwards, who lived year-round in Woods Hole and collected nearly every day, except Sundays, for forty years in the waters around Woods Hole.

The capacity to create models of highly complex ecosystems was many years away, but Baird's lasting contribution to science lay there. As Baird put it, "[a study of fish declines] would not be complete without a thorough knowledge of their associates in the sea, especially of such as prey upon them or constitute their food." He sought data on "the temperature of the water taken at different depths, its varying transparency, density, chemical composition, percentage of saline matter, its surface and under currents . . . and we must ascertain, among other facts, at what time the fish reach our coast, and during what period they remain; when they spawn and where; what is the nature of their food; what localities they prefer; what agencies interfere with the spawn or the young fish; what length of time elapses before the young themselves are capable of reproducing; for how many years the function of reproduction can be exercised; and many other points of equal importance."

Were fisheries declining in Baird's day? Undoubtedly. Atlantic salmon were gone from southern New England's rivers by the 1820s. One West Falmouth captain, Thomas Hinckley, seemed to confirm the state of decline of black sea bass (*Centropristis striatus*) in 1871 in the bay waters around the marsh: "They are much diminished—almost extirpated. We catch them with hooks in spring but they weigh half a pound apiece. The largest weigh from three to seven pounds and then the old seabass as they are called, weigh from ten to ninety pounds." Black sea bass are staging a small comeback only now.

Why were the fish in decline in 1870? Overharvesting was a factor. During Baird's day, the Pacific Guano Works in Woods Hole, using tons of menhaden caught annually from Buzzards Bay and Narragansett for nitrogen content, guano mined from Caribbean guano islands, and salt peter mined in Peru, produced superphosphate fertilizer at Penzance Point and shipped it around the world. It was a stinky and prosperous business; fertilizer production was for a time the largest manufacturing sector worldwide. But it wasn't only overfishing that was killing the catch. Power dams and the pollution of rivers, destruction of habitat, ill-timed harvests, currents and weather patterns, natural cyclical population fluctuations, climate and water temperature change, and changing migratory patterns all contributed to declines. In other words, it was, and is, complex. The year after Baird's report was issued to Congress, fishermen reported huge increases in certain fish populations, including scup. Who knows why? The removal of cod? The increases flew in the face of some of Baird's conclusions and made it all but impossible, politically, to implement conservation measures. Ocean fisheries, a nonplussed Baird concluded, are far more complex than initially imagined. To come to any sound understanding of them would take years of research. He set about creating an institution that could use cutting-edge methods of data collection and continuous research of the ocean as a system to find his answers. And he aggressively pursued fish culture and fish stocking, but rarely successfully.

The political atmosphere in which Baird operated in 1870 on the southern New England coast was not unlike Marsh's Vermont forty years earlier and weirdly echoes the contentious striped bass (*Morone saxatilis*) debates between fishermen and scientists in the 1980s. Marsh's Vermont legislature feigned poverty as its reason for ignoring Marsh's recommendations and skirted tough political decisions for a dozen years. Baird found himself in the middle of a regional dispute between hook-and-sinker fishermen and gill netters. The latter had been accused by the former of causing the declines by setting nets too near spawning runs and taking too many fish. In the 1980s, it was gill netters, trap fisherman, and seiners lined up against sport fishermen and regulators. Baird held up science itself as way to resolve conflict and determine the true causes and best solutions for fish declines. Not many fishermen or politicians were ready to hear him. It depended on whose ox was being more gored. The same is true today. While there are hopeful signs, we still lack the moral and cultural fortitude to say yes to science and no to rampant exploitation.

Baird became the second director of the Smithsonian after Joseph Henry died in 1878 and remained U.S. fish commissioner for another five years, successfully fighting off a congressional attempt to end the work of the commission, before handing over the reins. His fish commission became the Bureau of Fisheries in 1885 and eventually evolved into the National Marine Fisheries Service under the National Oceanic and Atmospheric Administration. Spencer Baird died in 1887 in Woods Hole. He is buried there, and there is a monument to him—a glacial boulder on the edge of the harbor, with a plaque bearing his name. We go there often. When they were toddlers, my children could just barely climb to the top of that boulder for a grand view of the watery world. My wife and I, weary with diaper changing and kid patrol, were satisfied with the more limited view from the bench and the bottom of a coffee cup.

Baird undoubtedly visited Sippewissett often. His interest in birds and fish would have propelled him to this place, since it was the largest marsh within several miles from Woods Hole. The marsh would have been a convenient haunt to witness shorebird and tree swallow migration—or the annual early summer spawning of horseshoe crabs. Baird has a sandpiper named after him, as well as Baird's sparrow—a very drab bird of arid southwestern grasslands, named in honor of him by John James Audubon.

I've never seen Baird's sandpiper on the marsh. Its range maps show a migration from breeding grounds in Alaska and northern Canada down the center of the country, but it does show up on the marsh from time to time. I like to imagine running into Baird at Sippewissett—he was a Unitarian, hedging his bets with the metaphysical. Like Agassiz, and probably like Marsh, he knew and admired the writers and thinkers from Concord shaping the new American transcendentalist philosophical paradigm. If I could see him on the marsh, I imagine he'd be walking hand in hand with his daughter Lucy and whistling an old Scottish tune. Like Agassiz, preoccupied by the question of origins and captivated by the simple forms of life, he likely would have been found continually kneeling down to pick up small precious things to show his daughter: feathers, shells, and stones—all things with a common beauty.

Reflecting on Baird's life, I find myself considering the worth of fish to recreationalists who don't rely on them to survive—those of us fishing the worm hatch and hunting the marshes at night. Maybe we should retire our rods. Commercial fishermen may have the deeper claim to the deeps, though a strange lot commercial fishermen make: quarrelsome, independent, surly, sure that they know what's scientifically best for the fishery, and superstitious. Maybe it's always been that way. Thoreau in his Cape Cod journals writes about the decline of oysters in Wellfleet. "I find that a similar superstition with regard to the disappearance of fishes exists almost everywhere—that when Wellfleet began to quarrel with the neighboring towns about the right to gather them, yellow specks appeared in them, and Providence caused them to disappear." Fishing, Thoreau notes, is by Providence— as, it appears, is much else. Marsh noted that declines in fish stock are by improvidence. Fishing is, either by providence or improvidence, a hard way to make a living, which most fisherman would never trade away.

I joined Roger in his float boat, and we drifted together, casting vainly into the dusk. We weren't catching so we talked natural history. We named the different kinds of fish we knew that come into the pond during the year. Our incomplete list included tautog, black bass, stickleback, menhaden, all manner of bait fish, and alewife. There are undoubtedly many others. Roger mentioned a kind of shad called hickory shad (*Pomololus mediocris*). I mentioned pipefish (*Syngnathus fuscus*), a relative to seahorses. You find them by the creek mouth or floating in small schools by the shore near the tracks—in certain light they look like suspended spears of glass.

What seemed like millions of small dimples of swimming worms covered the water. Dozens of fish continued to rise and splash on the surface long after the moon had risen. We did what all fly fisherman mostly do. We practiced our casting. "Try the double haul," said Roger, "and delay that forward cast. Like this," he said, casting to an eruption of fish right on shore. "I'm left-handed," I said, pushing a cast onto the beach. "Yeah," he said, "that's too bad. Drop the tip just a little more. With this rod, you should be able to lay out seventy feet with no false cast. There," he said, putting a fly on top of a splash.

My one long association with a commercial fishing guide has led me to believe that most are unlike the friendly and scientific Roger. In the mid-1970s, I was twenty-three and worked for a Nantucket charter captain who had a long-standing quarrel going with anyone who claimed to be a scientist. He was an island man—born and raised—a difficult person but a good man down deep, a barber by trade and the best fisherman around. He scoffed at the notion that bass were disappearing. They come and go in cycles he said, and in that he was right. Science had mapped those cycles by his day but hadn't determined fully what caused them. There were photos on the charter captain's mantel showing him as a boy standing in front of a model T pickup with small bass laid out before him like dozens of ears of shucked corn—small, school-sized fish. There were no small fish around, but large bass were plentiful during my early years with him, and our luck was very good. His boat was a twenty-six-foot wooden lapstrake MacKenzie with a 275-horsepower inboard Seamaster engine that had plenty of torque but no great speed. He called her *Possessor,* and the name fit him like a favorite fillet knife fit his hand. He was a man who measured success against the size and weight of his possessions, most especially the stack of fifties in his wallet. *Think and Grow Rich* was his bible. All spring, summer, and fall he took fishing charters. Then late in fall he switched to guiding goose hunters. He maintained a small camp on Tuckernuck Island for that purpose and for years was equally well known for his prowess as a goose hunter. I lived in his basement surrounded by orange-and-black slickers on hangers, hundreds of old fishing plugs, an enormous and flaking mounted striped bass named Charlie, and the washing machine. We left the house at all hours, depending on the tide. And if on return the fishing had been good, we'd drink vodka with a splash of milk and Kahlua at any hour, and if the fishing hadn't been good, we'd drink to that too. He was a man who felt an enormous pressure to succeed.

We took charters during most days in spring and early summer and fished for the market at night and on days without charters. In hindsight, fishing on the *Possessor* in the 1970s was like hunting that last herd of buffalo. I didn't know what a bass under ten pounds looked like, and we loaded the boat with large fish. *Possessor* drew only a few feet of water, could barrel through shallows and breakers both, and hold well on anchor in fast rips. In three seasons, we ran aground only once. Night and day, in every tide and every conceivable weather from heavy fog to driving rain, he could navigate us through the complex and shifting shoal waters off Madaket to the places the fish were to be found. Some moonless nights, we'd troll back and forth through the breaks between sandy islands—the shoal water there is vast and difficult. I'd have no idea where we were until the first light, and then more often than not I still wouldn't know. We'd look for stacks of white birds in the morning. We called them flying currency because they portended a boat full of fish.

That first spring we caught thousands of pounds of striped bass all on rod and reel. During all of May 1978 the two of us routinely caught 600 pounds of large fish in an afternoon. We had a few secret places—rips that formed at certain tides he called our honey spots and he'd put us into them. I'd throw a bow anchor and a stern anchor, too, sometimes, and we'd start casting, hooking up and hauling in fish. Woe be unto me if I snapped a line, lost a plug, lost a good fish. I'd look out for other boats, and if they came toward us, we'd avoid hook-ups, change plugs, and cast off the wrong side of the boat when one came near, feigning a lack of success or sometimes bolting if we thought it could fool them. At the market, we sold stripers whole for nearly three dollars a pound. I took a third share and thought I was growing rich. One particularly good night we came home in the morning with 1,500 pounds of striped bass in the back of the truck. He took the long circuitous route down the cobblestone streets to the docks with his tail gate down, talking to admirers through the open window all along the way. The biggest fish I caught that night weighed forty-four pounds. The smallest couldn't have been much lighter than fifteen pounds. The local paper, *The Nantucket Enquirer and Mirror,* took our picture. His six-year-old son Robbie rode with us. The camera caught him sitting on the roof of the truck pointing his toy bow and arrow at the sun. The last buffalo hunt.

By next spring, the fish were scarce. It wasn't a happy boat. He was sullen and took to popping something to calm an ulcer. Charter captains don't like to come up empty-handed. It's bad for the stomach and bad for business. I had arrived with no money and was eager myself to find fish. We spent long nights on the water. We'd anchor in a cove at slack tide for a few hours of sleep. He didn't eat and didn't talk much. Sometimes we'd leave the breaking shoal waters close in to the islands and head for Muskegut Island between Nantucket and Martha's Vineyard. Somewhere out there was a submerged bank he liked. He'd caught fish there once. It was deep water. Here, he said, is where bass spawned in the fall. He'd observed it and held onto the belief, though it was contrary to what science said about spawning stripers. We'd drift through that dark water, and he'd watch the depth finder then bark out the order to cast the anchor. And I would. But we'd miss and have to drift through again and again. This place, I realized, was his dream territory. His graveyard. His last-hope water. But nothing was going our way. The charters were way off and the people we took out were impatient. One morning, he buried a hook deep into his thumb and told me to push it through so we could clip the barb. On another morning, we pulled his nephew out of the water. He'd been there an hour, his own twelve-foot Whaler circling him like a shark. I watched him standing up in his small boat to head for land, the red gash in his butt where the engine prop had hit him looked like a red rag hanging out of a back pocket. Increasingly, over a "pop" at home, he'd talk about his own death. Bury me in a fish-shaped coffin, he once said, out there. Whereas I imagined, in half-sleep early in the morning, my own death as a hook dropping out the sky, skewering my lip, and hauling me up into the light. We were both depressed. But he was going down, whereas I was going up. It was here we finally parted company. Light and dark. One anchor toss too many, and I left broke and on bad terms with him, convinced I'd witnessed the end of the bass fishery. I never saw him again.

Once I sold a piece about fishing with him to a sport fishing journal, but they sent it to him for a review, and he killed it saying it would hurt his business. I wanted to go back and work things out with him. He'd been charitable with me, not a father figure—I had a good one already—but a life enhancer. "You have no idea," he said, "what you want out of life, so think it through." He dropped me off at Tuckernuck Island one November, having arranged for me to have the old Humane House there on my own for a week. I burned peat in the fireplace during the day and froze at night. It was like Thoreau's Humane House near Truro—not very humane. The only company I had was a flock of red knots facing the cold wind on the point, each holding one leg up. The striped bass were somewhere far to the south or disappeared off the face of the Earth altogether.

But I was wrong about my prediction of the end of the bass fishery. New catch regulations went into effect in the early 1980s, which brought about a robust recovery in the early 1990s. It has been twenty years since the charter captain I knew fished his own waters. Stripers are everywhere now; large schools have the run of the bay. We catch them off the beaches and in the marshes and salt ponds. Kids catch them on flies and plugs from canoes and

Boston Whalers, from docks, bridges, and points. In the evening out in the harbor, schools of hundreds of small fish in the ten- to twenty-inch range feed at incoming tides. Drifting through this plentitude, we sometimes hook the smallest imaginable striped bass—the size of large goldfish. These delicate littlest ones are my favorites. I think of the charter captain. Maybe he was right about the spawning grounds out there in the dark water between the islands. Who could imagine such small fish making their way up from the Chesapeake? There's a resigned fisherman's hope packed into their little shimmering bodies.

What changed in the intervening years? The main thing that changed was bass fishing regulations. Several years after my last season on Nantucket, I was running a coastal wildlife refuge in Newport, Rhode Island, and attended hearings conducted there by a citizen's advisory council on new bass catch regulations being proposed by the U.S. Fish and Wildlife Service. In Narragansett Bay, these regulations would put the last trap fishermen and commercial gill netters out of business. These were families that had been in the fishing business since the time of Spencer Baird. Much of the discussion bore on the same old conflicts between hook-and-sinker fisherman and gill netters. We listened to their testimony. It was disheartening. Sad. It would put new pressure on the likes of charter fishermen, too. Fishing is what these families had done for generations.

A year or so after the new regulations went into effect, my charter captain took a shotgun out of the gun case in his living room, drove his truck out to the Nantucket moors, and took his own life, leaving his wife, two children by a first marriage, and a thirteen-year-old son—the one holding the bow and arrow in the photo taken the morning after our big night. A friend who had worked as a mate for him after I left sent me the clip from a

Boston paper. It wasn't really a surprise to us. Those of us who had worked for him knew about his moods and suspected the recurring depression in this island man. I wondered whether it was depression or depressed fish stocks or a combination of the two that killed him. With the captain of the *Possessor* gone, I imagined the entire nation of Nantucket converted overnight to the picturesque carnival for the wealthy that it eventually became.

We live in denial of the world the science of home is carefully sketching for us. The full picture isn't there yet, but what we can see is clear enough to act on.

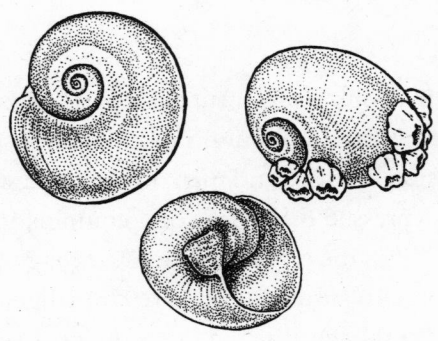

— 3 —

bird

A physical fact is as sacred as a moral principle. Our own nature demands from us this double allegiance.

—Louis Agassiz, 1873

On the Isle of Penikese
Ringed about by Sapphire seas,
Fanned by breezes salt and cool,
Stood the Master with his school . . .
Said the Master to the youth
"We have come in search for truth,
Trying with uncertain key;
Door by door of mystery.
We are reaching, through His laws
To the garment-hem of Cause."

—John Greenleaf Whittier,
from *The Prayer of Agassiz*

WHEN DID THE land actually stop being sacred to us? Did anyone record the moment or rather was it a dimming of awareness across years. Did we become modern producer-consumers by misattention, caught by time and opportunity while our meanings changed? Is that how we lost our way, moving nowhere but toward progress? Or is the land still sacred to us, and we just have to turn over more stones to know it? Is the soul of a place like the ugly larval form of a helgramite that creeps from under a rock at night and slips unnoticed into the stream to metamorphose into the graceful Dobson fly? Is the soul of a place the whole of the place?

Looking for birds on a salt marsh in May is turning over stones. All birds are like Darwin's finches, creatures of biological necessity shaped into behaviors, form, and patterns of color by environment and the need to avoid competition to survive. But are they something else, too? To scientists, they are barometers of environmental change and an endless source of field study. But gotten hold of by the poets, do they reflect a dual nature? The sacred landscape with dinosaur wings? They mean something more to us. They always have. To the great Louis Agassiz, perhaps the first scientific luminary to arrive in Woods Hole intent on building a scientific legacy, all biological diversity—all the various changing forms of birds, fish, clams, worms, crabs—reflected a divine plan. He, like many other scientists at Woods Hole in the later part of the nineteenth century, many with connections to Harvard University, worked under the glow of transcendental thinking coming from the not-too-distant Concord, home of Emerson and Thoreau. Science in Woods Hole and here on the marsh was illuminated by that glow. Natural science in the 1860s was still a philosophical undertaking. Agassiz was a Unitarian and friend to Ralph Waldo Emerson. They shared hunting rifles, and they shared friends and ideas. Emerson, at one point early in his career, during a visit to the Paris natural history museum of Cuvier, thought he would become a naturalist like Agassiz. And scientists, like Agassiz, wrote poetry. Religious and scientific forms were for a brief period in the mid-nineteenth century almost interchangeable—science had advanced far from the Natural Theology of the English theologian William Paley in the 1780s. But Divine Cause, for many, was still indisputable one hundred years later: God made us. The nineteenth century's natural philosophers watched or collected birds, or made collections of eggs, as much out of an interest in the new scientific paradigm as out of an interest in portents, a quest for original ideas, a hunger for the transcendent in nature, or a belief in the mystical landscape.

An interest in birds seems to foretell things, among them a man's career in science. E. O. Wilson, before, thanks to poor eyesight, focusing on ants, spent portions of his childhood tracking down birds. James Watson, codiscoverer of the double helix, was a boyhood bird-watcher. Charles Otis Whitman, first director of the Marine Biological Lab in Woods Hole in 1888, spent his youth looking for birds' nests in Woodstock, Maine. He was a staunch Darwinian but also an admirer of Agassiz's. Behind most scientists is a bird. The modern environmental movement was carried aloft in large measure on the feathery wings of birds. Consider that the formation of the Audubon Society near the turn of the century rested on the feathery plumes of egrets used to decorate women's hats. Consider the work of Rachel Carson, which led eventually to the flowering of environmentalism in the 1970s. Her ghost is here on the marsh: she came during her summers at the MBL in Woods Hole to watch birds in the evening. Hope is carried forth by feathery wings, according to Emily Dickinson, and a death in wartime is heard in the forlorn voice of a thrush by Robert Frost. And so is Walt Whitman the "curious boy, never too close, never disturbing them, cautiously peering, absorbing, translating . . . the two feather'd guests from Alabama . . . and their nest, and four light-green eggs spotted with brown." For Whitman an "uncaught bird is ever hovering, hovering," holding that unrealized "plan of Thee enclosed in Time and Space / Health, peace, salvation universal."

Transcendentalism, this light of Emerson that spread across a region that encompassed the Cape, Nantucket, Martha's Vineyard, Buzzards Bay, Narragansett Bay, Block Island, and Long Island Sound, had its roots in the Puritan religious tradition, though it was also a radical departure, with elements of indigenous and Eastern thought, English Romanticism, Platonic essentialism, and the German Kant's idealism. The branches of the transcendentalist reached far up into an atmosphere of individualism and personal revelation. The aim of the transcendentalist was, after all, to find his way back to God—to the godly relationship before the Fall. Plato's admonition to know thyself pointed the way. Emerson, like George Perkins Marsh, accepted the truth of natural law, but deplored the loud materialism of his age. Transcendentalism was Emerson's moral response, his jujitsu—turning materialism on its head, making what was material and ruled by the laws of nature secondary to what was original, primary, unchanging, a reflection back to God. To Agassiz as well, "A physical fact is as sacred as a moral principle. Our own nature demands from us this double allegiance." Neither Emerson nor Agassiz believed that dusty scriptures, or historical texts of any kind could hold sway over personal revelation or new information. In this brave new world of scientific discovery, the past no longer controlled the present. Except that the world was still holy and originally so. "Study nature not books," Agassiz wrote. These words are written in Agassiz's own hand on parchment hung above the entrance to the stacks at the MBL library. Who says librarians don't have a sense of humor? Write your own holy texts, said Emerson. Let the world become revealed through personal reflection. Agassiz saw science as enabling this view, so his scientific theories of life always put the idea of God as creator and divine will in front of the physical evidence before him.

There is a barely discernible path out the back door around behind our dilapidated shed. It leads through the woods to a neighbor's yard. These are beech and oak woods, interspersed with old field red juniper. The understory is dense; honeysuckle vines and bushes, a complex of shrubs and scrubby trees. Briars and thorny roses dense enough to entrap, bleed you, then drive you mad, make it great habitat for rabbit, fox, bobwhite quail, mourning doves, robins, and catbirds. The Carolina wrens love it too, and they were teakettling away around me. Stepping over a stone wall and then around the corner of our neighbors house, I stood on the edge of the marsh. In early May, the short marsh grass was a burnished brown and gold tinged with green. The cordgrass lining the creeks and channels was greener still and taller but still had gold in it too. Along the forest edge the high-tide bush that had gone to fuzzy white seed in the fall was greening. The glasswort was blood red and the sea lavender bleached frail purple to white. Glasswort in May is a burning bush enough for me. Standing in this place and looking south, the marsh stretched out its body full length—the beautiful mouth, dune lips, and brow nearly a half mile south. From here, this waving golden green grassland, with a rim of white sand and then the blue bay and sky, looked much more expansive than it really is. Almost any other public view—from the railroad tracks that run along its full length under the glacial moraine to the east, or from the beach road running on its west side—would make the marsh appear smaller. At its widest, it's only about a thousand feet across. Its total area, squeezing out every ounce of marsh-connected forest and beach, is a sinuous five hundred acres. At its mouth, the broad, sandy inlet passes over sands and out through braided sandbars into Buzzards Bay. A low barrier of dunes runs between bay and marsh. The dunes are hardly dunes now. They were tall and dune grass covered thirty years ago, but without a source for renewal, they've retreated and eroded away. The two-track road that took us out to the tallest sentinels of them is under sandbars now one hundred yards offshore.

As one would expect, there's a nice confluence of upland and marshland habitat in the back of the marsh. I walked by the edge of the woods over the creek that connects one of two salt ponds, listening to crows and to the keening of an osprey. A chestnut-sided warbler, a white-eyed vireo, and yellow warblers sang from the wood's edge. There was nothing uncommon about them, but each of the warblers was uncommonly fancy in its gaudy breeding plumage. Like the white candles of a blooming blueberry bush in an otherwise pale green undergrowth, migratory birds in May provide ecstatic relief to the eye. Up along the tracks, a shallow brackish marsh, nearly cut off from the tides, held a congregation of red-winged blackbirds, and chattering away invisible behind the prison bars of phragmites, a marsh wren and a swamp sparrow were singing. I am a lazy bird-watcher who is never bird watching but always looking at the birds, who uses his ears more than his eyes, who rarely writes anything down and counts only if forced to—habits that would make me a middling naturalist at best and a poor biologist. "How many" is something I don't usually care to know, unless it's the bank account and I'm paying bills to exhaust it. The Christmas bird counters would make a study skin of me after a season or two. But song does interest me, and I do use my ears well enough. Hearing birds is like finding Christmas presents that sing to you. They are a terrific puzzle besides—snatches of jigs and reels to try to remember. I've always wanted to buy one of those clear Plexiglas dishes—the artificial ears that magnify sound—so that I might hear better that distant thrush, or that high-flying loon. Donald Kroodsma, author of *The Singing Life of Birds*, reveals this secret to the reader: he sees song. His relationship to birdsong is built among other things on hearing sounds and simultaneously seeing sonograms, those charts that plot sound frequencies over time. How wonderful! My knowledge of sound is the mere memory of melody, I think, and with it comes a place association. I remember keenly exactly where I was when I first figured out I was listening to a hermit thrush back in college. And I still conjure an image of sky and reeds when I hear a white-eyed vireo. But Kroodsma is onto something. Were one to become a true collector of birdsongs, learning to employ the sense of sight to see sound would be a wonder.

Turning off the tracks and onto a carpet of *Spartina patens* cut by creeks and potholes and walking parallel to the creek that drains the pond across the tracks, I could see the far edges of the big pool—that near dead-center of the marsh where three creeks come together. The big pond, an acre or so in size, drains completely at low tide, leaving the creek to wind, deep in places, around the outside, undercutting banks of spartina peat. An occupied osprey pole sits at the mouth of the north creek. The north creek is the main branch, and up it is the way home. It's two lanes wide, and it narrows then opens again several times into white sandy pavilions good for clamming, fishing, and doing nothing. The east side of the big pond is low, wet, and sticky with silt and detritus. The west side is white and sandy. Shorebirds, gulls, and terns roost in here, though not in great numbers. The main creek meanders around the far side—the west side. The big pond is where our regulars hang out: the bright white statuary of common and snowy egrets off in their creekside pools, great blue herons stalking knee-deep by the banks, lesser yellow legs bobbing and weaving, and willets, semipalmated sandpipers, least sandpipers, semipalmated plovers, and black-bellied plovers probing. In the fall, the green-backed herons, sometimes ten or more, station themselves along the creek, heads cocked looking for fish. The seldom-seens were mostly absent—piping plover, whimbrel, pectoral sandpipers and solitary sandpipers, bittern, and glossy ibis—but scanning north I did see something unusual. A golden plover stood all alone on the sand of the main branch north of the deepest hole where even at low tide the water is black and the bank undercut by ten feet. I don't exactly know how I knew it was a golden plover, but I knew. I'd spent a week on James Bay in the fall years ago surrounded by thousands of them. I knew from the rare fall singles I'd seen on Block Island and Rhode Island mainland beaches. I'd never come across one at Sippewissett. I am not a birder living in the birding hot zone with a passion for finding and listing. I don't drive long distances for hawk owls. Although I've birded in Central Europe, Mexico, Latin America, the Southwest and Northwest, northern Canada, Texas, and Florida, the trips have been always about more than birds, and don't ask me for the numbers. I don't keep a list. It's boring. Birding for me is an element of knowing where I am, whether home or abroad. When abroad, it's knowing who travels with me and who lives there. Honestly? I'm a vain bird-watcher more interested in my backyard. My home. Drab sparrows interest me more than peregrine falcons at Hawk Mountain. Sparrows justify leaving the fall garden weeds—the ones with the tiny black seeds. The regular peep sandpipers on the marsh are as interesting to me as the rarity of a golden plover. So is the occasional kingfisher that comes chattering up out of Love Joy brook at home. Who are your neighbors?

I learned most of what I know about shorebirds from George Lawrence, who birded here every morning in summers during my teens. I learned just enough from him to get me into embarrassing trouble with the more high-minded birding types among us. Types like George Lawrence, who cared so much about names and distinctions. But what are birds really? They're too beautiful to be merely creaturely machines. Their wisdom seems deeper than their fitness to the demands of place and procreation. The question why creeps in. Am I looking at a least sandpiper, or a letter written by God? How can we profess to know their true names?

George, a thin, tall old Boston Brahmin, always wore his Red Sox baseball cap while on the marsh: he would have cared little for shorebird metaphysics. Take a second look, he would say. Calm down. Observe carefully. Count things. See the dusty copper on the shoulder, the white stripe over the eye that gives way to solid brown; or the three primary feathers projecting over the rump, the downturned tip of the bill? That's a western, or that's a white-rumped. Green legs? A least. Why shouldn't I do as he did? He knew birds and life better than me by sixty years. And he was charitable with his knowledge and loved the place. His morning birding rituals kept him alive. At his age, each day was borrowed time. The same might have been true for Rachel Carson, who liked to watch the birds on this marsh late in her life. She was a teacher at heart. George, withered like a winter phragmites stem swaying in the wind but still strong, shared his knowledge and love. I suppose I resist knowing the exact identity of things because of wanting to preserve my subjectivity in a world where the object has been elevated out of control. Things are not always what they seem in spite of discovered natural laws. DNA genome fingerprinting, the current best arbitrator of identity, is busy rearranging our life tree. The hawklike turkey vulture is really a stork, for instance, according to its sequence of amino acids. A more interesting physical truth than the fine distinctions of identity within genomes is the discovery of how genetically alike we are. Consistently, molecular biologists find more likeness than apartness. We life-forms are mostly alike—the relatedness of frog, human, plover, microbe astounding.

As to the truest identity of golden plovers, I like to think beyond their ploverness. George liked everything he saw. He would have especially loved this plover. Could love have turned him into something different? A better man? A plover, say? Was this bird, standing perfectly still, every golden feather finely etched, one leg up and beak to the breeze, George? I found myself remembering him and resolving in my mind the lessons he had taught. Keep going back to your favorite places. Stand up for the place as long as you can stand. Walk there if you can, then ride your bike, then get airlifted out of Otis if you can afford it. Know it as long as you are able, as sacred landscape with, incidently, numbers attached. Know it in every season. Stop wanting to be somewhere else or someone different. Lose your mind and life here but before you do, tell someone what you know.

Like George, a hundred years earlier, Louis Agassiz may have also lost his mind and life here trying to pass on what he knew. He certainly exhausted himself trying. When he arrived in 1873 to open a school on Penikese Island, he was perhaps the most famous scientist in America. A rival to Darwin, a founder of the American Academy of Science and the natural history museum at

Harvard, Agassiz, born in the village of Montier in French-speaking Switzerland in 1807 and an immigrant to North America in the 1850s, had unrivaled enthusiasm for the youthful enterprise of the biological sciences. He was already famous in Europe for his study of fossil fishes and his synthesis of ice age theory. In America, he was the Carl Sagan of his day, lecturing the masses, popularizing, teaching innumerable numbers of graduate students. The Anderson School of Natural History at Penikese was designed for science teachers, and Agassiz was a gifted teacher, albeit with an unorthodox teaching style. Nathaniel Shaler, one of Agassiz's Harvard graduate students, described his first encounter with Agassiz's bizarre teaching methods in a humorous fashion. His first assignment was to study a small fish, "a rather unsavory object," until he felt ready to present his conclusions to Agassiz. By Shaler's account, he spent two weeks of ten-hour days looking at the alcohol-soaked fish, while Agassiz all but ignored him. His initial words to Shaler were, "That's not right." This utterance was his only response to Shaler's extensive verbal report of his own observations and conclusions one week into the ordeal. At the end of his second week, scales must have fallen from Shaler's eyes. He was able to capture the scaly essence of fish and to impress Agassiz both. At last, wrote Shaler, "I had learned the art of comparing objects." I would like to have heard what Shaler said to Agassiz. I imagine that by the end of the second week, delirium had set in. Shaler might have seen angels dancing in the reflected fish scales, or had his own vision of the abyss there in the lab (Shaler went on, among other things biological, to conduct an inventory of salt marshes for the National Geological Survey throughout the Northeast that included Sippewissett). If you'd been a teacher spending a month on tiny Penikese Island with Agassiz, it might have gone something like that. Agassiz was sixty-six years old in 1873, a grand man of science approaching the end of life who had taken on the Promethean task of challenging Darwin while trying to secure his own legacy of theory and instruction. The summer school opened its doors to forty-four science teachers in 1873. Among those first class members was Charles Otis Whitman, who in 1888 would serve as first director of the MBL. Agassiz's first lecture on July 9 gives a clue to what was in store for those lucky forty-four. "I throw the burden to you," he said. "Don't come to me with questions. I won't answer them. . . . The study of nature is direct intercourse with the highest mind."

Mornings at Penikese were for wandering the island, drawing, and collecting things for dissection and description: gull bones, horseshoe crabs with eggs, an embryonic skate, and fish and shellfish of all kinds were the objects of deep scrutiny. Afternoon lectures by Agassiz and his teaching colleagues covered a broad range of topics from Agassiz's glacial theories, to the *Radiata* (an archaic classification of radially symmetrical animals including echinoderms and colenterates), to Darwin's theory of life—that species evolved out of themselves by force of natural selection over time—and Agassiz's own religiously infused theory—creation by divine plan, with immutable, fixed types as the profound ideas of God. "Even metamorphoses," he wrote, "have all the constancy and invariability of other modes of embryonic growth, and have never been known to lead to any transition of one species to another." According to Agassiz, God's genius lay in man, fully imagined from the beginning of time and reflected in the simplest of all ancestral organisms. His lectures at Penikese Island on the simplest marine invertebrate groups often turned into an attack on the "atheist" theories of Darwin. Corals, sponges, jellyfish, and starfish, he believed, exhibited proof of his theory. All were well represented in the fossil record, from the deepest fossiliferous strata forward. The chain of their existence, Agassiz claimed, was complete. Each, he said, had its own well-marked forms, and there were no transitions. "Nothing but a presiding intelligence could produce these wonderful gradations from the simple to the complex. Therefore I am opposed to Darwin."

Agassiz's own theory of development sank like the *Titanic* as soon as he floated it. Few today can recall or even understand his ideas of fixed and prophetic types. And the Penikese Island Anderson School, his first and last love, didn't survive either. When I was twelve, my father took us out for an excursion in the family motorboat on a foggy day and we missed tiny Gull Island entirely, ending up on more remote Penikese, wondering as we wandered over ruined foundations and around gull nests with their brown speckled eggs—gulls screaming overhead—what had been there before (after the Anderson School, it served as a Leper Colony and now is home to a boys' school). Agassiz had had grand designs for the school. It was to be his model and his monument, combining teaching, embryological research, and applied science along the lines of Spencer Baird's work at the newly formed U.S. Fish Commission lab in nearby Woods Hole. But he died not long after the first school of budding natural history teachers left the island, perhaps worn out by all the wrangling over evolutionary theory. His son, Alexander, ran the Anderson School the following and last year. Charles Otis Whitman was in attendance for that second year as well. But Penikese Island was too remote for a school in 1874 and perhaps too suffused in creationism—a "closed type" of thought that would have to be unlearned by Agassiz's students as they marched forward into the Darwinian era.

Many have pondered Agassiz's stubborn opposition to Darwin. Alpheus S. Packard, writing in 1898 in *The American Natural-*

ist about Agassiz's philosophical views, described him as moving right up to the edge of Darwin's theories by advocating ideas that underlay it (including ice age theory), and then, illogically, stopping, and failing to adopt the new view—the idea of "organic or genetic connections between forms." He pointed out that Agassiz's enthusiasm for embryology and Hackle's biogenic law was also fundamentally an interest in evolutionary process. Agassiz himself said on Penikese Island that "I should have been a great fellow for evolution if it had not been for breaks in the paleontological record." Agassiz, the master observer of bones, scales, feathers, teeth, and guts of comparative form, should have seen as well as anyone the relationships within various classes of organisms across broad stretches of time and could have done so without abandoning his religious perspective. But the confluence of reason *and* mystery swirled about him. He had the golden fog of Emersonian idealism in his eyes and ears and a deep faith in God and science both. Here in this confluence lay his enthrallment: that form and cause were held together in a unified cosmos that conjoined moral and biological realities. Things were to Agassiz not what they seemed. Harvard philosopher William James, speaking about Agassiz's contributions to science fifty years after the founding of Agassiz's museum at Harvard, said, "the truth of things is after all their living fullness, and some day, from a more commanding point of view than was possible to anyone in Agassiz's generation, our descendants, enriched with the spoils of all our analytic investigations, will get round again to that higher and simpler way of looking at nature."

Could it be that, with our most commanding ecological view of the world today, we may be returning to an Agassizian perspective? Ecological science has shown a unity in all the diversity of forms and in the complexity of processes in the world. Our experience of the whole, organic world builds a space for something bigger, something sacred. Something different than the bird that our eyes hear and our ears see. Does successful Earth stewardship—the science and art of caring for home—demand this double allegiance? Walking home up the main creek, carefully skirting the snoozing golden plover, I see Agassiz in his black frock coat stooping to pick up something common that he finds incredible. Amazed, he holds it aloft—the smooth shell of a moon snail. Moving forward, he stands for a long minute bent over the red *Cyanea capillata*, lion's mane jelly, pulsating like a heart and pushing—a fixed idea in the mind of a visionary God—against the tide and upstream.

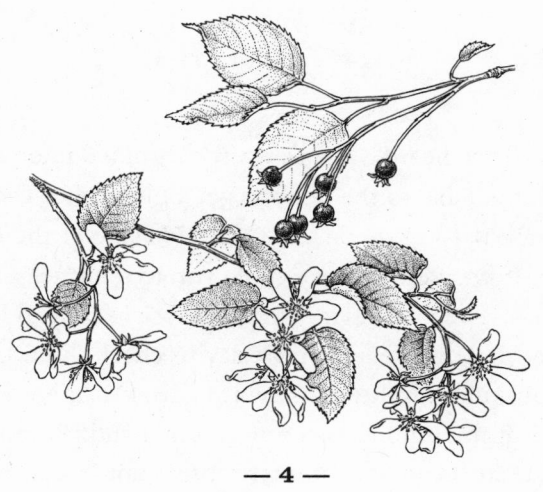

— 4 —

mud

AT NIGHT, ALONE, self-exiled from my family and living in an empty summer neighborhood, I found to my surprise that I had become bored. So I resorted to the mindless balm of television—a worthwhile, made-for-TV Louis L'Amour cowboy story with existential undertones. His courageous heroine homesteading with her teenage son on the vast western range waits, like Penelope, for the return of her gold-mining husband. She sends poems attached to tumbleweeds rolling out into the world to find him. But, unlike Odysseus, he has met his sorry end never to return. Unlike Penelope, a new cowboy rides in, and she rehitches. It's pragmatically poetic. An American reunion without all the risky years of waiting.

Growing up, we didn't have television here. We had roads and beaches to walk. We had a dock and small boats; and we had friends' houses, charades, and playing cards: crazy eights, hearts, spades, I doubt it, go fish, card houses, oh hell, and spit were games of choice. The grownups played bridge late into the night. If we were bored or wanted to escape in the evening, we went to the dock. If we heard a train's whistle during dinner, all six of us ran from the table to the dock to get a glimpse of the rickety three-car train passing by on the Cape Cod line at the east end of the cove. If we were fast, we could run to the tracks, beat the train, and lay a penny down. The dock was a central hub. We always went there a dozen times a day to check the tide, search for blue crabs, pull up the minnow trap, look at the mud, or, at night, swirl up bioluminescence with our hand. Boredom was easily staved. But an empty summerhouse is unnatural and full of ghosts at night. And boredom is not easily staved. Nor is midlife insomnia. My grandmother was reading in her old chair by the fireplace. Mary, her cook, maid, and companion, who at the age of fifteen with her sister left the tattered remains of her family in Ireland and came here to stay for good, was puttering over the kerosene stove in the little galley of a kitchen. Mary was family, but as both servant to my grandmother and best friend, the relationship was fraught with issues of class and religion that we never questioned. She was a devout Catholic set down in a family of Protestants. She read the *Herald*. Mimi and Grandad read the *Globe*. We kids didn't know much about her life outside our family. But she seemed to know everything about us as we trooped in and out of her kitchen through one swinging door and out the other, growing an inch every time.

It was lovely really that they were there in the house ghosting around, but I couldn't sleep with their tight-lipped immortality, so I took a beach chaise, a sleeping bag, a book, a bottle of cold beer, and a headlamp down to the dock for the stars' company. The tide was low and still dropping. Technically, it was already morning. There were no lights around the cove and no moon. The stars were bright in the sky above and reflecting up from the low water below. I could pick out the Dolphin and that funny keystone constellation our own galaxy is hurtling toward. The dock, a floating way station, with its vantage point of both mud and stars, was a good place to brood and feign sleep. The northern cross high over head and underneath the tintinabular bells of a small spring running fresh water through spartina into the cove and the splash of small bait fish. Thus suspended between the poles of a meaningful antithesis, I could direct my interior universe.

Children, according to the medical doctor, new age spiritualist, and author Depak Chopra, have an innate brooding complex—an abiding interest in the biggest questions of life in relationship to themselves. Class, privilege, religious intolerance may have been too close for us to handle, but what was the meaning of life? Who am I? Is there a God that cares? These questions do press on children. Childhood contains a window to the world before the Fall that closes as we get older. My experience of an earthly childhood paradise/home and experience as a father of three curious children bears out the doctor's claims of the childhood mind intuitively open to the mysteries of the universe. I remember walking barefoot down a dirt road here on a night in August with childhood friends Sarah and Ben. We were thirteen and big ponderings were afoot. That evening, young Ben, feeling romantically inclined, put his arm around blond and freckled Sarah. He had a crush on her. But she turned, slapped his arm away, and looked accusingly at me. "Did you tell him to do that?" she demanded. "No," I said defensively. Why would I have? I had a crush on her, too. Of course, I never told her. Ben laughed and, in one of the better non sequiturs I can recall, said, "Don't you love thinking about the meaning of life?" It was, he said, his favorite thing to do. We were in agreement and went on down the dark beach road, heads in the stars, leaving aside questions of romantic inclination, competition, and sexual yearnings for the moment. Childhood philosophers often came in trinities in summer, and there was wondering about God, life, and sex going on. Most of us lose the big brooding questions as we get older. Except for the question of sex, they fade, giving way to the more mundane, practical, applicable, and objective. Job security, taxes, and fortunes of the Red Sox. The history of biological science seems to me like that. It began as a brooding exercise, focused on the big metaphysical mysteries in relationship to "I." Who are we? What are we from? Girl, two boys. Answers often ended either in mud, sex, or stars. It's a fact of existence: good stewards of the home place ought to know and understand those polarities.

Mud, like crows, is common in a salt marsh, and even more common in the cove we lived beside. Ken Foreman, microbiologist and director of the Ecosystem Center's graduate studies program, likes to refer to mud—an iron-reduced gray, gelatinous substrate—as the ash of decomposition. It's considered an organic soil: at least 40 percent composed of life's finely milled carbon-based residue that, along with silts and clays—the smallest mineral particles—floats with the tides into the dead ends of marsh creeks, the pockets and edges of slack water coves, and settles out of near suspension. In a salt marsh, spring tides flood the upper marsh to the edge of the uplands, bringing the organic sediment load in to filter down. Slowly over the years, the spartina mat deepens and gives us a carbon copy of time. As life degrades, a marsh aggrades. The same is true in the cove. The mud becomes a type of book, recording drought and deluge, deforestation, young loves, and chemical catastrophe alike. It's a book that tells us who we are, answering at least half the question of a trio of thirteen-year-old philosophers. We are animals come from up from the real world of mud.

One of great scientific readers of the book of mud was Alfred

C. Redfield, associate director of the Woods Hole Oceanographic Institute in the 1940s and 1950s. Redfield, who had a prodigious appetite for research across a wide breadth of marine topics—from oceanliner paint to blue-tinted crab blood—conducted the first classic study of the origins of a Cape Cod salt marsh in the 1940s. His paper, "The Ontology of a Cape Cod Salt Marsh," includes a series of topographic maps derived from a systematic grid pattern of corings into the spartina peat. Each map took him farther back in time until he hit bottom—no more peat found in any of the corings—eighteen thousand years old. He found, as one would expect, that the deepest peat layers were from areas of the marsh closest to the bay—since the shoreline thousands of years ago was miles farther to the east, in an area now offshore. Our shallow upland fringes of marsh are its newest components. Redfield's maps show a shifting mosaic of marsh forms over time. In biology, form is said to follow function. A human arm looks like an arm because of what that arm must do. A finch's bill is conical because it cracks open certain types of seeds. The nature of particular seeds and the Darwinian struggle to survive shapes the bill through thousands of generations over time. A fish has a body shaped like a spear because it must move quickly through water to eat or to avoid being eaten. But the opposite is true when you consider the changing land forms of a marsh, a planet, or a universe. Functions follow land forms. First there was form. A glacier stopped its forward movement and melted away, leaving heaps of unsorted till. Water and rain eroded escarpments and sorted sediments and washed them into a barren plain. The sea level slowly rose to meet the land and kept rising, and as it did, the wet edge rose with it. All life on this wet edge had to conform to the constant change of forms. It's all written in the marsh book of life.

For today's marsh ecologist, mud and the many other sediment types that make up the floor of the ocean (the benthic zone) are the text, a vast linear black box in which microscopic life transacts biogeochemical change. Mud sequesters and transforms organic molecules, and equilibriums are maintained by microbial life that control atmosphere and ocean chemistry both. Microbes, we now know, birthed us and still rule us. But, for the earliest biologists, mud simply housed the invertebrates that they believed held the key to the question of the origins of complex life. In those early days, the debate over evolutionary process was fierce among men who basically agreed that Darwin was right. Woods Hole was in the thick of the Darwinian revolution. There was a kind of race to push beyond Darwin and apply his ideas to every corner of biological development. Competitive scientists were seeing red in tooth and claw.

Louis Agassiz's student Charles Otis Whitman, hired to direct the newly incorporated Marine Biological Laboratory, arrived in Woods Hole in 1888. He worked with sea worms and other mud dwellers. Described as kind, idealistic, "childlike in his unworldliness," Whitman was also a brilliant morphologist and a firm believer in Darwin and reductionist scientific method. A soon as he arrived at Woods Hole, he set about creating an institution that combined research and education and that could pursue not only marine science, but the study of human development and the human body. In Whitman's day, theories of embryological development were dominated by Ernst Haeckel's biogenic law. According to Haeckel (1834–1919), dubbed the German Darwin, evolution acted as a kind of oil painter putting down layer after layer of paint to get to the present set of living forms. The developing embryo, he believed, embodied each stage of evolutionary development. Biogenic law was a germ layer theory: ancestry controlled the developmental outcome of the egg. It was the layers themselves that somehow directed the outcome. Whitman and his MBL colleagues worked vigorously on an opposing theory of development. The epigenic view argued that creation occurred mechanistically, controlled not by ancient morphology but by chemical particles or enzymes in and around the cellular environment of the egg. Epigenics at its most radical said that anything could become anything else: development was just a matter of physics, chemical fluxes, and environmental manipulation. From his meticulously drawn observations of early cell cleavages of the leech, *Clepsine,* Whitman was able to cast doubt on Haeckel's dominant biogenic law. But it was his colleague at the MBL, E.B. Wilson, carefully tracing the earliest cell divisions of annelid worms, tunicates, and crustaceans, who put the old sacrosanct recapitulation theory finally to rest. Several decades later it was MBL researcher Thomas Morgan's work that brought back to the light Gregor Mendel's nearly forgotten genetics experimentation with peas. Eventually, Morgan laid out the function of chromosomes. It won him a Nobel prize in 1933. As a footnote to the lingering scent of transcendental metaphysics through all of this, listen to what the other Whitman—poet Walt Whitman, twenty-three years Charles Whitman's elder, though similar in white-bearded appearance—says about the source of being and Haeckel's germ layer theory. From "Song of Myself": "Before I was born out of my mother generations guided me, / My embryo has never been torpid, nothing could overlay it. / For it the nebula cohered to an orb, / The long slow strata piled to rest it on . . . Now on this spot I stand with my robust soul." Once again, science arrives to find that the poet has been there already, come and gone.

At the MBL, questions evolved from morphology and embryology, to physiology and eventually marine ecology. Mud always had a role. Every summer for ninety years the invertebrate class would make a trip to Sippewissett in search of specimens for study. Every summer researcher had his organism. Rachel Carson studied eels. Harvard physiologist Alfred Redfield had the horseshoe crab. He came to the MBL in his summers during the early years of the twentieth century and took up physiological questions of Darwinian proportions having to do with marine invertebrate blood transport systems. Among his creatures of interest were the mud-walking and burrowing spineless denizens of cove and marsh. Eventually it was Alfred Redfield's work that bridged from human physiology to the focus on ocean and global systems found at Woods Hole.

Initially, Redfield studied blood, the body's nutrient and waste transport system. His first papers reported results of his classic epigenic experiments on the developing egg. He used *Nereis*, a marine worm that was until recently hatching out of the mud of this cove and leaving tracers on the water's surface, and examined the physiological effect of beta rays, ultraviolet light, and radium on the developing eggs. By the 1920s, he had moved on to the study of respiratory proteins in blood, particularly the oxygen-bearing protein molecules containing hemocyanin—copper-based protein compounds. Hemocyanin gives off blue-colored spectra when exposed to oxygen. His species of interest included horseshoe crabs (*Limulis polyphemus*) and other blue-blooded organisms collected at Sippewissett and in the waters off Woods Hole. The transport of gases and gas exchange in the blood occupied his imagination, as did the entire notion of blood circulation in the bodies of marine organisms. He asked some typical Darwinian questions, but from the perspective of physiology. What, for example, might have been the evolutionary pathway to development of the respiratory functions of blood in marine animals: the origin, advantages and efficiencies of these copper-based gas transport systems? His mind was fixed, like his predecessors and contemporaries, on functions—how and why pieces of anatomy, organs and organelles, and molecules interact.

Redfield's research shift came in the 1930s with the founding of the Woods Hole Oceanographic Institute. He was one of the first scientists hired by Dr. Henry Bigelow, the first director of the Woods Hole Oceanographic Institute. Redfield's investigations into blood chemistry, gas exchange, and circulation in the body expanded to encompass the functions of a bigger body—the ocean. With his physiologist's perspective intact, Redfield began to view the ocean as a vast organ controlling climate. Seawater was the bloodstream. Changes in seawater—temperature, chemical makeup—reflected changing chemical processes in the world's body. John Hobbie, codirector of the MBL's Ecosystem Center today, points out that this idea of an interacting global system, or organism, is now held by many global systems ecologists some seventy years later. It was earlier researchers like Redfield who first described physiological interconnectedness in chemical terms—the oceans as the hub of the wheel. Naturally, Redfield worked to understand the physics of ocean currents and tides, the flushing of harbors and bays, and the movements of hurricanes, since these were analogous to a body's circulation of fluids. In 1934 he published a paper on the proportions of organic derivatives in seawater and their relations to the chemical compositions of plankton. He discovered that the proportion of inorganic, dissolved macronutrients in the ocean was directly correlated to the concentrations of the organic forms in ocean plankton. Redfield's discovery of this connection between the organic and inorganic is now referred to as Redfield's ratio. It says that the cycling of carbon, nitrogen, and phosphorus in plankton determines the ratio of these nutrients in seawater. Redfield's work has been invaluable to the development of the understanding of global carbon and CO_2 cycles—and to the understanding of global warming and sea level rise. Using Redfield's ratio, contemporary global ecologists have been able to estimate global sources and sinks of carbon and model the processes of exchange between them. The Redfield ratio has helped ecologists develop predictive models that consider the impacts human activity has on nutrient cycles—and changes in nutrient cycles on the health of natural systems. For instance, a near doubling of global nitrate levels due to fertilizer synthesis and the burning of fossil fuels in the last hundred years has had a devastating impact on eelgrass in shallow coastal bays, not to mention the impact on global temperatures. The loss of these systems has meant the disappearance of fish populations, the degrading of water quality, and the destruction of valuable scallop beds. Nitrate overenrichment is killing coastal ecosystems. These are, fundamentally, transactions made in mud.

Modern science has gone deeper and deeper into mud, finding worlds of organisms there from the macro to the meso and down to the microbial. More important, science has discovered that within vastly complex communities of marine sediments— the benthos—many vital ecological transactions occur. These are still unexplored worlds. Ken Foreman, my guide to the Ecosystem Center, bent his eye toward Sippewissett when it came to trying to understand the science of nitrogen loading. He sought to understand this microworld and the ecological roles of its middle earth inhabitants, those little-known multicellular monsters (meiofauna) that move between sediment particles, preying on microscopic organisms and protozoans that live on sediment particles (microfauna), and are in turn preyed upon by bigger organisms (macrofauna), large enough to displace sediments. He noted that these creatures contribute significantly to a marsh's overall production and asked whether their populations were limited by available resources or by the organisms that prey on them, all part of a larger effort to understand what constitutes health and worth in a salt marsh system.

I have often thought that messing about in small boats was an apt metaphor for growing up and out of the clutches of adults and childish things. But lying here on my chaise at dead low tide on a float now resting on mud, I am thinking mud walking may be a more apt metaphor. In the ideal, a child first leaves the safety of the dock in a small skiff, confined to the gentle water of the cove. Pondlike in appearance, our cove was safely fringed by tall cordgrass and woods. We spent countless sunny days circling that cove, pulling each other on ropes, racing each other, sinking and bailing, sailing back and forth, and exploring the little water. We learned how to tie bowline knots and how to pull up a sail. Under the watchful eyes of an entire neighborhood of adults, we ventured forth. By ten we were graduates beyond the green bridge to the middle harbor and to bigger boats, and then to the outer harbor where the likes of the white *Jade* and the sleek black *Aleria*, the harbor's most beautiful yachts, and other seagoing vessels are moored. Beyond the outer harbor, a long stone jetty juts out into Buzzards Bay, creating a barrier against rough water: our Colossus of Rhodes. At some point, the child is grown and ready to navigate beyond the breakwater, past its pull of cross currents into the storm-tossed sea-lanes of bright, endless possibility and progress. And that is essentially what happened to us. We post–World War II children, with every advantage, grew up within this model of the progressive ideal: life as progress, continual achievement—positive movement upward and forward out of the cove toward the bay and the light of the stars. If we lucked it out and survived the mud of the cove, we were to become inheritors—to become doctors and lawyers, corporate managers and kings. The star travelers. It was all mapped out for us—the sons and daughters of a conquering class. Modern Western science had a similar childhood—no challenge too great, only a matter of time before all the shadows were swept aside and mystery exposed. In time, every synthetic question, however small, was to be answered, and from this Babylonian edifice of scientific answers, the whole world would be understood. Positivism and pragmatism emerged together with the power of reductionist experimentation, rapid technological innovation, and the industrial revolution at the turn of the nineteenth century to reshape society and the face of the earth. What a hundred-year ride we've been on!

But perhaps mud makes a better metaphor for growing up, for existence, for the science of home. The cove as it is at low tide at night: a sheet of glistening, transformative mud, rank with its devilish sulfide vapors. The end point. The void. The abyss. Not all of us, after all, make the breakwaters and beyond. But all of us end in mud.

As children, we'd sometimes venture out into the muck on a dare. My cousin David, the most daring among us, and with him my older brother led the way. They ran with the bad boys, the boys who couldn't keep their hands off fireworks and engines. Who pulled live things apart. Girls were more attracted to them. They had an excess of boy energy to burn. The first to experiment. Going out there, thigh deep and gleeful in the sucking ooze. They were willing to run the risk of getting mired in mud too thick to escape. I had little courage for it. But David had heavy bones for trouble and a greater interest in pulling things apart than in putting them together. Hair in his eyes all the time, a big laugh and a wide grin, David was funny, charming, and a good athlete.

Hanging around him, when he let you, was a giddy, scary experience. Mud life and sand life moved out of his way. Sand crabs would skitter and bury in the bay, and he'd go after them with a fearless expertise. Blue crabs in the cove gave wide berth, gone in a gray cloud of silt smoke. What couldn't move fast enough came up out of the mud and, once examined, got tossed up really high or pulled apart. Sea cucumbers, a class of marine invertebrates called *Holothuroidea* from the phylum that includes *Echinodermata* (sea urchins and starfish), are little scrotal bags of jelly water that send up delicate, black, flowerlike filter tube feet and a madreporite, or sieve plate, that connects their circulatory system to water outside them. They were a favorite prey of his, and he was fast. Thrown up into the air, they made the sound of spit when they hit the mud's surface again. I always felt sorry for them. They needed protection. As long as there have been boys walking through the woods with sticks, all small lives have needed protection. George Perkins Marsh may have been among the first to make that rather scientific observation in his study of fish declines in Vermont rivers in the 1830s when he pointed out that the destructive potential of juvenile boys was not the *only* reason, as if it might have been a claim made by distraught mothers that he needed to debunk. The ecology of bad boys. Was this the beginning of my own environmental ethic? David's doing was always done full speed. No mud in the cove ever held him back. He danced on the edge of the muddy abyss, and I was in awe. Then we grew up and I saw little of him, and adulthood had its own kind of mud that took him, held him, and never let go. His life was short, but he lived it with a sense of gleeful daring. Always striding forward toward the new thing and unafraid or unaware of mud's deadly hazards. He got more per mile than most.

But, I am still here, playing it safe—afloat now on the thin water of the turning tide and watching the faint glow of the coming day over the glacial moraine to the east. I have not known suffering.

We all end up in mud to be biologically remade. This is truth writ small as a microbe and large as a mudflat that reflects stars. But do we have a dual nature? Is it a cruel light that remakes a soul? Was Agassiz right? Is there some perfect balance, a harmony of two that makes one? Is the science of home a mystical logos of equilibriums? Dark and light? What can be known and what can't be? Stars and mud a vital unity? I don't know. Out on this dock at dawn now, I think of my cousin David and a smile forms on my sleepless lips. Somewhere he is, I think, slurping his way joyfully to a green bridge and beyond, up to his thighs in mud. And I do miss him. That smile of determined, deranged delight.

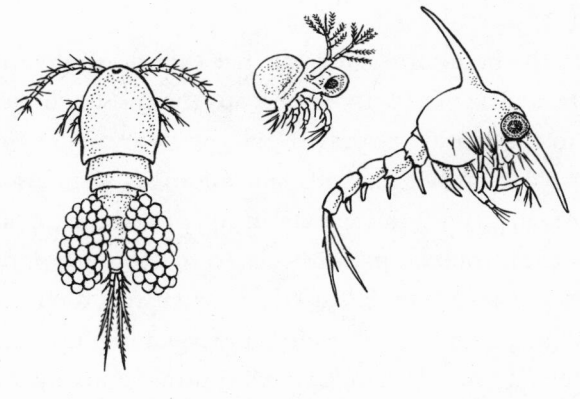

— 5 —

microbes rule

IT CAN BE hard, warming up to microbes, even the pretty purple ones. In June, at low tide, a lovely purple sheen lights up over the exposed sandbars in the creeks at Sippewissett. Up on the marsh peat just above the mean high tide, the sheen has texture and develops a matlike structure. Purple blends to pink and gold to curling black leaves of the same stuff. It's layered there like a slimy black pancake. At some point growing up, I learned that these thin leathery mats were sulfur bacteria, but I didn't go much deeper than knowing the name—since it was, well, bacteria, and bacteria is, as my son says, kind of icky.

In retrospect, the bacterial communities on the marsh were the prize passed over, the well-disguised and distinguished party guest nobody recognized. Microbes everywhere in the world are superstar performers in the oldest economy—the global ecological one.

At Sippewissett, beginning with John Teal and Ivan Valiela, microbial life had been center stage from the start. Not only were microbes the base of food chains that led up to fish, and one of the sources of productivity in perhaps the most productive ecosystem in the world, surpassed only by the productivity of the vascular plants in salt marshes, but microbes were also the mediators of nitrogen transformation, sulfate reduction, and a host of alchemical transformations related to the decomposition of organic matter. Certain bacteria, particularly in the genera *Nitobacter*, break down nitrate, using the oxygen in nitrate molecules to fuel cellular metabolism. Denitrification eventually transforms the nitrates back to atmospheric N_2 gas. Salt marshes are muddy chemical plants capable of processing tonnages of land-derived nitrate. This is good. Shallow coastal water ecosystems are extremely sensitive to additions of nitrate. Because we've been nitrate loading for the past one hundred years, the biogeochemical transformations occurring in muddy places like Sippewissett were, suddenly in the mid-1970s, very important processes to understand.

Woods Hole, in many respects, is a world away from the marsh. It is home to at least four great world-renowned research institutions and a handful of almost great ones. It has achieved a status of nearly mythic proportions in the annals of American biological science history, marine fisheries science, and oceanography. The Hole itself—a fairly narrow, rock-strewn cut where the tides daily rage between Buzzards Bay and Vineyard Sound—is dramatic. Dangerous. Across the Hole, treeless Menemsha Island, the first bump of the Elizabeth Island chain, is as mistily off-limits to the general public as Avalon was to mortals. But, for all its fame, beauty, and summer wealth, Woods Hole has always had the feel to me of a no-nonsense working town full of shipping businesses, sailboats, fishing, an undisguised distain for tourists, and surprisingly decent chowder. It's especially nice in the off-season when you can always find a parking spot in front of the red-brick labs and offices of the National Marine Fisheries, the MBL, or the Woods Hole Oceanographic Institute huddled around the harbor and still get a ticket for overstaying.

Up in the old brick Lilly building, the MBL has a small DNA lab called the Josephine Bay Paul Center for Comparative Molecular Biology, which is surprisingly full of state-of-the-art equipment and state-of-the-art people. I had wanted for many months to meet its esteemed and impossible-to-meet director, Mitch Sogin, because I understood that he had spent some time sequencing some of the microbes involved in the nitrogen cycle in the marshlands. When I finally met Sogin in his lab, I was both delighted and chagrined. I have found in my limited experience around highly accomplished scientists that they expect a lot from someone who calls himself a science writer and are let down when they learn that we actually don't know as much as we should. But Sogin was willing to take me on, for a limited time, as a sort of walking individual human genome project. He gave me a quick tutorial, referred me to remedial reading resources aimed at about the middle-school level, laid out the state of the science of gene sequencing for microbial IDs, and, most important, hooked me up with Ginny Edgecomb, a microbial researcher coming into her own, but currently mired in salt marsh mud.

But before going on, don't you agree that most of the microbiologists you routinely meet carry a bit of chip on their shoulder—seem a bit like they feel underappreciated? It may be the size-matters thing again, though I suppose that given what they know about what microbes do in the world and the general public's vast ignorance and indifference to microbes (unless it's the kind that make them sick and our medical industries thrive), it's easy to see why a microbiologist's life could be frustrating. It's too bad we don't listen to them. When Sogin began enumerating the values of microbial existence, I began to wonder where I'd been all these years. Microbes were the first forms of life to appear on Earth more than 3.5 billion years ago. Microbes can get energy for cell functions from just about any source of chemical energy imaginable, including rocks. For most of their evolutionary span, microbes were the only life around. Microbes produced our oxygen-rich atmosphere, and their primary production and respiration maintain it. Two groups of ocean-dwelling bacteria, *Synechococcus* and *Prochlorococcus* with a global biomass of one billion metric tons, provide 10 to 50 percent of the oceans' primary productivity and as much as 15 percent of the atmosphere's oxygen. Nitrogen-fixing bacteria, nitrifiers and denitrifiers, control global utilization of nitrogen, a nutrient essential to the structure of protein molecules in our cells. Sulfur microbes play a major role in cooling and warming the Earth, and sulfate-reducing microbes buried in the anaerobic muds of salt marshes may contribute significantly to the processing of vast amounts of sulfur washing into the ocean from the land and over the marsh from the sea, making sulfur, a critical nutrient, available to life-forms. Microbes decompose organic matter with its stored carbon and energy and turn it into mineral nutrients that become available to new life. In doing so, they mediate CO_2 levels in the atmosphere. In fact, microbes make up 50 percent of the total biomass of life on Earth. There are more microbial cells on Earth than stars in the universe. There are more microbial cells *on* you and *in* you than cells *of* you. And as far as microbial diversity goes, said Sogin, 80 percent of all biodiversity is microbial. Evolutionary distances separating plants, animals, and fungi are dwarfed by similar comparisons between lineages within the kingdom Protista (single-celled animals with nuclei) alone, said Sogin. In the current five-kingdom view of life on Earth, for instance, one small group of Protists called *Chrysophyta* contains organisms as genetically diverse, based on ribosomal analysis, as, say, a rhinoceros is to a banana tree. All of this Sogin said to me. In short, he said, microbes rule. I couldn't disagree.

Given the ultimate importance of microbes, why is it then that science knows so few of them by name and function? Sogin estimated that fewer than 1 percent of the microbes that keep the Earth healthy—its biogeochemical systems in dynamic equilibrium—are known. Part of the reason is that microbes are small. The most primitive prokaryote bacterium is one-fiftieth the size of one of our blood cells. It's hard to grow them in the lab. Bacteria living in the muddy organic soils of the marsh, inundated twice daily by salt water, live in symbiont colonial communities with thousands of other microbe species along complex and shifting chemical gradients. Re-creating these gradients and the symbiosis found in the salty and muddy natural chemical plants that salt marshes are is next to impossible in the lab. But knowing them, Sogin said, by their genetic signatures and linking these signatures to a vast and as yet unknown universe of functions microbes perform in nature could be a boon to our efforts to become better stewards of our world. We don't really know, for instance, said Sogin, which microbes are doing what in the marsh, or what, for that matter, constitutes a community of healthy functioning microbial life in the salt marsh. We know the by-products of their metabolism, but that's about all.

To date, said Sogin, ecologists have treated microbes in soil and water as a kind of black box. They have been more interested in the chemical inputs and outputs of the box than in the identities of the organisms in the box itself. Sogin and other microbial taxonomists working on microbial IDs are opening the black box by going back to ply the morphologists' and cell physiologists' trades, only with the developing Star Wars technology of the computer-driven genetics lab. But, of course, it goes way deeper than knowing the names of things. Learning the chemical functions and genetic identities of specific microorganisms is important to understanding how various places and localities like coastal estuaries, hardwood forests, salt marshes, tundra regions, coral reefs, grasslands, and salt marshes function biochemically, and how these functions fit into global-scale biochemical cycling. It is no longer adequate to be concerned merely about the loss of biodiversity. Ecologists are worried that Earth functions are failing: toxic pollution, global warming, ozone depletion, and the fertilization of vast areas of the coastline are, they fear, pushing the regulated systems that support all life into disequilibrium. Most, if not all, of these systems are microbe driven.

Many scientists and graduate students at Sippewissett worked with microbes in creek beds and spartina peat over the years. Bob Howarth and John Teal published studies of sulfate reduction in the marsh, and students in the MBL microbial ecology course conducted projects of all kinds at Sippewissett between 1972 and 1985. The pigments, structure, light penetration, and photosynthetic activity of microbial mats at Sippewissett have been studied in detail and published. Over the years, several Sippewissett scientists worked, like Sogin, on microbial identities. They worked on detecting visual and physical characteristics using powerful microscopes and chromatography. But chromatography had its limitations. Microbes, like people, look a lot alike. Gene research opened an entirely new vista in the microbial ID department.

Ginny Edgecomb, a microbial ecologist with the MBL, had spent a fair amount of her time mucking around in the salt marshes before I met her. Thanks to Sogin, I was able to tag along with her team to the Long Term Ecological Research Lab in the

Great Marsh north of Boston to find out what their work with denitrifying and sulfate-reducing bacteria in marsh mud was all about. Her team was part of a study she called the "Microbial Observatory."

The purpose of the Microbial Observatory, said Edgecomb, is to document seasonal changes in microbial communities and to consider human influences—the inputs of toxic substances or nutrient enrichment from fertilizer runoff and air pollution, for instance—on these systems. "We're trying to get a handle on both sulfate-reduction and nitrogen-fixation processes, in particular, and how they change over an annual cycle. We want to try to link these changing chemical processes and products to the groups of organisms that are responsible," Edgecomb told me.

I watched as Edgecomb leaned out over a bed of black creek-bottom mud and, with one arm extended to a colleague for balance, inserted a tube to collect a sample of cold black creek mud. Not a particularly glamorous undertaking, but it's DNA she's after, not mud. She and her team took the creek mud samples and more from just beneath the spartina mat, a zone of highly oxygenated mud, infiltrated by grassroot-like rhizomes called the rhizosphere. Back at the lab, Edgecomb went through what she described as cookbook stuff, designed to separate the DNA from the rest of the material in her samples and then amplify it.

Edgecomb atomized mud samples to separate and tease out living cells from muddy homes. Then she applied a series of chemical enzyme treatments coupled with organic extractions to isolate DNA molecules. Once they were isolated, she began making thousands of copies of the gene for the small subunit ribosomal RNA using a process called polymerase chain reaction, which splits the DNA molecules, combines them with a small DNA primer for that gene section, and amplifies new copies in a cyclical process. Within a few hours, the smaller subunit of the ribosomal gene had been amplified exponentially. This particular section is ideal for sorting out microbes because parts of it have evolved very little in three billion years, while other parts have diverged dramatically.

A final step she described is called gel electrophoresis, whereby the different genes she was expressing are separated into bands according to their unique base compositions. The gels are photographed using ultraviolet spectra, analyzed by computer, and used for a variety of further tests to identify the organisms that each band came from. What you end up with is not a name as we know it but a pattern—something deeper than physical appearance. And, said Edgecomb, since we already know where it resides in the mud and the by-products of its metabolism we can finally link who it is with its job in the world.

It will be a big step forward when school children know the names of the microbes that, say, mediate the level of CO_2 in our atmosphere or turn nitrate back into atmospheric nitrogen. Because it's likely that they will be putting as much energy into connecting the world back together as we currently expend taking it apart. Keeping our microbes happy appears to be a prerequisite of the first order.

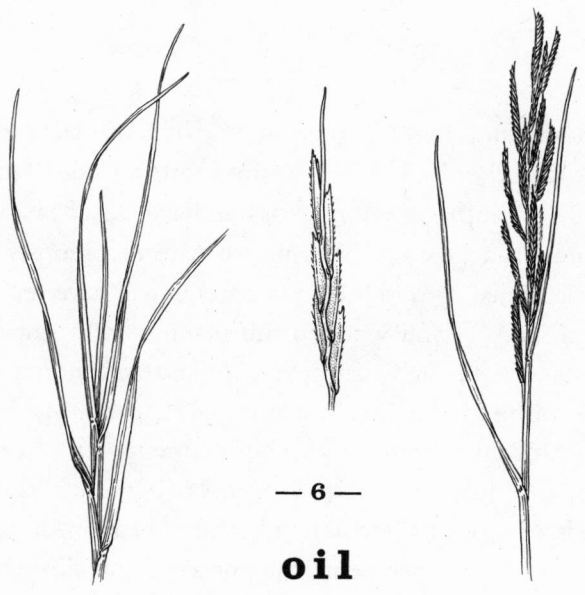

— 6 —

oil

The true men of action of our time, those who transform the world, are not the politicians and the states-
men, but the scientists. . . . When I find myself in the
company of scientists, I feel like a shabby curate who
has strayed by mistake into a drawing room full of
dukes.

—W. H. Auden

EVERYONE HAS PARENTS. Sharks, people, and microbes do. My
kind, good parents just arrived here at their summer dwelling, as
they have been doing for sixty years. They are two who are one.
How can my siblings and I, six who are many, possibly do as well
by this place?

They came in around noon, bearing boxes of perennials for
the border garden inside the low stone wall that circumnavigates
the small front yard. It's an old garden first established and cared
for by my grandmother Mimi and her Irish cook and house companion Mary for years. There is a marble statue of the Virgin

Mary without hands in the corner—a relic of a Wellesley garden of my grandmother Belle Hart on my mother's side. And yes, she grew up a Southerner. Pink roses and a Rose of Sharon by the gate and, inside, clumps of primrose, asters, coreopsis, lilies, phlox, crane's bills. By mid-June, my parents will have replanted the hanging baskets and wooden tub planters with impatiens. This year they've brought trumpet vine and vine honeysuckle for trellises on the back shed and another clematis. My parents are the opening crew, arriving well before the march of families troop through in July, with minnow schools of grandchildren and their friends. My parents retreat in July and return for August and September. At September's end, they become the closing crew, putting the house to bed, somehow still managing most of the work of washing the mildew out of curtains, hauling boats, and reseeding the terrible lawn, in tandem, in spite of replaced hips, bum knees, fuzzy eyesight, and the irksome faculty of come-and-go memory. They are the truest stewards and soul of the place. The elders—sharp and active and beloved by family and a large multigenerational surrounding community, with fewer of their generation by the year—are still here and an original pair.

It is possible to discover the fountain of youth at home with parents like them on one side and children growing up on the other. Three generations taken together is a time span long enough to detect a trend—something indestructibly youthful hidden inside human nature. A resilience in spite of the way things are. It's a time span wide enough that time itself begins to dissipate. At home among the generations, what is common ground trumps what is different. What is long trumps what is short. Good parenting enables difference and growth by holding sacrosanct what is not different and what is enduring. My parents and I don't see eye to eye on many things. They are Republicans—though not of the fraudulent type in power today. They are faithful liberal, non-literalist Episcopalians. They see biblical truth as the metaphor and poetry and reflective guide that it truly is. Adaptive and un-changingly eternal both. I am not an Episcopalian anymore, but have gone deeper down their liberal grain. And as far as life and work is concerned, we differ. My father spent twenty-five years at a bank. I am a not-so-gainfully-employed fifty-year-old writer who has left his wife and children for a month; who is strung out on words, subsisting on small grants and freelance crumbs; who is currently considering clams, the universe, and everything else in a salt marsh, except how to pay the bills. He is a money guy. I have worked in the nonprofit sector for twenty years. I taught children off and on in canoes, on mountains, and knee-deep in bogs. Had bees up my pants and held gray jays in the palm of my hand. My mother held down a classroom for twenty years. They are conservative in their ways. I am a liberal conservationist in my way. During the American Revolution, they might have come down as Loyalists. I'd have been smoking hemp and scattering tea on the water. And yet, they accept and welcome me. They trust something about me—I don't know why—knowing what it is I need now—to write, to finally give what I've always wanted to give. And we are a family. That's the way it has always been. I know that the very best gifts I received came from them. Thus, I have been free like woodbine to climb my own way toward the light.

Their arrival necessitates that I clean up my act, repent my slovenly ways, give up my habit of wakefulness and pacing ac-tiveness at all hours of night and day; that I forego fishing when I want and spreading out my scientific papers where I want; that I stop sleeping on the living-room couch, eating out of the pot, and writing into the wee hours. Not reluctantly, I give over the kitchen to my mother, who has brought real food that must be prepared and cooked before it is eaten. I give myself over to formal sit-down meals. We dine at their preordained time. They have funny little rituals leading up to dinner: a game show they like, or news. TV is rarely on in my house. Then, just the three of us there in the evening at the big table that fits many more. We talk about small important things. The Carolina wrens prattle from the window of the shed. The catbirds meow. We talk about my father's minidune restoration project going on where our path to the beach cuts over a dune. He puts snow fence in a zigzag to capture blowing sand. We catch up on other family members: Abbie in Rome; my brother's new job. There is always something for dessert. My father and I wash the dishes. My mother reads. When they're around, I don't miss the solitude but get more of it. They hold down the fort, and I get out and about on the marsh or into Woods Hole. One afternoon in particular, I make a trip by rusty bike to another harbor and another salt marsh only a few miles away as the crow flies. Wild Harbor was the landing site thirty-six years ago of one of the worst oil spills to have occurred in Buzzards Bay. I was in high school when the spill occurred, and I've saved the note my father wrote me about it. I wanted to see the residue of it with my own eyes.

There is something about time that home dwellers, like my parents, and a home scientist, like John Teal, should have in common. They have an interest in the long view, in what good can outlive them. Upward or downward ecological trends can't be well detected over the short term, and dwelling—knowing and loving the place—is a long-term venture with plenty of short-term risk. Toward the back half of life, why not think long term? We arrive at our own state of the eternal now by very different means. Whereas, in the reflective moment, or absorbed by the life of working and being in a place, I get a fleeting glimpse of timelessness, a home scientist seeks out time—crawls through the agonizing minutes, hours, months, and years of it—with probes and dials to measure the minutiae of change. By so doing, he approaches what is beyond time—a picture of how a marsh, a world, maintains itself in constant change and in endless equilibrium.

What happened in Wild Marsh? On the evening of September 15, 1969, at the brink of Richard Nixon's—that most unlikely avatar's—environmental decade, a tugboat, pulling the oil barge Florida through Buzzards Bay from an oil storage facility in Tiverton, Rhode Island, to a power plant on the Cape Cod canal, lost its radar, veered off course in the thick fog, and came aground. One hundred and seventy-five thousand gallons of number two heating oil washed out of the broken barge onto beaches and into the harbors and marshes nearby. Sippewissett was not hit directly. But Wild Harbor, a narrow and shallow gut of tidal water surrounded by spartina marsh farther north in the bay, bore the full brunt of the spill.

According to newspaper accounts, the immediate effect of the spill swamped the senses. In the water the oil formed a "coffee-colored emulsion" visible for several miles. Because of the powerful petrol smell, residents far inland woke up thinking their furnaces had failed. Within hours, dead marine life began piling up on nearby beaches.

George Souza, the local shellfish constable in 1969, toured the scene and was overwhelmed by the windrows of corpses. Onlookers described miles of beach littered with the dead and dying: decaying lobster, finfish, scallops, soft-shelled clams, mussels, marine worms, and other benthic invertebrates. And the numbers seemed to increase exponentially as a stiff wind and waves washed remains ashore. The impact of the oil on ocean life was immediate, catastrophic, and long lasting. Over the weeks, benthic sediments once teeming with diversity were overtaken by a single opportunistic species of red worm. In a piece about the spill in the November 1973 issue of *The New Yorker* magazine, Souza described Wild Harbor as "a waste land, a massive graveyard."

The scientific study that began nearly immediately was the most comprehensive ever to date to be focused on a spill. A scientific team led by Dr. Howard Sanders, George Hampson, and Dr. Max Blumer, all from the Woods Hole Oceanographic Institute, set out to study all the impacts of the spill. In all, over twelve scientists conducted studies that included surveys from top to bottom of the marine food chain, sediment cores, and long-term trawling for benthic organisms in affected areas offshore and sampling far beyond the affected areas. While earlier studies, paid for and often conducted by oil companies, were limited to measuring fish kills and dead birds, the scientists from Woods Hole sampled the worms, crustaceans, and micro- and macroscopic creepers and crawlers within the benthic community at the base of the food chain. Benthic invertebrates aren't mobile over wide areas so are good pollution indicators. By running chromatography analysis on samples, researchers were able to fingerprint the hydrocarbons they were seeing inside organisms and thereby differentiate spilled oil from naturally occurring hydrocarbons that are widely produced and persistent in nature. And Woods Hole scientists were in it for the long haul.

One of the scientists in on the study was Dr. John Teal, the Woods Hole salt marsh ecologist and marine biologist who'd just published, with his first wife Mildred, *Life and Death of the Salt Marsh*. Having studied salt marshes up and down the East Coast for fifteen years, he had the long view in mind. What, he asked, would be the impact of the spill on the marsh long after the harbor and bay looked normal again? He set long-term monitoring plots at Wild Harbor and began visiting them regularly and long after other researchers had closed up shop.

Oil spills, it turns out, have short-term devastating effects on coastal ecosystems that spread across a widening area as hydrocarbons disperse. It is also true that natural systems do recover, though it may take them many years to do so. Most important, the study of the Florida spill proved that independent ecosystem science could be an indispensable partner to environmental policy making. The following decade produced the bulk of this country's most important environmental policy. Government started listening to ecologists. This is when my generation came of age: those of us who graduated high school and went to college in the early 1970s found ourselves in the thick of new environmental studies curricula and daily headlines on the latest disaster, disaster response, and policy initiative. Thirty years after the wreck of the *Florida*, domestic oil spill volumes had been reduced from a high of twenty-two million gallons in 1975 to less than two million gallons in 2000. But what about the impact on the marsh?

Teal kept going back. And he kept finding oil. Through the decade that saw the resignation of Nixon and two Middle East oil crises, that heard Jimmy Carter's pleas for conservation and alternative fuel research, oil was still oozing out of Wild Harbor. Teal kept going back through the 1980s that elected Reagan and saw a rollback of environmental protections and a stall in clean energy development. He kept going back through the 1990s and the rise of the SUV and an uptick in violence in the Middle East. He kept going back through two Iraq wars and through the oil war genocide in Sudan and the shutdown of wells in Venezuela, through the effort to open the Arctic Refuge for its drop of oil in the early years of this century. The oil in Wild Marsh is still there.

Salt marshes have a long memory. Humans have a short one. Like sponges, salt marshes hold onto things. But for us, it's out of sight, out of mind. Over our dinner that evening, I described my trip into Wild Marsh. I parked my bike by the outlet bridge where the marsh flows into the bay and walked back on the squishy peat mat to find the subtle markers of forty years of observation, and there it was, the stained black pitch of time eternal, the stuff that sustains hydrocarbon man, leaching its beautiful little rainbow slicks. It's likely, I told my parents, according to what I had read, that the microbes that live around that oozing ground have long since adapted to life with oil, modified through random mutations to endure the stuff—maybe even live off it. Like us, they may now need it to survive.

What did the biblical prophets say: fire next time? Will the oil that sustains us become the fiery death of us who are willing to drill up the last best place, home of the last greatest free-migrating caribou herd, to extract every drop? While oil wars, global warming and the inherent instability of a world economy that runs on oil that is running out beset us, so does the paralysis of vast profit prevent us from changing. It's not just the oil itself that is strangling us, it's what oil makes. While the incidence of oil spills globally is down, toxic chemical pollution of the ocean has increased. Increased fertilizer production and usage worldwide is the other sign of global overenrichment. Fertilizer takes a tremendous amount of natural gas to synthesize, but it's the nitrates that cause the biggest problem when they end up in our harbors and bays and increase algae growth that upsets the chemical balance of these nitrate-limited waters. Seventy percent of the world's harbors and shallow estuarine bays, the world's most productive natural fisheries, are now badly degraded by nutrient pollution.

About time, Teal said, we need a lot of it to understand what's going on, and yet we don't have the luxury of waiting until we are certain before making policy and management decisions. I had visited with him earlier in the year. John Teal is a healthy, vigorous man in his early seventies. He and his wife Susan live off-Cape in the colonial village of Rochester. Their home is full of books, wooden banisters, and clean swept floors. It's lit by natural light and cooled by trees he planted that grow right up to their windows. The plantings keep the house warmer in winter, too. He is a numbers guy, keeping daily tabs on wind speed and air temperature around the house to show what happens when homeowners work with nature. His wife is an ecologist, too. Home, it appears, is both the source and the extension of their work. They make great coffee between them, too.

Teal has been thinking about salt marshes for a long time. He got his first dose of salt marsh in 1947 at Harvard University from Harvard physiologist and Woods Hole oceanographer Alfred Redfield. Then Georgia-based ecologist Tom Odum recruited him fresh out of Harvard for postdoctorate studies of a salt marsh at Sapelo Island in the 1950s. Teal arrived at Woods Hole Oceanographic Institute in 1961 after a stint in Halifax and spent the next forty years working as an oceanographer there, spending half his time on salt marshes. With Ivan Valiela, a younger ecologist from the University of Massachusetts, Teal began a full-fledged marsh ecosystem study at Sippewissett in 1971.

"No," said Teal, "we didn't know where this thing was going when we started. But we established a very well-controlled long-term experiment. This allowed things to grow along the way." The first purpose was to try to understand the effect of the things that reached the marshes from land by happenstance. At the time, pollutants were pouring into the oceans and atmosphere. "We knew natural systems were being severely impacted," said Teal. They also knew that salt marshes had the capacity to sequester many pollutants and render them less toxic—the idea had even been floated in some civil engineering circles that salt marshes might be used as a final step in sewage treatment. Then there were the basic scientific questions about production and energy flow in salt marshes. Teal had already published an influential paper hypothesizing a model for salt marsh energy flow in *Ecology* in 1962. If anyone was going to prove his model wrong, he said, he wanted to have his name on the paper, too.

Teal and Valiela established twelve permanent nitrate fertilizer plots on the marsh. They used Milorganite on one series of fertilizer plots—a sewage sludge product from treatment plants in Milwaukee, Wisconsin. Each Milorganite plot had a threefold increase of nitrate applied over the last. Traces of heavy metals in the Milorganite remained ten years later and became the basis of studies that traced the pathways of heavy metals, which are toxic to many life-forms in salt marshes and adjacent aquatic systems. Researchers made their weekly forays to the marsh for years, applying fertilizers and studying the long-term effects as added nitrate worked its way through each trophic level, from grasshoppers feeding on spartina, to snails and other macroinvertebrates, to microinvertebrates—including a splendidly complex array of arthropods—down to unicellular life. Vegetative composition of the plots changed over the years; the peat grew deeper and at a faster rate. Nitrate levels were recorded in creek channels, in anaerobic creek muds. Fish populations were also carefully studied. The conversion of nitrate to nitrite—denitrification going on in anaerobic peat layers and creek bottoms—was carefully assessed.

For years and years, they kept going back—observing, recording change, and in the process coming to understand how the entire system works.

"We went into it thinking of marshes as simple systems, and in some regards they are—of course, as far as the higher plant community is concerned they are. But at the invertebrate level and the microbial level, there's a great deal of complexity we hitherto knew little about. Of course, there are great difficulties. The only things you can really understand are those whose functions you can figure out in a controlled lab situation. But what about all the things that don't grow in labs? Taxonomic systems of microbes are still not well understood," Teal said. "Without very detailed knowledge of what microbial organisms do, without knowledge of microbial ecology you probably don't understand enough to link functions properly. There is a great danger in being too certain about what your computer models tell you about complex systems."

"We've learned over the years that salt marshes are robust: they have the ability to resist a good many insults," said Teal. "But today something is happening that is causing marshes to lose their robustness. Salt marshes are receding. Researchers on Long Island suspect changes in sedimentation rate, and sea-level rise may be responsible for salt marsh recession there. But we don't know why yet," he said. "In thirty years of study at Sippewissett, this isn't something we've seen. But thirty years may not be long enough."

How long is long enough? "Long," said Teal. "It's very likely that dredging that occurred in the marshes of Long Island forty years ago for JFK airport may be the major contributor to the decline we're seeing there today. In hindsight, if we had begun monitoring marshes much earlier, long before the dredging began for

JFK, we might have been able to detect the very first indications of decline and know the culprit.

"You never have all the answers—but scientists can no longer use that as an excuse not to give advice. . . . The fact is you know more than the manager knows. If you don't give advice, his decision will be based on greater ignorance. This is a conclusion that comes out of my entire career. People who have information need to share it. And managers and policy makers need to listen."

"The threats to marshes are the same today as they were in 1960," Teal told me. "People are moving in greater numbers to coastal areas, so direct marsh losses still are taking place. The losses are occurring more frequently but usually involve smaller areas of marsh. . . . To save marshlands, we need to do things at all political levels. All politics is local, all ecology is local in one sense too, and on the other hand, all ecology is worldwide. Our actions, in the richest country in the world, consuming more of the world's resources than anyone else, make us responsible for what goes on in Amazonia and Indonesia, too. And what goes on at Sippewissett. We need to take responsibility for our actions. . . . There really isn't a moment to lose."

— 7 —

quahog

CHERRYSTONES, OR QUAHOGS, are hard as rocks. Finely ribbed, the small ones fit in the palm of your hand like a cold heart. I had some in my pocket. You find them in the deeper channels of the marsh that hold salt water even at low tide. I had poached them early in the morning for scup bait and now, with a box of books and a collection of scientific papers from the MBL Library, I was on my way out to a one-room cabin loaned to me by the local land trust. We can't clam here anymore because some of our own homes, with inadequate septic systems, send fecal matter into the marsh. But we can quietly poach, and I should not publicly declare that we do so. But I speak only for myself. Yes, I am a terrible poacher and probably a polluter as well.

But at least I am not a realtor. I wanted to throw my cherrystones at the realtor, whose hair should have been gray to match the color of her soul and her age, but was blond. We stood talking on the little concrete bridge that crosses the tidal steam where it enters the pond at the end of the lane. She had a delightful smile.

Behind us was the last house, where the shell-strewn road turns into two dirt ruts and the ruts into a grassy path where the green woods begin. She had recently sold this last house. The new owners were suing to close public access to the woodlands, cabin, and trail beyond. They had legal toehold enough to believe they might prevail, and enough money to cause the land trust that owned the property to bleed. Why shouldn't they deserve their privacy? she argued. They'd paid dearly for their privacy. Burdened as I was by a heavy box and headed toward that woods and that small cabin hidden there, my new place of work, I couldn't reach my cherrystones to stone her. That's good. I would have been a murderer, and that's worse, in some ways, than being a realtor. Really, where do these people get off, arriving from outer space with millions of dollars and trying to close us out of our own land? Logic would dictate that the little woodland, protected forever, added significant value to the house next to it. The woodland would never be developed. Not sold for all the silver and gold. The owners of the last house would have the run of it, the buffer of it, the beauty of it as their own. The look-what-we-live-beside bragging rights. As would we all. Then she had the gall to ask where all the fish were. Just last night, she said, they were rising here in the pond. They must, she said, have gone through an underground connector to the other pond that's a quarter mile away. And I felt I had just gone down the rabbit hole. Realtors are our Mad Hatters. They are not real, in fact, at all. They are our unrealtors. The fish do not have an underground passageway, and money can't buy what they promise it can. How soon before we set land mines around what we think we own to keep the world at bay? We'll probably blow ourselves up. How dearly do we pay for our privacy?

Privacy and ownership. Who owns all of this? No one. And as a wise friend, Dana Meadows, once said: you need what is mine and I need what is yours to be whole. Around here in these little summer home kingdoms, full of happiness for that brief season of joy before plunging back into work or school after Labor Day, where neighborhoods are interknit with informal sandy paths and the property lines are invisible, it isn't always clear who owns what. Could we have inadvertently created something communal over the years? A sense of clan sharing? If so, it's worth preserving that culture of a shared place. In fact, to save these physical places, we may need to cultivate an understanding of the importance of shared pathways and a type of privacy that invites some level of public participation without lowering standards to the worst insults of the mass mind. This *is* our place after all. There are rules here in this dirt-road paradise. And they apply to everyone. The new homeowner who sues to keep out the riffraff—us included—is breaking some law, something unwritten and important.

That last house on the road the realtor was so proud of selling for such a high price will one day be razed. A taller, larger house will be built there out of economic Darwinism. But the current home is already too large, and it has a domineering view of the marsh and the bay. The oyster lady of my youth built that house and lived there. She, too, was particularly sensitive to encroachment, to privacy, to the sense of her exclusive ownership. Her sensitivity was at least as strong as my enthusiasm for eating clams and oysters. After all, a healthy spirit needs to taste a fresh clam or oyster gotten by its own fingers and opened with its own knife. As kids in old Converse tennis sneakers, we looked for clams at low tide in the marsh by searching out the small holes indicating their presence in sand, then dug after them, piling the gray sand and their white ovate bodies on the flats, and sometimes making large holes that filled with seawater just for the fun of it. This was a kneeling activity, something of an act of prayer. Intent on finding the next one, we were unaware of the passage of time. This was our childhood science. Messing around on the marsh confirmed that we came from clams, and in some ways, that knowledge is the sum tally of the science of home. That awareness of the relationship we have with nature is how we come into our truest inheritance. But a clam ancestry notwithstanding, there remains the problem and reality of property lines.

My first brief encounters with the oyster lady occurred some thirty-five years ago. I had no concept then of land possession or private property. We were not an especially private family. There is little privacy in a small house with six children. This first encounter so surprised and shocked me, I nearly fell down. In a booming voice and holding what could have been a rifle or a wet mop—it really didn't matter—she ordered me to drop that oyster and get out of her creek and off her property. Shocked and afraid, I did drop that oyster, and I did leave—"the way you came in, mister."

I had always been drawn to the creek that runs out of Oyster Pond and along her house through the upper marsh and into Sippewissett. It flowed clear over stones and gravel more in the manner of a freshwater stream in Vermont than a creek in a salt marsh. Mummichogs darted into the shadows beside stones, and spider crabs picked their way daintily along the seaweeds of the bottom. The orange sponges grew in abundance there, looking like polished stone baubles on display under glass. Toward the mouth of the short creek, where the bottom substrate changes from stones to silt and sand and then mud, lay a secret stash of quahogs. I'd scoop a few from there and be on my way. The entire creek also ranked as the best place for oysters. Herein lay the problem with the oyster lady, compounded by the rumor that she packed a Remington 16 gauge.

For a time, the oyster lady's family farmed oysters in the salt pond drained by the creek. To farm oysters, you need clean water. Farming them in the pond must have been marginal at best. Like many creatures of land and sea, oysters produce fantastic amounts of embryonic material. Lots of spawn escaped her floats and seeded the creek. I always felt these were fair game. The oyster lady disagreed.

There are many invisible property lines in the world and in the marsh. There are rights-of-way and easements, contour lines, and something called adverse possession. In a marsh, the tide and storms own it all. But there is the federal "ownership" of waterfowl, fish, and migratory birds. There are the ecological boundaries, and that ineffable sense of ownership beyond property line all users and dwellers of places develop over time. What we think belongs to us often doesn't. It's strange what we come to believe we own. Common law lays out some guidelines. According to the Public Trust Doctrine, which dates back centuries to ancient Roman law, tidal lands and the water itself are held by the state "in trust" for the benefit of the public. While in most states, private property rights extend to the mean high-tide mark—which would have left much of the marsh available to public purposes—in Massachusetts, private property extends to the low-water mark. This old provision of land-use law enabled landowners to develop and protect docks, wharves, and other commercial structures along the shore. The good news is that colonial lawmakers did write up a few exceptions to the rights of landowners to control access to tidal lands. They reserved the rights of the public on these intertidal lands to walk or otherwise pass freely anywhere to fish, fowl, or navigate. According to the attorney general's office, fishing and fowling generally includes the right to clam and the right to birdwatch. So, for instance, as long as I was below the high-tide mark on the oyster lady's property—and this extended practically to her deck—and as long as I carried a few oysters and had binoculars slung around my neck, I was legally within my rights there.

In hindsight, I shouldn't have been so bothered by her, or perhaps so resolute in my desire to flout her rule. After my initial encounter, my shock turned to youthful contempt. I kept daring myself back to her creek. At night, she lit her home with floodlights. To me, these lights, and the imposing presence of the house on the marsh seemed like a much worse encroachment than I had made. I resented her for it.

Usually I stuck to the lower creek, the outer limits of shouting and accurate shooting distance. But soon, intentionally, I began walking closer to the house—ignoring her in a vaguely taunting fashion. Her voice would boom out like a cargo crane's arm trying to lift and displace me. Over time, she stopped shouting and stopped coming out onto the porch when I passed by. She became resigned. She never even tried to shoot me.

What lingers now is the knowledge that she probably *was* a little crazy. Replacing my youthful resentment is a grown-up sense of lost opportunity. I carry the odd desire of wishing I had known her better. Of wishing she were still here, defending her place as if it were a homestead on the high plains. There are worse crimes against the public good. In fact, she committed them. Not only was she threatening me and defending the invisible lines around what she had bought, it was she who first thought up this notion of closing public access on the little road that crosses the bridge and turns into a path into the preserved woods. The road to the cabin (*my cabin*) and to the last bit of woodland on the marsh went past her driveway. She believed it would hurt her property value to have the public pass so near. Apparently, this is a common fear, more common than I wish. Still, I feel more charitable to her memory than I would have expected. After all, she was growing oysters, unlike so many of our new neighbors who are only growing privacy fences. I could have learned something useful from her: how to cultivate what I liked to gather. I was just a summer kid crashing around, oblivious to property rights, consuming pieces of the place: an animal scavenging free lunch.

Where does the view of the world come from that amplifies the need for control and privacy to such a high level? Not from microbes I think. Microbes are inherently communal. They appear to colonize and borrow from each other all the time. We've nursed and nurtured our selfishness. She's gone. She sold her house and moved away. I have the sinking feeling that I will never even meet the new owner, but that instead I may someday hear from his attorney. The court fights over privacy and access continue, and the spoils go to the lawyers. But who could fail to see that wild land full of cedar trees, where the occasional owl can find refuge, where poison ivy and old stone walls ramble, where only a handful of walkers, bird-watchers, and children pass through, accrues benefits directly to us and ours, forever?

There's something in the world that doesn't love a property line. We rely on them to protect us. But they can't. We confuse what we own with what composes and owns us: clams and sun, community, family bonds, the inner stories that sustain us. An excessive focus on boundaries leaves open the possibility that we'll privatize ourselves out of existence.

All of this that I have written I wish I had spoken to the realtor who, when I left her on the bridge, looked perplexed and mad about fish. Meanwhile, onward with books to the little cabin in the woods.

I approve of trespassing and poaching. That's why I tell my kids, go find a marsh on someone else's property and dig a damn clam. Call it common ground. Just don't get shot. Don't contract salmonella poisoning or paralytic shellfish poisoning either. Obey the spirit of all reasonable laws. Stay healthy. Here's my brother's childhood quahog recipe. It's the only one we ever needed:

Open fresh quahogs, careful not to cut off fingertips.

Do not drain!

Place open quahog on cookie sheet.

Place bacon on quahog.

Place small bit of horseradish on bacon.

Place cookie sheet under broiler and broil until bacon begins to smoke, just!

Take out and eat right away. Do not burn your tongue. Of course, there's only one way to fix and eat an oyster. Raw, in situ.

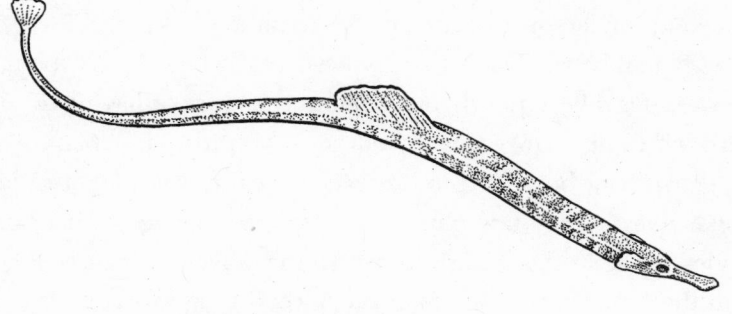

pipefish

> The man who built her so well, said, "This little house
> shall never be sold for gold or silver and she will live
> to see our great great grandchildren's great great
> grandchildren living in her."
> — Virgina Lee Demetrios, from *The Little House*

THERE ARE SO many of us now that share this one small Cape home. We have become a flock. Or a can of sardines. Between my parents, who spend most of June, August, and September at the house, my five siblings, and our combined seventeen children, some of whom are old enough to want the house on their own with friends, the problem of how to divvy up summer is not without its hazards. Fortunately, we are a civil flock, generally flying in formation, and we love each other well. But we now face the even more difficult question of how to pass ownership of the Cape home to my generation. The legal work is complicated, involving the establishment of a trust and a limited liability corporation. It progresses, and a transfer should occur in the fall.

But long-term success—the staying power of our name here—depends on factors outside the legal realm.

My family has a week to ourselves in early July. We try to make a week feel like a month, but without the sense of having to rush around to do so. My three children—two girls, fifteen and nineteen, and one boy, thirteen—already have their own set of rituals: bike rides, a high-tide plunge off the green bridge, ritual boats rides, a sail in the sunfish, a trip to the waves of Nauset Beach on the outer Cape, picnics at the inlet, fishing for scup, days on the beach, barefoot night walks down dark wooded paths to test one's fortitude, and racing around on go-carts one night out on Route 28 in Bourne. A bike ride to Woods Hole. Some of these are our traditions, some theirs. This year, I have had the luxury of long weeks alone here already. For me, vacation week isn't vacation—it's sociology and a kind of worshipful play with a purpose, plus research and writing. During it I have to balance the feeling of being invaded with the desire to spend as much time with family outdoors as possible, doing the things with my children that I did as a child; that I know are fun, that I know how to do; and that reflect the inherent playfulness of this place on the marsh.

I've always been ambivalent about the Fourth of July, not because I don't believe in what it stands for, but because the Fourth seems to give license to the astonishing number of pyromaniacs living among us quietly most of the year. It's really their day. Vermont Fourth of July celebrations always start out small scale, what you would expect given the modest size of our rural communities. Families have tailgate cookouts together in local parks with their swing sets and swimming holes. But then at dusk, they morph into these gargantuan fireworks displays paid for by locals passing a can and managed by the volunteer fire departments. Vermonters, it would seem, scrimp and save all year for the five minutes of sonic blasts on the Fourth that will rock your soul and turn you deaf if you're not careful. I flee them. But even here on the marsh on the night of the Fourth, big explosions woke me at 2:00 a.m., and I began to realize that the explosions were coming from some place out in the woods behind the house. Probably the cabin. And I was sure it wouldn't stop with bottle rockets and M80s. They'd probably end up burning the place down. Pyromania is like gambling: it accelerates and accelerates until the powder abruptly runs out.

So at 3:00 a.m., I walked over the creeks and through the wet grass to the cabin to assess the collateral damage, expecting to find a smoldering ruin, but all I found was a broken window and some harmless graffiti on its fine cedar walls. They had snapped the broom handle trying to force the sliding door, but the new padlocks I'd installed held, and it was just a matter of sweeping up glass and measuring for a replacement pane. They hadn't even stolen the birding scope. There were powder stains on the floor of the deck above, but everything seemed to be in relative order inside, including my books.

The cabin—a simple open room, twelve-by-twenty feet, with a hardwood floor, shiplap cedar interior walls, no electricity, and a woodstove without a chimney—is a wonderful and strange phenomenon, surrounded, as it is, by homes valued in the million range, yet removed and hidden in its wood. It was used as a hunting retreat in the 1930s, then given to the Massachusetts Audubon Society along with more or less ten acres of land around it. It languished for years and slowly began falling apart. The small yard grew up with cedar and roses, the paths grew over, and the old stone walls around it disappeared under viburnum, cat briar, and honeysuckle. Audubon deeded it to the Salt Ponds Land Trust in the 1980s, and the cabin underwent a face-lift. New shingles and paint, a deck with benches all around it, and up on the roof a widow's walk. The idea was to use the property as an environmental education daytime retreat for local school groups, a place for day camps and workshops, with a particular focus on understanding Sippewissett: a great idea that was not particularly well received by some of the neighbors. Today, Marshlands, as it is called, is a fine little gem of a place that sits mostly empty, caught up in a legal dispute with a neighbor over public access rights. Its paths and meadow are mowed regularly; its cedars and a towering white oak give shade. Out of the mainstream and nearly forgotten.

Not withstanding the morning after the Fourth, there were frequently small dramas to witness at the little cabin on a scale I find more engaging. One morning, I found the floor littered with dead black ants. On another, there was a live wasp struggling in a window web made by a small yellow spider trying tentatively to wrap him. Usually there were clacking wrens and chickadees two-noting from the dead branch of a juniper off the deck, and a robin, churr-lupping from the stone wall. Once, three red birds—finches—came rushing through the open sliding doors and hovered, a twittering trinity, a fluttering little mess of essence, spirit, and holy chaos. I prefer this to explosions.

In his essay "Nature," Emerson noted that the world, when viewed from between the legs, took on a very different character. When I was a child, we called this act of peering backward between the legs "purpling." We would look at the setting sun that way until our faces and the sky both grew purple. How nice to learn that this was an Emersonian exercise, too. Emerson relied heavily on the new angle of view. His enthusiasm was for the spiritual touch and the cultivation of intuition that transcended created nature. Through reflective practice and mystical extension, Emerson sought an experience of the divine essence—what was above nature. From what is created to the creator. From what is earthly and secondary to what is original. For me, a cool morning in a cabin on the marsh gives that new angle of view and ties together head and heart. When the sea breeze swept through the cabin's open doors, it carried with it a worldly resurrection. I welcomed that waking up to the astonishing and magical presence of a transcendent world around me.

That July morning, as I was getting ready to leave the cabin for breakfast at the house, two teenagers walked into the clearing. Visitors were rare. Standing quietly in the doorway, I startled them enough to induce looks of defensive dismay, as if they believed they'd been caught trespassing. Or maybe I looked like a derelict and they were afraid of me? Children cannot know that people over fifty are often terrifyingly young. They couldn't know that I approve of trespassing or that I do it whenever I get the opportunity. Poaching, too, is OK by me as long as you only take a wee little fish or a clam or two from someone's so-called private property. And don't get caught. And besides, this wasn't trespassing—this place was public in all the important ways. They couldn't know that I approved of vagrancy, in this age of optimizing productiveness and preserving objectivity. The vagrant subject has the better chance, however slim, of knowing who and where he is and what is subjectively true than all the busy people on Wall Street and in the malls.

They were cousins, and both grandchildren of my shorebird teacher who years ago had passed away. They may have been too young to have known him. The boy was born to one of his two sons who spent part of his summers here. The girl was half-Saudi, a ninth grader, just one year older than my middle daughter, born to the daughter who now owns the last house just back across the bridge—the source of the current legal battle over access to the woods and cabin.

We exchanged pleasantries. I asked about the boy's college and the girl's life in Saudi Arabia. Knowing the preoccupations of my own children and the way that children talk to each other today—the importance of style and stuff, music and success—I suspected they didn't know anything about the chic and successful natural world that surrounds them. Today, most of us move through it but don't play with it the way kids and adults used to when I was growing up here. Parents perceive too much danger and so advise and direct from a center of fear and ignorance and obsessively program their children's time to eliminate vagrant time—danger. Of course, we ultimately fail. Our intent, I suppose, is to optimize investment in future conventional success and guaranteed happiness. I would wager that children of the iPod culture know less today about where they are in space and time even though it has been pixilated for them. My view is arrogant, self-righteous, boring, stuffy, and old-fartish, I know. But a parent worries.

I found myself wanting to ask these children questions that felt essential to me, on that day, about their experience of growing up summers in a place like this: What is universal to our experience? Do they feel safe here, safe walking these paths at night? Do they feel safe enough to allow an upwelling sense of wonder and awe as they look at the sky or a fish? Is there ecstatic gratitude waiting to be born in them? Or just the drug Ecstasy waiting? Do they want to know the mud, sand, stars, wind, trees, birdsongs, roses, bugs, smoke, rain, fish, eelgrass, water, and sky that surrounds them? What is the world asking of them today? What river will they have to navigate in this age of the Internet? What quiet can they drink in? Do they notice wind? Can they notice reality one bite at a time if they want to? Is a bird just an image on a screen?

Has Emerson's great intuitive eye upon the world become a blue flat-screen television eye? A Tivo or PlayStation? Did they love *Moby Dick* or hate it?

We carried the birding scope up to the platform on the roof and watched ospreys for a long time—one adult bird and now three young. With a silent nod to their grandfather, I told them the essential osprey story: DDT, thinning egg shells, Rachel Carson, the Ferandez's stewardship work, the loss of Cape habitat, the loss of birds, the eventual return from the edge of the abyss. I told them about Rachel Carson's visits to this marsh and about how important she was to changing the ways our society treats nature. Basic stuff. I tried to convey the hope that is in the osprey story and some of the simple evolutionary facts of bird-ness. Birds are dinosaurs with feathers. Our air is dinosaur air, and we breathe what dinosaurs breathed. They are vertebrates like us, but they lay eggs, not like us. They raise their young like we do, but they do not eat as we do. Ospreys eat raw, wriggling fish. Ospreys are raptors, birds of prey with large talons and hooked beaks for tearing fish flesh. We are extremely close to them on the phylogenetic tree. In fact, we are all cousins. We and the cedar tree. We and the osprey. We know in our gut this to be true.

I talked too much. I overwhelmed and ultimately bored them. But the osprey story, and Rachael Carson's triumphant *Silent Spring*: These stories must be passed down. And it was their grandfather who passed something of the place's knowledge on to me.

It may be that we underestimate our children. As they left, with me promising to drop the book called *Fish Hawk* off by the Ferandezes, the girl looked over her shoulder to say good-bye, smiled, and added that she had seen pipefish in the pond.

Pipefish! She'd been holding out on me. What else had she seen?

It isn't that pipefish are particularly unusual, but one does have to look carefully to see them. Somehow this gave me hope. This place, she was saying, in her manner of speaking, was her ground, too. Someday, she'll show her children a pipefish, dwelling in the native place her grandfather roamed. It's not much to go on. Just a thread from the hem of Agassiz's invisible garment. The possibility for her of a future familiar place. Of carrying it on.

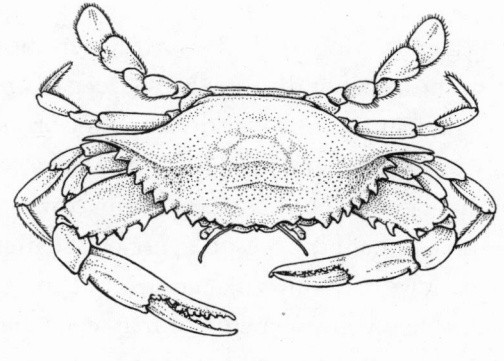

— 9 —

blue crab

We look at the world once, in childhood. The rest is
memory.

— LOUISE GLÜCK, from *Nostos*

THREE BOYS, A dog, and a boat could combine for a perfect
scientific adventure on the marsh. Or not. The boys, my thirteen-year-old son, Toben, his cousin, nine-year-old Sam, and his
friend Tom, also thirteen, found the boat, a nine-foot inflatable
Zodiac tender, bumping in and out with the waves lapping the
sand far down Black Beach, waiting for us to claim her. Likely, it
had been sliced off a cabin cruiser's loosed stern line—its painter
was shredded. We claimed her under the international laws of
salvage we had construed, at least for a day, or until we could
find out who owned her. Then we waited for the tide to turn.
My plan was to let the full force of an incoming tide carry us,
to literally go with the flow and snorkel our way through the
marsh to home. I wanted—in an informal way— to repeat the
studies of two Sippewissian fisheries biologists, Christine Werme

and Linda Deegan. Werme worked on her dissertation here with Ivan Valiela in the 1970s and early 1980s. Deegan arrived at the Ecosystem Center in the mid-eighties to work on questions of marsh energy production and flow. It seemed like a good enough plan, except that dogs and boys have so many common impulses that tend to run at cross-purposes to the scientific method. Natural phenomena have natural explanations, but to children they may be explainable only by alchemy or magic. Children visit the world still fully possessed by their wild dog natures. They wonder as they wander, lapping from the tidal pools of consciousness, picking up the random objects that wash ashore, and getting wet without having a thought for towels.

Imagine, if you will, the marsh as a tree of water lying horizontally, each winding creek a branch of that tree. Fish, like birds, dwell in those branches and graze in them. Much like birds gleaning beetle larvae from inner bark or plucking aphids from leaf surfaces in a tree, fish find their sustenance in these creeks along sandy channels, against mud banks and bottoms. At high tide, when water spills over the creeks and floods the spartina mat, minnows swim out into this watery air and feed among the roots of the mat.

Christine Werme turned the marsh into a tree and fish into birds in her research. She began her doctoral work here in 1975 and presented her dissertation thesis in 1981. During the intervening years, she snorkeled her way through the branches of the marsh day and night and, at regular lunar intervals, followed two distinct six-hundred-meter transects. Her aim was to learn which fish species were using the marsh; their seasonal occurrences, abundance, preferred habitats, and food; and their breeding cycles and behavior. She wanted also to determine the behavioral and morphological mechanisms of selective feeding among three resident fish species—two species of the very numerous salt marsh killifish and the Atlantic silversides, which together make up over 90 percent of all fish biomass found in the marsh. Which fish, if any, she asked, were moving out onto the marsh mat, and once there, what were they eating? Which fish were morphologically suited to herbivorous foods and how did they feed? What differences in behavior and morphology allowed these fish to coexist in the marsh, and might these differences lead to slightly different roles in the dynamics of energy flow through the marsh? Finally, how do marshes affect the ecological structure of adjoining marine systems? What is the nature of fish species that aren't dwelling in a marsh, but invade it from the bay? she asked, and how might they influence the economic value of a salt marsh?

Picking up on Werme's work, Ecosystem Center ecologist Linda Deegan, in the early 1980s, began asking how important marshes are to fish production. Since John Teal's early studies of carbon production in a salt marsh, ecologists have debated the role and importance of salt marshes as producers of fish. Do marshes actually produce a net surplus of fish? And what role do fish play in the process of converting the primary production in the marsh—spartina roots and shoots—to secondary production that moves beyond it and into the open ocean? Deegan's research at Sippewissett helped answer these questions.

The boys, our dog, a golden retriever born to the water, and I had some time to kill while the tide turned—that's the loveliest kind of time of all. The boys searched the clear warm water of the inlet channel for interesting things. They shadowed a sand crab and watched it bury itself several times. I stepped up then to provide an impromptu testament to the effects of a powerful pinch by a sand crab when I demonstrated the improper way to snatch one out of sand. Thrust aloft into the deadly air, the startled crab reached back and seized me by the pinky. The boys found my shout and the points of blood dripping down the inner part of my finger quite hilarious. Do not do it this way, I said. Then they spied a large blue crab working down the channel and captured it by boxing it in with my once-dry shirt. They found oysters locked to each other in fat clumps in the peat walls of a pothole the tide was spilling through. I opened and ate a few, offering them some. The boys would not eat them. Oyster shells, encrusted with algae, look dirty, so it seemed impossible that inside the meat could be as clean and pure as it appeared, white delicate flesh free of sand and slippery and good to eat. Farther up the inlet, with its flooding wavelets coming over the sand, the boys found dozens of nickel-sized flounder moving from the white sand below their feet, where they were nearly invisible, to a dark seaweedy substrate in deeper water, where they became instantly obvious. My son held up a horseshoe crab bent into an angle at its hinge and cradled it like a cereal bowl, peering into its upended body of bristling legs. The horseshoe crab is all legs, sword, and shield. We considered his primitive, shell-covered eye before releasing him, and then had to scold the dog who fetched him for us again. On the flats the boys found pencil eraser–wide holes and dug into the sand after clams. I explained why we couldn't keep them. But then had to explain why I had eaten oysters. There was no explaining that.

They took great delight in digging up clams. We practiced catch-and-release clamming, but not before I considered aloud the difficulty of that. Does one need to restore the clam's siphon hole? Can a clam, so cut off, survive through to the high tide and then push through to the surface, to restore its hole and home to proper order? No one knows, my son said, why a clam really moves about in the sand at all. It might just want to. We found a lethargic clam worm in one of the larger holes. Going back down the inlet to the boat and sand spit by the low hump of what remains of the dunes, they noticed shrimp, as clear as glass, jetting through the blue water.

Though the tide had changed, it was still too low for a marsh-length snorkel. But that didn't matter to the boys. They were in no hurry, knowing that a real boat demanded a shake-down cruise. They dragged the boat out into the shallow bay. I had brought Werme's doctoral thesis, Deegan's papers on marsh fish, and my binoculars back to the nub of dune. Alternately, I looked down at my reading, then out to the terns massing on a sandbar—there must have been two hundred least terns packed together on a bar that would soon disappear with the rising tide—then back to the boys. Terns joined the flock in a steady stream of twos and threes flying up the channel off the inner flats, now being inundated. The boys floated the boat past the crowded tern sandbar then pulled ashore above them. My nephew disembarked and, with the dog keeping pace, ran toward the terns, scattering them with his mighty shout. There is little peace with boys and dogs.

Another hour went by this way. We ate our sandy sandwiches. Then the tide was up enough to float the marsh with masks and snorkels. The crew needed little convincing. A salt marsh, underwater, has some of the visual appeal and habitat qualities of a tropical reef system—imagine a long brown coral reef with mud banks, instead of coral, studded with ribbed mussels and perforated by fiddler crab holes harboring tiny fish. From my reading of Werme's work, I knew that sandy channel bottoms were preferred over the muddy bottom substraits by all the minnow fish—resident and invader alike. I pointed out to the boys the ubiquitous killifish darting in small schools around us and the two common mummichogs: *Fundulus heteroclitus* and *Fundulus majalis.* We also saw sheepshead minnow, *Cyprinodon variegates.* It's *F. heteroclitus* and the Atlantic silverside, *Menidia menidia,* that make up so much of the minnow biomass here. But silversides are not true marsh dwellers. Though summerlong residents, they move in and out of the marsh daily with tides. The striped bass follow them. *M. menidia* only live a year, but I suspect they are the most important prey food for striped bass here. Most of our successful fishing flies imitate them. Werme found that striped killifish feed on benthic invertebrates from creek bottoms, chiefly the small bivalve *Gemma gemma* and the gastropod *Hydrobia minuta,* and on other tiny invertebrates living in algal mats. Sheepshead minnows (*C. variegates*) are morphologically better suited to eating plants. Together with the mummichogs, they head for the spartina mat at high tide—feeding more heavily during this part of the tidal cycle on detritus and algae but less for the plant foods and more to exploit invertebrates living within them: eating the algae then spitting out most of it once the invertebrates had been sieved out. To test whether these apparent differences in food choices were statistically significant, Werme designed and carried out experiments in the lab with live fish. As she measured fish mouth gapes, analyzed the contents of tiny fish guts and fish feces, and probably contracted migraines gazing so many hours into high-powered microscopes, she was looking to link morphological differences to food preferences. For instance, striped killifish are more slender, making them stronger swimmers than mummichogs. They have pointed rather than rounded snouts and use these to poke into sandy substrates for invertebrates. Werme likened these differences in body and head shape to the modifications of beaks in birds, corroborating other research that shows that body and mouth forms of fishes influence diet preferences. All these little dwellers of the marsh are remarkably adapted to the physical extremes of marsh life—the high temperatures, high salinity, and low oxygen of shallow water habitats. *F. majalis,* in fact, is able to flip-flop himself like a walking catfish across the spartina mat, for several yards at least, to find a new puddle, should the one he is in dry up.

Picking up on Werme's work and following up the questions that John Teal's work on marsh energy exports left unanswered, Deegan studied Sippewissett's resident small fish and transients in the 1980s. Teal's earliest studies of salt marsh production concluded that overall photosynthetic production by vascular plants in a marsh—among the highest per acre production values of any land system—was nearly twice the level of consumption and respiration going on there. He calculated that 45 percent of the total production occurring in a salt marsh was in excess of what was consumed there. This excess production, he proposed, flowed out of the marsh and was then available as an outwelling of nutrients to the fish and invertebrates of shallow marine ecosystems surrounding marshes. His was a model of detrital export—the energy in dissolved organic carbon molecules and semidecomposed plant matter together with its colonizers of decomposing bacteria, algae, and fungi all being swept out to sea. This, he hypothesized, was a marsh's major contribution to offshore fisheries—marshes were producers of vast amounts of fish food in the form of decomposed plant fibers, dissolved chemical nutrients, and bundles of organic nutrients. His work suggested that, for this reason, marshes were important economically beyond their open space value, and his findings led eventually to the legislative protection of salt marsh systems throughout the nation.

Deegan confirmed Teal's model in some ways and in others changed it significantly. The outwelling of detritus, it turns out, is less important than Teal's research showed. Much of the detritus in a marsh is respired by decomposing bacteria and fungi before it leaves the marsh, it's eaten, or it's buried to become part of the growing peat mat itself. There isn't a lot of nutritional value left in it. The real contribution of marshes to energy flow and export has fins and scales. It's not detrital fish food that flows out into shallow bays to feed offshore fisheries. It's fish. Marshes really are the nurseries fishermen suspected them to be. Deegan showed how and put a number to it. Marsh waters are warmer than coastal bays, so growth rates are much higher—high enough, Deegan found, to offset the slightly higher mortality rates there. Marshes, she found, are hazardous places for small fish, some 90 percent of which are eaten before they turn one: but they compensate through higher production.

While salt marsh grasses are the obvious and most visible source of sun-driven primary production in a marsh, what's invisible is equally important to fish. Some researchers have referred to the benthic microalgae production that happens in the marsh as "secret gardens." Just like vascular plants, microbial producers—diatoms, green algae, and cyanobacteria—are sun driven. They contain chlorophyll and "evolve" oxygen during photosynthesis just like the vascular plants we see. These organisms divide rapidly, are extremely light sensitive, and are found on surfaces throughout the marsh and in the water column. These groups of organisms provide the most important food sources to fish.

To irrefutably link certain fish to certain nutrient sources, Deegan and her fellow researchers went to great technological lengths. In the late 1970s and early 1980s, Woods Hole researchers Bruce Peterson, Bob Howarth, Deegan, and others experimented with methods at Sippewissett using stable isotopes to do the job. Stable isotopes are nonreactive forms of elements essential to life. To simplify a complex technology, the idea is that isotopic signature variations are preserved as nutrients move through the various trophic levels of a food web. By looking at the isotopic signatures found in various marsh animals consuming plant foods, we might better understand the primary producers they are relying on. Using stable isotopes to trace food webs in poorly understood and complex ecosystems can shed light on relationships that one might think shouldn't exist.

Peterson first determined the signatures of isotopes of carbon, nitrogen and sulfur for a number of salt marsh plants, including *Spartina*, floating macroalgae, benthic microalgae, and phytoplankton. In some cases these were plants somewhat delinked from marshes because they float in the saltwater column in and out with the tide and gain nutrients from salt water and energy from the sun. For instance, he could show that consumers were getting sulfur from a variety of sources in a marsh: organic sulfur from detritus, sulfides from the sediment, or sulfate from seawater. In some cases, the sulfur from detritus was less important than the sulfur flowing into the marsh from seawater and phytoplankton. Even microscopic animals at the base of the food chain are flexible and adaptive, feeding opportunistically depending on what's in season. When Peterson deliberately added a stable isotope of nitrogen (^{15}N) to the water column, for instance, he found that the N tracer showed up quickly in the phytoplankton—diatoms living and dying in the water column—and after a lag time, the N tracer showed up in the planktonic copepods that live in the water column and feed on those diatoms and in the fish (alewives) that feed on the copepods. But surprisingly, tracer showed up also in mud-dwelling amphipods and crabs—detritus eaters—who were eating the nitrogen-containing dead cells of diatoms floating down to collect on mud surfaces.

Why do we need to quantify how important salt marshes are to growing fish? Because we live in a society that bases its decisions on the economic values of things. For years marshes were perceived as having no economic value. They were places that bred illness and disease. They were used as dumping grounds or were filled in and built on, ditched and sprayed. Over 60 percent of the land Boston sits on was marshland. New York City is built partially on salt marsh as well. So are the extensive landfills across the river in New Jersey. Some 70 percent of all pre-European settlement salt marshes in America have been destroyed. Some knew all along what we were losing. Food, among other things. Marshes provide habitat for up to two-thirds of the commercial and recreational fish species we catch and eat. When we eat fish, we're eating salt marsh. Clammers and fishermen know that. But the voice of reason has too often been drowned out by the voice of greed.

The boys, the dog, and I began floating down the channel. I tied the Zodiac to my foot. The boys floated for twenty minutes then got tired and climbed aboard the Zodiac to direct scientific matters from there. The dog and I stayed in the water. His dog-paddling legs kept milling up the bottom or tangling the painter tied to my ankle. We pushed on. The boys scouted for crabs. For a half-mile we floated like this. Occasionally the wind blew us up a side creek, or we'd "anchor" over a deep hole. I had my hand net ready for blue crabs. It was difficult to observe feeding behaviors of killifish and silversides on the creek bottom three feet below me with dog legs stirring up sand. Never take a dog into the outdoor lab. But I did learn a few things. Fish activity seems to be busiest around those places where shallow channels connect to drain surface ponds and puddles entering the main channel. The minnows seemed to congregate there. And I know from night-fishing forays that these places often hold large striped bass as well. I also learned that the juvenile tautog (*Tautoga onitis*) are dark, nearly as black as the black mollies you buy for the aquarium at home. They stay close to the mud banks, sometimes disappearing into the larger fiddler crab holes. We all saw more winter flounder (*Pseudopleuronectes americana*) than we ever believed could be in the marsh. Bottom-feeding flounder eat shrimp and polychaete worms, especially *Nereis* sp., here in the marsh. We saw dozens and dozens in the sandy channels, each the size of a quarter and camouflaged with flecks of gray and brown.

In the deep pools, we found schools of menhaden (*Brevoortia tyrannus*), each fish like a silver spoon with a small black spot on the gill. Juvenile menhaden enter the marsh in great numbers in late summer. They dwell at midwater depths in these creeks and, according to Werme, partition food types even in this restricted habitat. Menhaden have finely spaced gill rakers that form delicate sieves capable of filtering zooplankton from the water. Alewifes are filter feeders too, but Werme found that they fed more selectively and on larger prey, like postlarval shrimp—swimming in one direction until they encounter prey, tipping their heads quickly to take the prey, and then swimming in another direction. Silversides feed in a similar manner, but because their mouths are much smaller, they take smaller organisms like copepods and isopods from the water column.

We were surrounded by legions of nursing fish; a marsh really is a kind of multispecies nursery. We managed to capture a three-spined stickleback off the bottom of a sandy creek with our small handheld net. *Gasterosteus aculeatus* is only an inch or so long but weirdly alienlike in configuration, with sets of sharp spines that come off the dorsal and ventral fins. The boys peered into the net with a mixture of awe and disgust. They feed, according to Werme, mostly on zooplankton in the midwater habitat. Another stickleback, the four-spined, feeds on benthic macro- and meiofauna in creek bottom sands. Werme found that zooplankton is the high-tide preference for the four-spined; the three-spined prefer copepods, foraminifera, and other tiny invertebrates that inhabit the middle of this benthic food chain, feeding on the microscopic. These meso-faunal animals become available as shallow areas are flooded at high tide.

I wondered if Werme had ever brought dogs or boys on her swimming forays. They had begun to think about how nice it might be to live as animals here in this sandy creek bed with its undulating bottom. My son said he would be a blue crab. Blue crabs were numerous and proved very hard to catch, in spite of the tactile and analytical advantages we had. The survival instincts of crabs are hard to overcome. They sit still until you are nearly on them, and then fly down the creek bed, claws waving menacingly. We missed most, but with the boys as spotters up top, we managed to catch five.

My nephew, Sam, preferred to be a bass. They are big and no other fish can eat them, he said. I reminded him of the ospreys overhead. But his resolve was unshakeable. Over the deep holes, the bass's favorite habitat, the clear water grades to black. There we saw flashes of their dark backs and striped sides. In these holes we also found rock bass and more moving walls of menhaden. Tom said he would be an oyster firmly attached to the back of another oyster and clumped deeply into the bank—filter feeding, growing big and hard so nothing could eat him.

We floated deeper into the marsh. The wind dropped and the water became shallow, the substrate increasingly brown silt and mud. The boys had collected things—crabs, a razor clam, mussels, old shoes, lobster floats. I poached three enormous quahogs for scup bait. But the final prize was a giant blue crab. His carapace alone spanned my fully outstretched hand. I found him deep down and perched on a peat ledge under an overhanging chunk of peat that had calved off the marsh. The perfect hiding place for the king of all blue crabs. I caught him with a lucky scoop of the net and held him aloft for the boys to admire. From claw to claw he stretched a full eighteen inches. The boys were astonished by this unblinking blue-and-white monster who would not succumb to the crab bucket. His outstretched arms spanned the edges and held him in a crucifixion limbo that the boys must have felt. Victory presents the victor with the opportunity for sympathy. Thumbs up went the boys, and plop, back into Sippewissett went the crab, and with a flash of his scimitar claws he was gone.

Finally, we were paddling with our hands toward the woods. The muddy bottom of the inner marsh a foot below us was littered with shells and feathered with delicate branching algae. Having spent an energetic afternoon, most of it underwater, I ventured to ask the boys what they liked most about it. The dog, said Sam. The orange sneaker we found, said Tom. My new boat, said my son. Small wonders, I thought. The general mood of the explorers was tired, salt-encrusted, sunburnt joy. We had seen a marsh laid out like a watery tree with fish turned into Darwinian birds. Here's to Christine Werme and to Linda Deegan, I said, holding up the orange sneaker flotsam, who gave us both information and joy. That, I think, is what the science of home places can do: shed light and preserve joy to the fullest extent. In that union is our hoped-for communion.

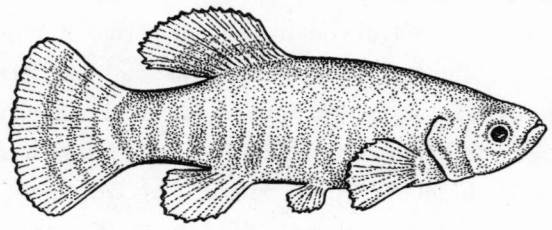

— 10 —

night

MY BROTHER-IN-LAW WAYNE has often been my fishing companion at night. With Wayne you never know who else might be coming along—it could be Darwin or the Enterprise Institute, or the entire Republican Party's religious right, conspiracy theorists' wing. Wayne is a strong Christian, tending toward literalist bedrock ideas. He goes to a charismatic church. There isn't much grayness in Wayne's spiritual attitude, but there's enough gray matter inside his skull for political issues to arise between us. He's a big guy with a PhD in computer chip design—a senior engineer at IBM. That all makes him interesting and perplexing to me, his opposite, linked by a marriage and fishing alone. My own probing Unitarianism, sprinkled with skepticism, rationalism, an interest in transcendental essentialism, combined with my Anglican, liberal Episcopalian roots, leaves me vulnerable to claims from people like Wayne that I don't know what or where my self is. He may be right. Unitarian Universalists are universally ill versed in scriptural dictum. Hallelujah for that. But we do take personal responsibility for our actions.

It used to be that Wayne and I couldn't discuss politics without getting agitated, and we avoided religion altogether. But we've learned some common ground over time. Fishing is a salvation, of sorts, for our relationship. And, usually, he brings along decent cigars—a fishing tradition that goes back with its companion, good whiskey, to caveman times. It used to be that I was the fishing master in this improbable duo, but Wayne's engineering brain has slowly taken fishing apart to learn it the way only an engineer can. I knew that very soon I'd be getting flies, leaders, and fishing tips from him. And I knew it would aggravating.

I've often pondered the old hostility between religion and science. It cuts deeper than we know since we don't know what we don't know. That hostility was amplified with the publication of Darwin's *Origin of Species* in 1859. It was like the Berlin Wall coming down. Darwin and empirical science won out, turning man entirely natural, as the anthropologist Loren Eisely put it, red in tooth and claw and increasingly terrified by that reality's loneliness and meaninglessness. Science came of age and along came Existentialism, proof of the abyss, and the age of anxiety. What if it's an empty universe save for us and the TV evangelists? Lately, I've begun to realize how glad I am that the evolution debate is still here. I like that our collective imagination is still caught up by mystery and a belief that life has mysterious direction and meaning beyond the material, beyond the chemistry of the interacting world, and that a God might exist somewhere above the earthly fray; that God and nature are injured but not dead. Just don't make my kids say a Christian prayer in school or listen to Robertson on TV. Let's keep it separate and clean.

Science has not disproved the existence of God, and it never will. The world as calculation only is half complete. And our age certainly shows that highly learned people can reconcile in their minds that the atomic bomb and God can coexist. In fact, such a reconciliation should be easier to achieve today, thanks to the advances of science. But we continue to struggle. And we continue to plunder, even in the name of our various gods. Even with all our science and our trumpeting about holiness and our big god, we're screwing up down here big time.

It helps to go fishing to gain perspective. At this inauguration of our summer night-fishing outings, Wayne had been promoting the latest argument for intelligent design and creationism. Wayne would believe in intelligent design. He invents computer chips and so has the designer model in his head—and the father, son, and holy computer analyst trinity model, too. I suppose I could be a believer in intelligent design myself, but a design belief, I suspect, quite unlike his. We argued as we picked our way down the dark railroad tracks, gazing at stars and stumbling as a result of looking up while walking over ill-spaced ties. Railroad tracks were designed by engineers like Wayne for railcars, not reflective walking. It is a shortcoming of engineers and perhaps all of science, this ignoring of the human gait. Reason provides a limited set of tools for the kind of meandering a soul requires. The whole world, I said, seems intelligently designed to me. The marsh reeks of it from low tide to high tide. Intelligence, intelligence, intelligence beyond the scrutable matters at hand. Yeah, said Wayne, knowing that I was preparing to disagree with him again. Try this cigar.

The arguments for intelligent design are old, beginning with the Roman Cicero in the first century to Thomas Aquinas in the thirteenth century and William Paley in the eighteenth. Louis Agassiz, a scientist/morphologist first and metaphysician second (and a phantom on this marsh), argued for the hand of a creator/designer. We talked that night, though, about a book written by molecular biologist Michael Behe. *Darwin's Black Box* had caused enough of a stir when it came out to prompt a number of responses by evolutionary biologists. Wayne explained that Behe proved that cellular functions, even at the simplest molecular level, are irreducibly complex, and therefore they could not have been the product of single random mutations of genes' base structures. Unlike other creation theorists, Behe neither disputed the ancient age of Earth, nor the evolutionary age of *Homo sapiens*. He didn't dispute the evolutionary facts of common descent, though he complained that the spotty fossil record doesn't prove it. As a biochemist, he directed his arguments against the Darwinian theory of random mutation-driven evolution by looking at the development of biochemical cellular machinery. Multiparted molecular machines, he wrote, because they are irreducibly complex, could not possibly have arisen through gradual random mutations of the individual genes that produce them because if one part were missing or incomplete, then the whole would fail. And in his mind the entire edifice of Darwinism would collapse, too. Thus, he wrote, there must be a designer—a creative power at work with an end in mind, capable of causing the instantaneous formation of complexity. A visionary.

I knew from the little I'd read that evolutionists have had little difficultly shooting down Behe's arguments. Individual components of complex systems turn out to have value in and of themselves. Cells are constantly evolving new ways of doing things through small modifications and tinkering. Through constant fine tuning, evolution works to build very complex things from very simple things. Given the vast stretches of time available to evolutionary processes, all kinds of improbable monsters become possible. The whole world itself seems to deem it so. Many complex biochemical machines have simpler versions found in more primitive cells—so molecular evolutionists have traced the evolutionary journey of cellular machinery. Biochemists have watched bacteria repair damaged genes through random mutation in the lab. An eye began as membrane. It and all sense organs came out of the very notion of a cellular identity separate from everything around it. An eye develops from a single cell's ability to sense light. The process may take a billion years. But nevertheless, any ability to sense light is valuable. And time is on evolution's side. Hearing and sound making evolve separately in the same organism, but then through a gradual process begin benefiting each other until a highly refined feedback mechanism is developed, like echolocation in bats.

The tracks we walked on crossed next to Quahog Pond. There, a skinny guy came hurriedly out of a hidden path in front of us and began tossing quahogs into the pond. Illegal, I said to Wayne. Wayne knew him and stopped to chat. We could hear music coming from the bar on the highway. A drunk was singing in the parking lot. It was getting close to closing time, but for us the night and marsh was just opening up for business.

At the midpoint on the tracks' journey through the marsh, a path slants down the bank of railroad scree, through a brackish puddle, across the spartina mat, worn wet from our nightly forays into the marsh, and out to the land of flowing creeks. From there, on a dark night you really have to know your way. There's a bush out on the moor where a yellow-breasted chat sings. You have to know that bush, and this meandering creek, and the depth of certain potholes, some of which are very deep. I thought then we should be moving beyond the discussion of intelligent design and on to the placement of our footsteps and on to fish, but when we arrived at the edge of the first creek, Wayne stopped and said that it was very hard to design and build the computer chips he built. And that we are asking evolution to build complex living organisms—randomly. He didn't buy it, but he wouldn't have his hackles up so much if the evolutionist elite wasn't so intolerant. So blind, to use his words. Evolution is scientific theory, not like a quartz crystal set in stone. He didn't care what anyone said. Someday, something will come along to sweep it all away.

Huh, I thought. I said, I didn't think Darwin's discoveries of selection, of a theory of fitness, would ever be swept away, but I thought there would come a time when Darwin's ideas, extremely useful as they have been, would be joined by something bigger. Darwinian theory was being bolstered by new evidence nearly daily from every biological discipline. Still, it could be enlarged and deepened, rerouted, and rerooted. There is no sound Darwinian explanation of the whole, or of human consciousness for that matter, I said. Just as there is no human experience across several billion years of life on the planet. Better to look into Goethe or Whitman, or the Tao, I said, for what life and the human are and might become.

But enough speculation, we agreed. On to something quite agreeable and tangible. Between low tide and mid on an incoming tide is the best time to fish the marsh in July, and we didn't want to miss the prime. Wayne took a casting position on the edge of the channel close to a sharp turn. Here the shoal water drops into a deep hole milled out by water coursing around a bend. The main channel into the marsh pours through there and had dug the deepest hole in the marsh where fish can find refuge through the hot midsummer days. There was a big fish splashing there. I walked up the channel to another corner and stepped off the bank, still thinking of the ramifications of intelligent design. It appealed to me. But so did the notion of a struggle and a journey that forges growth and change over time. I liked the idea of a creative design *process* providing tools, shaping the structure of things for the purpose of better fitness to the tasks at hand, but no end, other than that, in mind. And no designer, per se. Alfred North Whitehead termed this "actuality." "Value," he said, "is the soul of actuality." John Cobb put human evolution in these Whiteheadian terms, too. He said, "We have been selected in the evolutionary process for particular capacities of language and thought and mutual affection. To exercise those faculties is our calling." Mutual affection—and that from evolutionary thinking from the ground up—from rock and microbes upward. Couldn't we expand on that some to say that understanding was our calling? Understanding the whole. Isn't there an element of knowing where you are and knowing you belong to our calling? And isn't there some element of topdown to that? Divine wisdom poured from above into a creation that results in self-awareness. I confess liking the idea of a distant all-knowing absolute, Emersonian essentialism, an all-seeing eye—an intuitional universe that human rationality can't begin to approach, but feeling can. All the self-callings taken together create a mysterious unity—a world that, defying all logic, works excellently well. This marsh world is intelligent and irreducibly complex. The stars and the crabs crinkling in the banks, the invisible trillions of microbes, the minute creatures of the mesocosmic world buried in benthos belong here. Could all of this complexity really have arisen only by the Darwinian forces of competition and selection? Maybe. If so, then connecting the unpredictability of atomic motion and gene mutation to the very purposeful striped bass doesn't diminish my reverence for the bass and the process that made it, or my sense of responsibility to this place. Life *is* better felt with the tingling suspicion that there is something else going on here, something that a debate with fundamentalist literalists won't ever resolve. That particular conversation we're caught up in isn't large enough. Today, precious few of us have any real idea what the creation looks and feels like or tastes like: we need to listen to the ecologists and we need to go fishing.

Wayne had moved off the corner and we were wading toward each other. Big smart ole Wayne with his know-it-all PhD was handicapped by his lighter rod. It was a small trout rod, stout enough to bring fish in but too short and light to cast long in a strong sea breeze. His line kept falling short in puffs of wind. Privately, I was snickering up a storm at him, so that I lost my own concentration and spooked the big fish that is almost always holding on the corner where I step into the creek. Here the narrow channel opens into a shallow embayment that often holds many fish. A bar stretches the full length of the channel that runs along the far bank and fish are always working on the other side of it. I began casting into that trough. A fish popped on the surface within casting distance of Wayne, and I saw him move to face that fish.

When I'm with a friend, I want that friend to catch a fish. Especially a fundamentalist Christian brother-in-law IBM engineer with a doctorate degree, even though he'll retire ten years before me. That's my heart talking. Of course, I'd like to catch a bigger fish than him. That's my skin talking. Damn it all! This size-matters debate gets extremely tedious. Big fish equals . . . what? More hookups with female striped bass? Bragging rights? Trophy fish-wife: trophy-wife fish? Anyway, we both caught a fish, almost at the same time. A double hookup means something I think. That Darwin was wrong? That it's a cooperative and fair universe? My habit is to quickly bring a large fish to shore hoping it will be above the twenty-eight-inch legal threshold for keeping and eating. There are certainly fish bigger than twenty-eight inches here. But this summer I haven't caught one.

Wayne brings his fish up into a shallow creek ten feet from me, then walks his fish over. We lay them side by side in shallow water. Each is twenty-seven inches by measure of a mark on my rod. Fat, healthy, silver bodies. We tied, just under keeper size. We admire them and release them and shake hands, happy to disagree on just about everything but what really matters.

Of course, it is true that we fishermen are disturbers, regardless of our religious beliefs. When we lumber through the marsh at night, the fish tell us by going down. But if we are quiet and sneaky, then the fish come to our flies. The run has produced fish consistently for twenty years of summer nights. The marsh keeps giving and giving, yet one miniscule example of the world's fecundity—its capacity for ever-renewing, ever-transforming, ever-becoming. If we want to keep fishing, then we may need to learn how to be very quiet. We may need to learn from our calling for affection how to act on the knowledge that we are all bound up together—that the welfare of fish and clams is our welfare, is our calling.

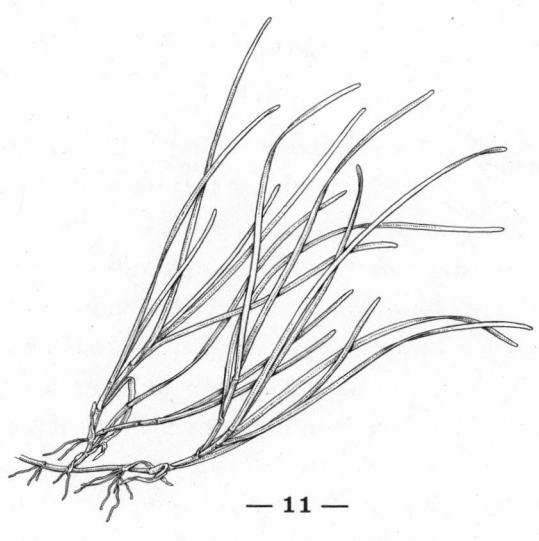

— 11 —

eelgrass

Zostera. DELIGHTFUL WORD. It's the Linnaean name for the genera of eelgrass. I planned to undertake a major expedition to the eelgrass beds at the mouth of West Falmouth harbor with my thirteen-year-old son, Toben, and my six-year-old nephew, Sam. They were game, too, to go fishing. To see eelgrass. And I wanted to once again suspend myself between the impossible blue sky and the watery green fields of eelgrass—that mesmeric waving sea of sea grass we usually skim unsuspecting over in a boat on our way out into the bay. These are among the last vestiges of eelgrass beds in the harbor, and they are dying.

We could not take the dog with us since we were going by sailboat and there wasn't enough room for him. All morning, from the wee hours before dawn until 10:00 a.m., I had been assembling neat piles of scientific papers. They covered the floor and desk of the cabin in the ten-acre woods. Each represented some significant node within the weblike map of biogeochemical transformations that go on in the mud, water, plants, and animals of a salt marsh, linking salt marshes to eelgrass. If there are two principal ecological conclusions about the functions of a salt marsh drawn from the years of research at Sippewissett, they are these: (1) salt marshes export an excess of energy into shallow bays in the form of fish; (2) salt marshes buffer: they intercept the flow of things coming from land to bay; they hold onto pollutants like oil; and they bury, transform, and convert nutrients like nitrogen that are vital to plant growth and yet lethal when overabundant. Where a bay's fringes of salt marsh are intact, the fishing is better, the water quality is better—and we are better. These functions are hard coin to us. We can take them to the bank.

Since 1900, we have produced a surfeit of nitrogen in the world. Scientists calculate a doubling of the amount of fixed nitrogen available to plant growth in the past hundred years. Thanks to the German chemist Fritz Haber, we learned how to turn atmospheric nitrogen into ammonia and ammonia into nitrates. This and other oxidized forms of nitrogen are applied as fertilizer to soil to grow plants. It is how the planet has managed to support a human population that doubled nearly two and half times since 1900. The human population is now concentrated in cities located on coasts. Our nitrogenous waste leaches from sewage treatment plants and septic systems into the coastal bays. Nitrates are sent up into the atmosphere by power plants and by cars burning fossil fuels that then filter down as dry deposition. Dry deposition unwittingly fertilizes our lawns and further pollutes our shallow salt bays, harbors, and estuaries, which are prehistorically nitrate-limited natural systems highly sensitive to human inputs of nitrogen. Higher nitrate levels radically change shallow marine ecosystems. Among other things, the eelgrass dies.

The science that connects nitrogen-loading and all its various sources to eelgrass decline is convoluted, complex, and the result of years of study. Salt marshes fit into the equation. I thought that by making neat piles of scientific papers on the floor of the cabin on the marsh, I could understand how. In a marsh you have your hierarchy of systems: rhizosphere; phototrophic bacteria; nitrifying and denitrifying bacteria; anaerobic and aerobic sediments; inorganic and organic molecular forms; the entire family of amines, from ammonia and ammonium to nitrous oxides, nitrates, and nitrites; oxidation and reduction; and why not throw in tidal fluxes and chemical gradients of all kinds and the niggling paradoxes—including the fact that sea water has plenty of inorganic nitrate only it appears to be unavailable to plant growth. It's confusing. And neat piles don't necessarily lead to well-ordered thoughts. By the time late morning arrived, a wind came up off the bay in through the sliding-glass doors of the cabin and blew the piles and my thinking into disarray.

If I were to attempt to summarize nitrate biogeochemistry in salt marshes for a child with attention deficit disorder, I would begin and end with a small table in a textbook edited by Ivan Valiela on marine ecological processes. In some ways, this neat little rectangle of data encapsulates thirty years of mapping nitrogen flows at Sippewissett. It's the nitrogen budget for Sippewissett Marsh. Simply put, the table quantifies the inputs, outputs, and net exchanges from various sources of salt marsh nitrogen, including ground water, fixation, tides, denitrification, sedimentation, and atmosphere. It shows that salt marshes intercept added nitrogen—convert it to plant tissues, return it to the atmosphere via denitrification, bury it in creek bed mud and salt marsh turf and peat, and turn it into fish and crabs. Less free nitrate flows out of a salt marsh and into a bay even when it's coming in at elevated levels. Life gobbles it up and transforms it. This is good for eelgrass beds and scallop lovers alike. It's good for eelgrass lovers, too.

Today, our eelgrass is reduced to a few beds inside the breakwater at the mouth of our harbor. At low tide, a sandbar forms just behind the jetty on the sheltered side, and it gives us a sailing destination that's both close and exotic—exotic because it's hard to get there by land. We can more easily beach a boat than drive, and once there, we can explore water-filled crevices between rocks, or snorkle out into the beds of eelgrass to see what we can see. We often combine a trip to the jetty with scup fishing. We brought with us a fishing rod and two boxes of sea worms for that purpose. Sea worms are three- to six-inch-long annelid worms, cousin to our old friends, the smaller benthic clam worm that striped bass devour in May. Their two rows of flagella and the tiny pair of black pincers protruding from the head give them a fearsome appearance. The pincers run in and out in a threatening manner, and who could blame them for trying to reverse their fishhook fates? Fish do love to eat sea worms, and we like to try to catch them at it.

It's half an hour sail to the jetty if the wind is right. We had to drop the mast to get under the green bridge, where tradition dictates a hearty shout is given. In the second basin, we passed a dozen sailing dingys rounding a mark in competition. These boats had names like *Redwall* and *Aslan* and are commanded by ten-year-old salts—tanned, blond-headed boys and girls who can splice lines, tie bowlines, and know a jibe from a coming-about.

Beyond the inner harbor around the little pier and into the outer harbor we went. The boys sailed, and I dangled my feet. An outgoing tide and a southwest wind carried us to the breakwater separating harbor and bay where we beached the boat. It was very hot. The boys jumped ship and set off to climb the big glacial boulders on the shore, collect mussels around the jetty rocks, and play at pirating. I hauled the boat up on the parched sand, with the boom swinging and the brass ring that attaches the boom to the mast making a cricket song against the aluminum mast, then lay myself down like a marooned sailor under the blazing sun and, cap over my face, dozed and dreamed a fishing dream. In a typical fishing dream, you either catch or don't. In this one, I did catch fish and in another place so familiar that when the boys woke me up with offerings of a dried sand eel, a dozen blue mussels, and the real prize—a blue-eyed scallop—at first I thought I was there on that other point and that the dream was true. But then I found their offerings arranged on my stomach. The scallop slowly opened up, little blue eyes sparkling. Huh! I said, still remembering the dream. But all they wanted was for me to eat the dried sand eel. So I did.

At the age of fifty, there's nothing to eating a sun-dried sand eel—we've all eaten plenty worse at McDonald's—and I still find scallops fascinating. They live under eelgrass. When eelgrass beds disappear the scallops disappear. They don't burrow into benthic sediments like clams, but rest on the floor under an eelgrass canopy. They're far more mobile than clams—which move significant distances only as larvae. Scallops swim by using their shells like butterfly wings. Once I heard a taped recording of the sounds they make with their shells underwater—a weird muffled form of clapping. What were they saying to each other? The voice of eelgrass is the drumming of scallop shells at night.

I don't think I appreciated eelgrass very much as a kid. We plumbed the depths of deeper water beyond the breakwater, spending hours snorkeling, spear fishing, exploring on the other side of the rock jetty in water too deep for eelgrass. But the eelgrass world is one not to be overlooked. Finning through eelgrass is like what I imagine floating down the Zambezi is like. It feels exotic, tropical somehow, more lush than the rocky bottom of deeper bay water, and richer, more full of living surprises. Eelgrass is a different sort of marine plant than those seaweeds we know that float in and out with the tides, that coat rocks and clog props. It's different too than the microalgae we don't notice unless it's blooming into a red tide. It also reacts differently and at different times to inputs of nitrate and to the streaming sunlight hitting the water. Eelgrass is rooted in benthic sediments, having solved the problem of low nutrient availability in the saltwater column by taking up nutrients, the way terrestrial grasses do, largely through their roots. They then store substantial amounts of nutrients in their thick leaves, stems, and rhizomes to parse out as needed. Eelgrass isn't nitrate-limited like the marine algae in the bay. It's light that it craves, and eelgrass growth is limited by the sun. It doesn't grow in deep water, but only in the bright shallows of harbors, bays, and coves, whereas floating algae have all the sunlight they need, and not able to get the nitrates they need from inorganic salt water, they are nitrogen limited. Nitrogen-loading, or nutrient enrichment, of harbor waters causes floating seaweed populations to explode. Blooming microalgae murk up the water. Large macroalgae also reduce the amount of light available to eelgrass. In nutrient-enriched seawater, tiny green branching epiphytic algae also attach in profusion to the stems of anchored eelgrass, and these further rob light from eelgrass fronds. Soon the lights go out for eelgrass. When eelgrass goes, so goes the neighborhood. An entire complex community disappears. Scallop beds vanish; fin fish, flounder, and juvenile striped bass have no place to hide, the diversity of the invertebrate benthic community plummets, and so do populations of lobster, blue crab, hermit crabs, shrimp, and mussels. It takes very small elevations of nitrate—several parts per million—above ambient levels to bring about these changes.

The boys went up onto the jetty to fish, and I put on mask, snorkel, and fins for a float out over the eelgrass bed. Just off the sandbar in deeper water, a thick crop of green vertical stems waved back and forth in the current. The water was shallow and bathtub warm by the sandbar. A few kicks from the fins, and I was suspended over eelgrass and let the tide take me slowly into the center of the large bed. All under a blue sky. Weightless, peaceful. Sun on my back. Eelgrass gazing is the ultimate in passive observation. The lens of the mask bends reality ever so slightly so that you see a slight curvature to things, as if you float at the top of a round light-penetrated globe. A fish swims by occasionally. You get a glimpse of shells on the sandy bottom, but generally the bottom is hidden by that swatch of thick green grass, light fed. I have to come out here at least once in a summer to be reminded that the created world isn't a busy one. Not busy like ours. Sure, lots of things happen, but the excitement—a marauding school of snapper blues, a small flock of terns diving on bait—quickly dies down, and life returns to the center of its being—restful, snooping, looking, growing. Above in the blue sky, a contrail bends and breaks up and drifts slowly north— the jet so high it can't be heard. But here is where we live. Down here. Suspended between what's above and below—the silence of the eelgrass beds, broken only by the occasional whirr of an outboard engine spinning through the channel. Sometimes I find the silence great enough that all I hear, given the slight changes in pressure a shallow dive down to the sand for a scallop shell can bring about, is the pulse of blood in my veins and the beating of my heart.

Healthy eelgrass is bright green, but here the color seemed a little greenish-gray. And there was plenty of that epiphytic algae fastened to eelgrass fronds. This last island of green fronds seemed precarious, too small to survive. I suppose there are serious economic implications, but what concerns me more is the loss of this light-craving thing we call home.

When I came ashore, the boys shouted down from the jetty that they had caught some big scups. Scup are beautiful pumpkin seed–like fish, showing bright lines of aquamarine along their sides. The bigger ones sport wider dark bands over the silver. Scup are very good at getting bait off hooks. My son can catch them, but he has no interest in hurting them, and he'd rather not eat them because, as he says, he's a vegetarian who eats chicken and hamburgers. So he let most of them go. My nephew, on the other hand, kept his and wanted me to clean them, cook them, and eat them for him.

We were ready to push our boat back in just as a small dingy came up, piloted by an old woman with a slightly off-kilter look in her eye. I did not recognize her, and she came up to us with some suspicion, it seemed. Her eyebrows were raised, and her mouth hung down a bit.

Who are you? she asked. I told her who I was. She remembered my grandfather, she thought. We shared some common acquaintances. We can be so provincial here, and without such a check-in, we're just other people.

Everyone has a community. The island people have their community—this woman's father or uncle built the watchtower we liked to sneak into on those roving summer nights. Our community, down its dirt road and less than two miles from her house, is different altogether from hers, or I like to think—lacking the same pretensions of wealth and history. Was there some overlap between our perceived communities? Certainly. She pointed to the *Aleria*—a sleek black yacht sitting on the mooring where it has sat for forty years. Hers. She turned and looked back at the island and began telling me a brief family history in houses. Her hand swept through the air, stopping here and there to point out what was hers, to take in, eventually, the entire gentle rise of the island's spreading oaks and beech trees; the long green lawns that run to the harbor edge; and the enormous gray shingled houses with their curving dormers and winglike cantilevers, their gleaming roof peaks and their clipper-ship weather vanes. The whole island, I was sure, she'd come to know as her property, including what surrounded it—the sound of the bell buoy and the boom of Cleveland's Ledge in the fog on an August night. Even the white birds that hovered over the fish were hers. Don't we all come to feel equally possessive about the places that set the contexts of our lives? And isn't that a good starting place? What about our problems? Do we own those collectively, too? The loss of our eelgrass worlds, our salt marshes. Isn't that home, too? What if we just go with that? Expand that sense of place ownership outward. Own what's beautiful and what's ugly both, until the island that our community is drops away, and we stand on the still blue-green globe?

The tide had long since turned, and it was time to go. The boys had staked their own claim to the strand, old claims be damned. They trailed their legs in the water, and as we sailed away, we looked back to the ephemeral world we had inhabited. It would soon be gone, under water again. We could see our new acquaintances, an old woman settler and a middle-aged man I took to be her son. They were standing fifty feet apart on the bar. She had put her arms out from her sides like a cross, and he was tossing plastic rings so that she might catch them on her outstretched arms.

Is there something wrong with her? my son asked. No, I said, there's nothing wrong with her. She's as sane as any of us. What's Alzheimer's disease? he asked me. It's when old people lose their memories and other abilities, I said. They begin growing younger again. Like Tom Thumb? he asked. Exactly, I said. Like Tom Thumb. And Merlin. People generally grow younger on vacation, too, I said. See her son? Yeah, said Sam, starring down into the bucket of his expired fish and then back at the woman with her arms outstretched. She's old all right, he said. Then he was quiet for a long time, looking back at the sandbar and the woman and her son. But those rings, he said. Throwing those rings at people, that looks like fun.

Now the tide was running hard with us, and the afternoon breeze had freshened to fill our sails.

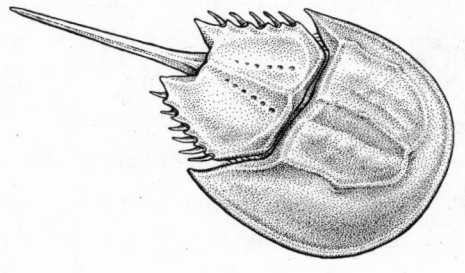

rachel carson

And there have been other shores where time stood still. On Buzzards Bay there is a beach studded with rocks left by glaciers . . . behind the beach is a narrow rim of low dunes, then a wide salt marsh. This marsh when I visited it on an evening toward the end of summer, had filled with shore birds since the previous night, and their voices were a faint, continuous twittering . . . farther back in the marsh a score of night herons stood motionless. From the bordering woods across the marsh a mother deer and her two fawns. . . . The salt marsh that evening was like a calm, green sea—only a little calmer, a little greener than the wide sheet of the bay on the other side of the dunes.

—RACHEL CARSON,
from *Town and Country* magazine

I HAD A love affair here on the marsh. With Rachel Carson. She is the most distinguished feature of this place. Her ghost. She loved coming here to watch the birds and ponder the imponderable beauty of the world. Linda Lear in her biography of Carson finds that Sippewissett was a favorite haunt of hers. She came often in the evening. The quote above is an unmistakable reference to Sippewissett—from the glacial boulders on the beach side, to the dunes, to the herons and forest edge, behind which, invisible from the marsh, is our house. I know precisely the places she stood in her mind's eye when she wrote those words. It makes my chest tingle to think of Carson pondering the imponderable on the marsh. When I told all this to my wife, she eyed me suspiciously. Rachel Carson was Athena and Helen both—a godly ideal and the ideal of romantic love of place—an immortal mortal. She was a scientist with a poet's sensibility and recognized Sippewissett immediately for what it was—a place of biochemical alchemy and wonder—as vast as a splendiferous green sea, quieter still, with a deeper reflective surface. What's not to love in Rachel?

Rachel Carson was born May 27, 1907. She first came to Woods Hole in 1929 to work as an MBL summer investigator, having graduated from Pennsylvania College for Women and gotten accepted at John's Hopkins University, where she would earn her master's degree in zoology. John's Hopkins had a chair at MBL, and she was invited down for summer course work and research. She returned to the MBL again in 1932 and made many subsequent trips to Woods Hole. She worked before and during the war, writing pamphlets and articles for the U.S. Fish and Wildlife Service. Her books about the sea made her famous. *Under the Sea Wind* was published in 1941. *The Sea Around Us*, a decade later, spent nearly two years on the *New York Times* bestseller list and won the national book award. In 1955, she wrote *The Edge of Sea*, completing her famous sea trilogy. But it was *Silent Spring*, her environmental manifesto, published in 1964, that secured her place in history and had a far greater impact on the world than she could have imagined.

Carson began *Silent Spring* at the urging of her friend, Olga Owens Hewitt, who told her in a letter of the deaths of many songbirds in her sanctuary from aerial spraying of the pesticide DDT. At first she balked. Her dream for years had been to write a book on nature for children, and if she'd lived a longer life, she'd have written for children. But she felt called to write *Silent Spring*. The evidence of the assault being waged on nature by our industrial style of growth and development couldn't be ignored. Carson felt that if a popular book about pesticides and their "rain of death" *could* be written—her editors and friends doubted it could—she had the best chance. She also knew she didn't have a choice. It took several years to research and write, but when *Silent Spring* came blasting out of her sense of moral outrage, it rang across the land clear as a bell.

When *Silent Spring* came out, first serialized in *The New Yorker* magazine in the late spring of 1962, public reaction was tumultuous. Carson found herself the object of fierce attack and derision by petrochemical industries, farm- and food-processing interests, and the U.S. Department of Agriculture. She was "that hysterical lady"—that little old lady in tennis shoes—standing against progress, against science and technology, against everything the country stood for, and her path, though she never advocated a complete halt to the use of pesticides, was the path to famine, pestilence, and financial ruin. Like Darwin challenging the church, Carson challenged the industrial paradigm.

And Carson was prepared. She had a mountain of evidence and was a master of organization. She stood firm in the firestorm. On a TV special airing the two sides of the debate, like

Joan of Arc she slaughtered the white lab-coated enemy. And the public stood behind her. President Kennedy formed a scientific advisory committee to look at the issue of pesticide use, particularly DDT. There were Senate hearings as well. Carson testified, and the committee's report, though considered balanced, broadly supported her positions. Thus the ball of environmental activism began rolling faster. It would take another ten years for a newly formed EPA to ban the use of DDT in this country, so firmly embedded were the values and dollars that demanded heavy inputs of pesticides and fertilizers on farmland and mosquito-infested salt marsh both, but the die was cast.

Sippewissett is a good place to see some of the fruits of Carson's life and celebrate them. The osprey, for instance. In *Silent Spring*—a vast referential work—is the research of ornithologist Joseph Hickey. Hickey was one of the earliest scientists to link DDT and its residual DDE to the phenomenon of eggshell thinning in birds of prey, including osprey. Eggshells became too thin to take the weight of brooding females and broke. There were no osprey on the Cape when I was growing up—a combination of loss of forest habitat and a poisoned food web. But now in August we can see as many as eight birds wheeling around the marsh, salt basins, and ponds, and an osprey plunging after fish is a common sight on this cove. There are three platforms on the marsh, and each spring and summer we watch the progress of osprey pairs raising young.

It's possible, just possible that on an August afternoon in the late fifties or early sixties, when I was out on the clam flats with my parents, Carson, fighting an ironic and losing battle to breast cancer and on her last visit to Woods Hole, came to visit Sippewissett to say farewell. Everything at the marsh would have recognized and welcomed her as she had recognized and welcomed it.

I imagine the tide would have flowed quietly around her dune, slowly emptying the entire body of winding creeks and ponds back into the gold light of the bay. Spread across the exposed sand flats would have been the dark forms of southbound shorebirds each standing one-leg-up together and facing the sun. Sippewissett, like every marsh, was part of Carson's eternal Earth home, eternally welcoming. She would have had no fear of death since she knew that in her marsh, as in the world, everything is born, everything is transformed, and everything dies and is born again. In her mind, she would have been floating out on that ebb, held by that sun-dappled water—the soul's river—the river of her own words, language imbued, as Emerson liked to think, with earth and spirit, and all singing their way back to the source of light.

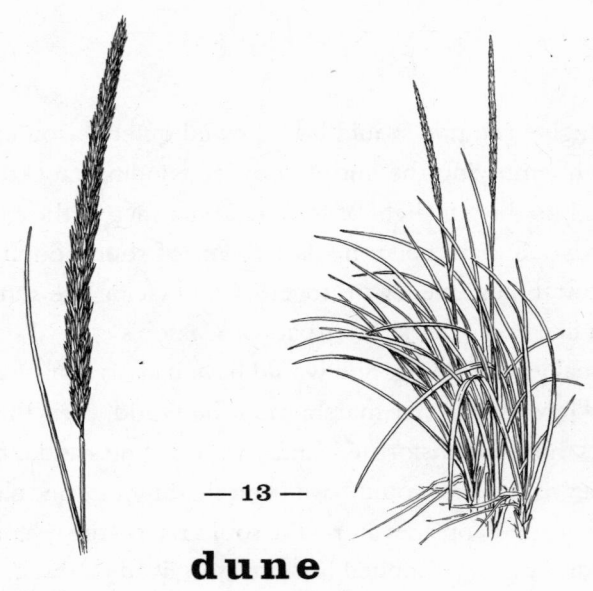

— 13 —

dune

One and One—are One—
Two—be finished using—
Well enough for Schools—
But for Minor Choosing—
—EMILY DICKINSON, from Poem number 769

THERE IS A party every night somewhere here in July. This was the first party of the summer that my wife and I would get to. Maybe our last. We are social marginals here, having lost touch with many of the friends, families, and summer traditions that define this place. We were invited by virtue of my sister, who maintains her network of summer friends through tennis and a near nightly gathering somewhere. The party was at a grand stone house on Chappaquoit Island (not really an island, but islandlike, and people like to think they live isolated from the mainland), home to many old friends and acquaintances, though we, of the nearby salt marsh clan, do not live there. The house overlooks the mouth of West Falmouth harbor, and its lawns stretch right down to the rocks on the shore. All day one can sit on reclining chairs and watch a colorful procession of boats coming and going while imbibing. We found ourselves there in the early evening drinking horribly strong rum drinks with ruddy-cheeked guests dressed in white slacks while the sun dropped toward the bay. My sister allows that you can wear anything these days to a summer party and it fits, so I had taken her advice and was wearing my orange shirt with the tiny duck logo, two buttons open, thinking myself as fitting in rather well. In the early evening, the bay was golden and full of boats. There were sails on all the western horizons, and motorboats on the move in and out, sport fishing boats, sleek cruisers, small knockabouts moving fast and slow, a handful of yachts, hull up and racing in from Cleveland's Ledge.

But, truthfully, I feel naked at parties. My wife feels fully clothed. Ted, the new millionaire, was there—everybody, even me, knew that—and so was Rainer. My wife struck up a conversation with him, who let drop that he invented the Nike swoosh logo, I think, but anyway, he worked for a national advertising firm in New York—a handsome, smart, and hardworking young man, who, even so, gave the air that he didn't seem to need to work very much. Once my wife strikes up, she keeps up, and does that thing you're not supposed to do at a cocktail party. She stays engaged in one conversation for a long time. What a Vermonter, I thought, thinking this behavior may be a rural affliction—a virulent combination of sincerity and curiosity. The men seem to love her.

I, however, found myself drifting around and hooking up with lamps and other inanimate things. I traveled once too often to the punch bowl, but then, circling back around to the hub of the party, which had reached its orgiastic pitch, I saw an old friend. At first, I thought she was her mother. When I was a boy I used to go to her mother's house to look at the amazing shell collection there. For a few summers, a small gang of us roamed the marshes and beaches together. She with her long blond hair was one of the gang. We'd spend hours snorkeling around the rocks, fishing from small boats, right around that tender middle teen age of fourteen. She was one of us when life was perfect. She said, My my, for a moment I thought you were your father!

My wife and I left early because we had plans for a night of floating. We left laughing about the way we had become our parents, and at the preponderance of tall tanned blond women at the party. How many of the blonds are real, do you think? my wife asked, who almost never wears make up, but does have a secret thing about her hair. All of them, I said. And it was true. I knew because I had known them when they were twelve.

In the driveway of the stone house, three large men were squeezed into the backseat of a compact car with its doors open like moth wings. Brother-in-law Wayne, the advertising wizard, and a wickedly naughty real estate developer named Johnny were tight together in there, like rugby players with shoulders locked, not talking. Waiting for their wives. Why are they sitting in there? my wife asked, after we had moved down the drive. They are friends, I said, and they are wealth peers. The stars were coming out. We named the constellations and the summer planets: Scorpio was rising; Jupiter was very bright.

On wealth, Ralph Waldo Emerson wrote that "a snow storm is soon blown into drifts." Here on the island is some grand old wealth, I think, with these elaborate homes built in the obnoxiously misnomered "cottage style." And there is plenty of new wealth as well. One morning over breakfast last summer, my father tossed down the *Wall Street Journal* and said, "Read this." It was a brief article about the recent sale of a publishing business in New York City. The owners lived nearby. "That's John and his father, Ted," my father said, "and I think there's an uncle who's in it as well. Thirty-five million dollars." I thought he sighed with admiration. He's a retired banker after all. What popped into mind was "indictments." I can't seem to shake the conviction that great sums usually accompany great crimes in life, and I wondered how many of the enormous homes here have their hidden bone rooms—were built on insider trading, inflated profit statements, graft, embezzlement—trivial means, some might think, to the ends that matter most. How wealth is acquired doesn't seem to concern us, only that one has it. Wealth appears to be its own justification. Our own cape houses, as modest as they are, have been made valuable over time, by the rarity of their location, by their quiet privacy. Certainly, they are out of reach, monetarily, to the likes of me today. Recently, young gazillionaires have been moving into them, occupying the neighborhood with bright-eyed children, nannies, and slobbery black Labrador retrievers that poop on our bipolar lawn. The original lots were laid out here on abandoned farmland in the 1940s. People of the new business class, like my grandparents, who simply wanted to be among their Boston area friends in summer and surrounded by water, built these places. Ours cost about $18,000. My grandfather was a salesman. He loved old Cadillacs, golf, and the Republican Party, and he joined up as a naval pilot in both wars. My grandmother, a small, dark-haired, not particularly effusive woman, came from Tennessee of Welsh miner stock and Irish grandparents. She played bridge shrewdly and was a meticulous paint-by-numbers lady. During her reign here, the house was adorned with her black-and-gold floral trays hand-painted from precut stencils—and her collections of china figures. Her paint-by-numbers Gloucester fishing boat still hangs in the dark hall by creaky stairs that go narrowly and steeply up to the second floor. We cherish it, like the other nonpecuniary things that give real value: dirt roads and sandy paths through the dunes and woods, the inky-black nights, fog, fish, and clamming—the oldest wealth—and we were fortunate to have the use of it all simply by virtue of being here. The world is a marvelous storehouse: a quirky, crumbling, ever-renewing mansion, a work in progress loaded with riches. The rights and responsibilities accorded to the living to use and preserve the storehouse for the future living cuts across socioeconomic boundaries. But today, when so much of the storehouse is controlled by so few in the world, the inequality diminishes us. One would hope that Emerson's snowdrift of money could buy good Earth stewardship. It is so, but only if you believe that ends can justify the means. When great monetary wealth appears to be its own justification, what really matters, our oldest green land capital with its beauty and fecundity, leaches away. Vast wealth could buy stewardship by worthy means, but it would have to end poverty and hunger at the same time. We all could be happy with less, I'm sure.

We found the beginning of the long beach. At the end of it, two miles east, the land turned into the marsh. The tide was flooding into it, and the small fish were spawning there. Would you rather have been a Wall Street banker, she asked. A man with an IPO? Yeah, I said with a smile, looking straight ahead. I'd buy the Jade. Does that excite you? She looked at me long and hard with mild disbelief, and then a smile grew into a little humming tune "me husband's got no courage in him." It was a taunt and a challenge both. Just checking in, she said. Ahead of us was the end of the beach and its perfect night destination. *Amophila breviligulata*—Italian opera, sandy coverlets, and grass rooms with their turned-back beds of dunes.

My wife is a sixth-generation Vermonter whose ancestors were among the early inhabitants of the tiny hill town of Glover, Vermont, settled in 1783. Glover is still rural and isolated. Dairy farms predominate. Everyone knows everyone else in Glover, and many are related by blood or marriage. Many Glover families come from people that fled Quebec after the defeat of the French in the 1750s, but her Staunton side was English, migrants from the wilds of Machias, Maine, and the little towns west of Cobscook Bay. The family says there is a bit of Abenaki blood on that side. Who knows? I wouldn't doubt it. Perhaps a wisp of Abenaki DNA resides in my wife. In the early years of our marriage, she would come south to the marsh only reluctantly. She's a lake person. The Cape had too much family for a Vermonter. If you haven't grown up in it, a summer community can be stifling and tough to penetrate for the outsider. Now, well into our third decade of marriage, she's more family than I am and loves to visit the house on the marsh, though it's a rare occasion. We have been married for twenty-five years. We divorced numerous times *before* we got married. So, we have stayed together. I recommend to my own children early premarriage divorces and living together first to work things out. If you saw us walking down the beach today, you'd notice our matching gaits, since we've walked twenty-nine years of miles together—and also that we walk long sections of beach far apart, too, and alone.

Her biggest fear used to be dark-things-looming-underwater. She grew up on Lake Champlain. There was a sunken boat off the point. But hers was generally a sunny childhood around boats and boys. If there was darkness, it was mostly in her ancestry. There had been a string of suicides in nearby St. Johnsbury, Vermont, during the first half of the twentieth century. Almost all were women. No one knows why. Isolation? Depression? Abuse?

Two of these suicides were in her family on her father's side: first her father's mother and then his grandmother. The daughter was hauntingly beautiful, a red head with sad eyes. My wife has her wedding ring and her Bible. Inside the Bible is her picture. I've always wondered if my wife's watery fears were connected to those suicides—the ribs of sunken boats a reminder of a not-too-distant past and what was buried deep in the family psyche. She's over the fear of dark water now, she says, and even wants to put old fears to test. I wouldn't have chosen a full moon night in July to test her fears.

The moon was as bright as a lantern, and the marsh was thick with the matings and mergings of living things when we set out: insects and crabs, fish and bacteria—cell division goes full tilt in July. Songbirds call out in the middle of July nights—yellow-breasted chats, Carolina wrens, and catbirds. The ospreys keen away on their platform nests, herons and crows bleat, black ducks in a flurry of beating wings fly nervously from one pond to another. The birthing, consuming, and decomposing of the marsh on a full moon night in July were further aroused by the hint of a north wind above us. The glow of the sunset lingered nearly to 10:00 p.m. Moonlight made that night one long extended day.

We carried the kayaks down to the place on the beach road where the Beach Pond—the last embayment of the marsh—came closest, and dragged the boats across the private marsh to the edge. It was just enough of a trespass to quicken the pulse. I can never get enough trespassing in a summer, especially on the beach where there is the lingering sense from childhood that we own everything. Fiddler crab nations were scrippling and scrilling through the spartina stems, and the sea, on a spring tide, had begun spilling over the rims of creeks and ditches and flooding across the flat spartina meadows of the upper marsh. This would be the highest high tide of the year. I timed our departure so that we'd launch the boats an hour before high tide. We'd have the slack tide to explore the upper marsh, and then the growing ebb would take us out and into the bay, if we chose to go there. And, if she could bear it, we'd paddle out to the metal flag at Barn Rock a mile offshore—the most looming dark-thing-under-water I knew.

All the marsh mergings going on that night had us thinking about Lynn Margulis's work. Margulis, a most potent scientist, collaborated with James Lovelock shortly after he first stated his idea of the Gaia hypothesis in 1972, a revision of the very ancient philosophical idea of Earth as a whole being. Their work introduced the world to a new scientific view that the environment and the interacting organisms on it evolve together as a living, energetically open, materially closed, self-regulating system. The Gaia idea, that Earth has a physiology, is now nearly 40 years old. The lucid picture global ecologists are assembling today is Gaian by any other name. We are one.

Several years earlier I had met Margulis at a conference in New Haven called *The G[o]od in Nature*. The purpose of the gathering was to bring together scientists and theologians so that there might be some fruitful discourse and discovery of the common ground between them. Conference organizers, including the Yale Divinity School, the Yale Forestry School, and the Wilderness Society, believed that solutions to environmental and social problems needed the synthesis of science and spirit: that Earth stewardship required both numbers and the numinous, the sacred merged with the profane.

Margulis studies the phenomenon of living fusions and has developed a symbiosis-driven theory of the origins of evolutionary novelty, including new species. A melding of science and spirit is decidedly not the kind of fusion she talks about. At the conference she did not buy into the idea of nature's goodness. She saw no sign of any moral universe, written into the material laws of nature anyway. She and Lovelock went to great lengths to point out their belief that Earth's emergent self-regulating system had neither purpose nor direction except survival to multiply. From many observations and experiments with microbes, she showed evolution to complexity over long periods of time to be a process of integration of symbionts that become genuinely new individuals subject to natural selection. A "big long result of forbidden fertilization," is how she put it.

Margulis has long had the reputation of a maverick thinker. As early as 1977 she was known as "one of the most unsettling figures in her field." (Kronenberger, John. "Lynn Margulis." *Bostonia* Autumn, 1977.) Her work challenged long-held neodarwinian evolutionary theory. That she was young, female, and smarter than many in a field traditionally dominated by men did not help her scientific reputation. At the core of her revolutionary thinking was the notion that species of nucleated organisms never originated only through the slow accumulation of random mutations. Most evolutionary novelty was produced by symbiogenesis: mergers between members of different species of organisms in physical contact with each other. Specifically, different kinds of prokaryotes (bacteria composed of cells that lack nuclei), created the complexity we see. All fungi, protoctists, beach plums, bees and other animals including us, composed of cells with nuclei, came into being through the fusion of once-separate bacteria. Margulis's ideas often appeared to flow in opposition to the mainstream. The scientific community rejected her first scientific article on the symbiogenetic origins of cells over twenty times before it was published in 1967. But today the mainstream has been turned, rerouted in part, toward her vision of evolutionary processes. During her years as a graduate student at Berkeley in the early '60s, Margulis was married to Carl Sagan. While Sagan worked to expand the public's appreciation of the outer universe, she worked out of the public eye on the inner universe. During her doctoral work in cell genetics, she collected data and made observations that didn't fit the current neodarwinian assumptions about evolution defined strictly as "changes in gene frequencies in natural populations." She, with others, showed that chloroplasts in algal cells contain their own DNA. Chloroplasts absorb sunlight to convert it to chemical energy—a vital function for all algae and plants. The chloroplast DNA suggested that algal plant cells have at least two different ancestors. One chloroplast cell type, a photosynthetic bacterium, had been ingested by another, a swimming consumer, but had survived digestion. The marriage between these two different life forms, in this case, survived to thrive and produce more offspring. Margulis made field trips with students to Sippewissett in the 1980s while she was a biology professor at Boston University. One of her many interests in the marsh were microbial mats dominated by blue-green, photosynthetic, oxygen-producing bacteria. In summer, up on the high marsh, these grow thick like slimy pancakes. Layers of brown diatoms and other algae cover green layers of photosynthetic bacteria. Underneath, purple layers blend to pink and gold. Each layer represents a structural mixture, complex communities of different types of interacting bacteria growing in profusion. Fossilized bacterial mats like these, when in the odd case they are preserved, are called stromatolites. Such layered rocks of former bacterial communities are among the oldest fossils known. Some in southern Africa and western Australia are 3.5 billion years old.

In the 1980s researchers at Sippewissett used microscopes, grew microbes in the laboratory, analyzed pigments by chromatography and other techniques to identify particular types of cyanobacteria. New techniques for the identification of microbes have been developed in the molecular genetics lab. Still, science has described less than one percent of the estimated bacterial and protist kinds of life. Vertebrate genomes, including ours, are yet the major preoccupation for most scientists, though the microbial kingdoms continue to regulate the planet's soil and atmosphere. No wonder Margulis is still interested in them.

Our tool of choice to experience the wholeness of the world that night was the kayak, not a DNA primer. What a wonderful invention! If you don't have much to carry and you don't mind the lack of stability, kayaks give you access to tiny creeks you'd otherwise never visit. Kayaks are speedy when you want them to be and maneuverable. With the tide turning the entire marsh into a moonlit pond, every creek became navigable. That night, my wife and I could explore the mosquito ditches and winding channels normally too narrow to float and too muddy to walk. These turn back on themselves to run opposite and parallel to the main channel, causing the appearance of a tide flowing in opposition to the main creeks. What was so unusual that night was the juxtaposition of sounds—the noise of a night of marsh love. We heard wood thrushes singing together with the contrapuntal quocks of night herons flying overhead and the high kilping of the ospreys. Under us, moonlight had penetrated through five feet of water to reflect off white sand, and over sand we saw the long shadows of bass moving. Moonlight lit us from below. Popping and splashing up near the boats and swirling along the grass banks, bass had moved up into the smallest creeks to feed. The entire back marsh was a busy labyrinth of love and feeding. There was nothing chaste about it. We inched along its quivering banks, poking into dead-end creeks and then backed out. For an hour we progressed nowhere except back to the edge of beach pond and then into another corner of the labyrinth—our kayaks often clicking together—touching then separating. We had entered the night together and merged, and we had not noticed the tide shifting into reverse almost imperceptibly at first, the grasses bending slightly on the creek corners where the water had milled pockets of deeper water. Slow, I said. If we take our time and wait for the full ebb, we'll get a great pulse out through the inlet, and the tide will take us over the bars without a single paddle stroke.

Well before the outgoing tide really began to pick up, we pulled our kayaks up the flooded creek into Quahog Pond, then onto the two-rut road there. In the culvert there, we saw the white ventral side of a blue crab shell reflecting moonlight and the quahog and oyster shells littering the bottom of the pond lit up like pool lights. An eel languished under the bridge. A spider crab picked along the bottom around the bright orange sponge, *Microciona prolifera,* that always seems like an exotic bauble.

I'll show you something else, I said, but I could tell that my wife, who is a Cancer—a crab lady herself—and strongly influenced by the moon, was getting moonstruck. Come on, I said, I'll show you something scary to snap you out of your moon trance. We waded back into the upper marsh. The water was dropping out of the marsh, but still it came up over our sneakers. The moon had reached the top of the sky. Out on the upper marsh, connected to the channel by its own creek, is a six-foot-deep perfectly round hole—twenty-five feet across. In it the moon was captured, like a pearl resting on gray silk. Looking down, we saw a silver school of mummichogs moving around and around and under them a pair of horseshoe crabs connected and moving slowly in tandem. It's like an inverted looking glass, she said, and there is the caught moon.

We are grateful for Margulis and her colleagues' symbiotic view of life. We like the notion of a marsh and a world made by fusions, by dynamic couplings. And we like the model they have given us of one world linked by necessary metabolic interactions, by the recycling of elements – that the spent gas of microbes is our balmy air. We witness here at the turning tide a world of emergence, of the evolution of the physical with consciousness.

Grace buoyed by scientific understanding is the essential idea for gathering what the world is and how it works. Of Earth's delectable body, science may detect no purpose or direction other than toward the more complex, but that has never been science's role. Science, in the end, is a long conversation. It's a way of knowing, based on physical evidence, many small things for sure, that when pieced together, by testing, by talking, by many people like Margulis, add up to something grand. For us, two ordinary people on a salt marsh at night, that grand thing is love. It's simply impossible for us to think of it in any other way.

The rush through the inlet was short but powerful. We shot out over the bars at the mouth of the inlet and into the calm bay and floated there, like island-bound seeds drifting east down the beach with the disk of moon high overhead.

Do you really want to paddle out there, I asked, trying to pick out Barn Rock.

No, she said, I don't.

How about this, I said, let's go explore the dunes. I can tell you all about sand.

No more telling me anything, she said, only showing.

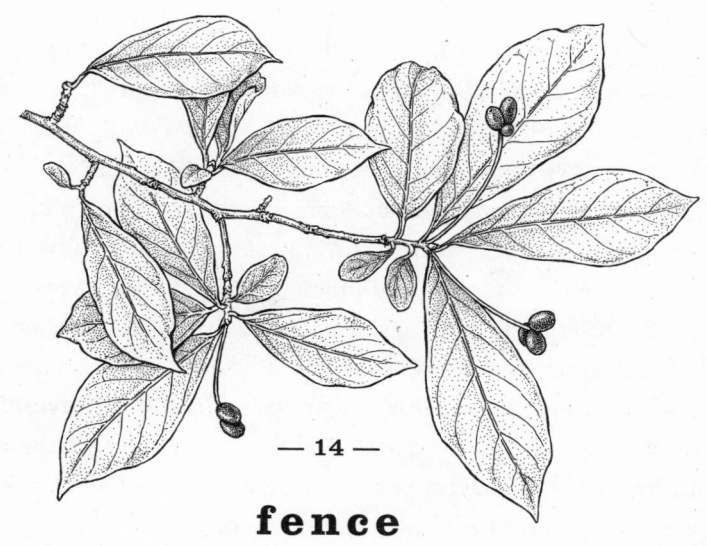

— 14 —

fence

OUR WEEK, OF course, had zipped by in a rush of blue skies, hot days, and cool nights. This was our last full day, though I would be coming back in August, September, October, and November to see what the marsh looked like at the end of its year. On this last July day, I had been up six hours by the time 10:00 a.m. rolled around and walked down the road with the hollow craving for a second cup of coffee in me. The day was hot and it felt deliciously long already. Low tide had been ebbing from the marsh since 4:30 a.m. when I walked there. I had counted twenty-two black ducks on the upper beach pond. And caught ten small bass. Coming home along Black Beach Road, beach plums hung in pale clumps by the path that goes over the dunes to the bay. The sky had that hazy, everlasting blue to it. Fat red rose hips, yellow clusters of poison ivy berries, and pale blue *Myrica* berries—the blue waxy myrtle used by colonial candle makers—were coated by the gray dust of the lane. Coming out of the marsh I had taken the path inside the dunes. This area, with its mosaic of sparse beach grasses, microvariations in topography, saltwort flats, shallow miniponds, meandering creeks, and high marsh grass, is a world onto itself. There's always something new. Once I saw a pair of horned larks. Once a single piping plover standing in a shallow pool, with a half dozen of its darker striped cousins, semipalmated plover scattered about. It was the only piping plover I've ever seen in the marsh—though they did nest on our beach not too long ago. Today, I had found a dead salt marsh vole and stooped down to pick up and examine its small body, sharp teeth, and tiny eyes. How do they survive a twice daily flood here? I thought of the thing that loves to hunt and eat voles—harriers—the owl-like hawk that glides slowly and lowly over prairie lands looking for mice and voles, sparrows, larks, and plovers. Then looking up, I saw one: a large female was sailing east like a child's kite skimming above the marsh. This, too, was an unusual sighting here. It seemed to portend a noteworthy day.

Trails, paths, rights-of-way, it seems to me, hold an importance to our sense of place that belies their small scrubby stature. Around here, paths, trails, bikeways, sidewalks, railroad tracks, abandoned roads, horse trails, and deer paths knit communities together. We all use them. They reduce our dependence on the cars that clog our communities. Once pathways begin to close up, grow over, get either fenced off or policed, the community begins to fracture, to lose track of itself. In addition to the legal battles over the public's right to walk into the woods around the cabin, there's a contentious battle around a short path down at the end of the road that runs past our house. The dirt road ends at the railroad tracks, turns at that point into a short narrow path through the scrub, then joins a private driveway built over the old road bed before hitting the old roadway again. The owner of the driveway wants to fence off this path. We all use it. It's a shortcut for the bike trip to Falmouth. My aging parents walk it to get their mail. Neighbors and friends living on the other side of the tracks ramble up it and up our road to get to Black Beach. We're not talking heavy traffic here, not even a steady stream. Now, to stem this light flow of humanity past his drive, the owner proposes to erect an eight-foot-high, forty-foot-long chain-link fence. But, who wants to be fenced out, or in, for that matter? He needed permits, of course. His neighbors opposed him, though some of us on this side were tempted to side with him—fences after all, they reasoned privately, keep the rabble out. The hearings stretched out over months, and numerous agencies were involved.

Much ado about nothing? Yes, but truly, a fence across this little path does disturb the universe. Only a people gone mad for privacy could want it. Perhaps only death could hold more privacy than we think we need. And the fence, our neighbor Chris Collins once asked, will it be electrified? Like a concentration camp?

There are few who can speak to the truth of a fence, who can go quicker to the heart of the matter than Collins. She is an unreasonable visionary with an uncommon view of history and a hopeful view of the future—an idealist who holds onto ideas that connect to community values in spite of all practical considerations, current legal contexts, and definitions of private property. After lunch, I walked down the abandoned tracks past Oyster Pond to the short path that connected the overgrown railroad line to Cottage Lane to visit her. Collins, I suspected, kept this poison ivy–lined path mowed—this little stretch through woods at the top of Cottage Lane. And I was right. Her shingled house with its small tower—her writing studio and elegant screened porch—is the last one on the lane. It's the old Smith Farm place. Plum and apple trees grow up out of the scrubby understory of the forest. Collins is a historian of urban planning and civic architecture.

With advanced degrees from Columbia University and a senior Fulbright scholarship to her credit, Collins, in her midseventies, who claims to have bitten a New York City policeman, is officially retired as director of the Gimbel Library of the Parsons School of Design. She and her husband authored *Camillo Sitte: The Birth of Modern City Planning* (1986), and she has been a visiting professor at Cornell University and lectured widely during her career. For the past fifteen years, she's been writing about the life and work of Werner Hegeman—a German urbanist and economist who came to America during the first decade of the past century and helped establish the field of city planning.

Hegeman's appeal to Collins? His belief in the early tenets of American Progressivism as they related to city design: that regional planning built around citizen participation could lead to the betterment of all citizens, including the poor, minorities, and women. He believed that planning was a way to awaken and direct the natural but latent civic consciousness among citizens.

Collins, here in Falmouth, had put Hegeman's beliefs in good citizenship to practice. Her notion was that rational planning, cooperative effort, and the cultivation of a public aesthetic could create towns and cities that were both functional and beautiful. Her years of activism, of speaking out at public meetings, of giving land, and of working to save places and pathways all reflected Hegeman's thinking. Hegeman had returned to Europe after World War I, but then began to see the danger in the rise of Hitler and Nazism in the late twenties and dropped his urban planning work to focus on the political situation, publishing articles, often under pseudonyms. His books and articles were included in the book burnings of 1933. He sought exile from Germany in 1934 and died, a soul in turmoil, in 1936.

That afternoon Collins showed me her own paths through the woods to the edge of Oyster Pond. Over the years she and her husband had created paths and had pushed the lawn out, saving wild trees, mostly tupelo (*Nyssa sylvaticum*)—a swamp-loving tree that turns bright red in early fall—and juniper. They also saved small specimens of English white oak and red maple, which now spread their great branches over the lawn to the edge of the forest, thinned in places for a view of the crescent of salt marsh at their end of the pond. Herons and egrets rose up out of it when we approached.

In the forest, her paths wound through small cedar groves and by the black trunks of cherry and under pitch pine. They ended on a small rise at the edge of the pond. Here is where her son Nick pitched his summer tent. One summer he stayed there nearly every night, she said. I remember him, I said. And did her husband like snorkeling? I asked, remembering the man who would show up sometimes on the beach with his son. He did, she said. He came with his mask and snorkel, donned them most unceremoniously among the proper sunbathers and tennis men, and would enter the water backward. I had admired him as a kid, his un-self-conscious behavior at the beach club and his unapologetic interest in our so-called zebra fish and jellies, since I had spent so much time peering at things underwater. I would think to myself, is he the geek I'm becoming? Of course he wasn't a geek, but a well-respected architect and architectural historian in his work life, but here on vacation, another person emerged, full of childlike glee. I remembered his big warm smile and the occasional astonishment on his stretched, rubberized face behind the glass disk of the mask. If I did what your husband used to do, I said,—snorkeling at the beach club—my daughters would be terribly embarrassed by my behavior. Even more than usual. Eventually, said Collins, we lose all our inhibitions, don't we? The sooner the better, I said.

After our walk, we sat in the quiet of her screened porch and sipped a concoction of cranberry juice and orange juice and listened to the gold finches and robins singing in spite of the heat of the midafternoon. Yellow daylilies were in bloom along the stone walls, along with tall red Asiatic lilies and the purple flowers of hosta. A skylight in the porch roof let in some yellow light, and the cedar by the porch was stirring just slightly in a breeze coming off the pond and through the oaks. I watched Collins's face, small, attractive, and trimmed by her short silvery hair, as she remembered the struggles of caring for her husband in his long and lingering decline from Alzheimer's disease. Her family roots are Austrian, but she was born and raised in Chile and met her husband in college in New York. At the end of their life together, he was twelve years an Alzheimer's patient, and she kept him home for all that time.

George was a generous man, she said. Before he died he gave fifty acres of land—part of the old golf course—that had become overgrown to the town for a town forest that now bears his name. The deed was one of the last papers he had to sign, and though he couldn't talk much by then, he knew exactly what he was doing—giving land away. He was smiling when I helped him sign the deed. He knew that he had done a good thing.

Collins had recently continued that tradition of conserving land, this time by giving a conservation easement on her homestead, which was only twelve acres but included the forest and a thousand feet of frontage on the salt pond—land that today is worth millions with its development values still intact. Property value she had just given away.

Property values, she said. We can become overly concerned about preserving property value when what really needs preserving is something deeper.

Why is a path so important? I asked. Collins didn't need to think too long or hard for an answer. Paths, informal and formal, she said, knit our places together, like webbing, connecting all the disparate ground, even in the smallest towns, even in the largest metropolitan places. The way we design pathways, or allow the public to design and define them over time, has much to do with how well our civil society works.

Then it was time to go back over small paths, an old railroad line, and the dirt road home.

Underneath the dream of civil society are individual lives and dreams—spirit journeys if you will. I thought of the physical pathways I usually walk in life, most of them crowded and many paved over. So often it isn't walking but driving I do on them, through a landscape lost to all but memory. Why was a dirt path hemmed in by honeysuckle and poison ivy so important to me and to so many people? It wasn't, I suspected, because it saved us time or got us somewhere; though it did that, there is usually another way around. It was because the walk itself through an informal landscape informed our inner lives. We remember that thing learned. The thought long ago held. The iron smell of first rain. The labyrinth of paths is our memory palace here. To lose it is to lose our memory. Consider all the thoughts that have occurred to people when they went walking the dog or the baby, or walked hand in hand with a girlfriend or a daughter growing up in this place. What story would they tell? On these paths did we not daily remember our dead? A fence blocking a path might be viewed as a Berlin Wall of local memory. Paths connect us to the past, not only to the post office. I would like to know what new directions the lives of walkers took on account of all their walking and thinking along this path and all the sandy paths and empty landscapes that are becoming closed and filled up as we grow up and lose that sense of what we are.

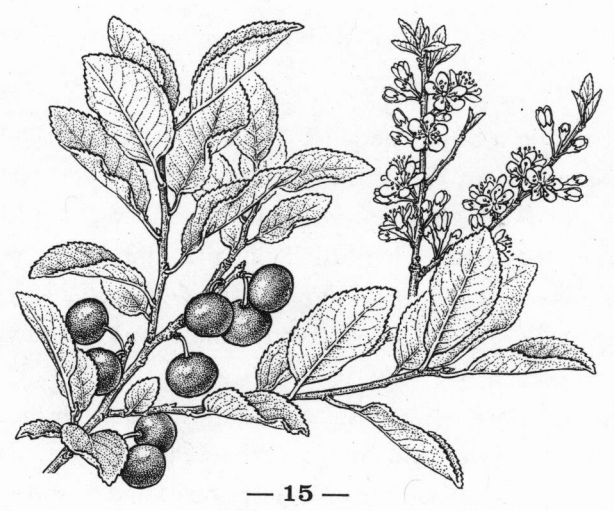

beach house

I PREFER A party I can walk to in bare feet over a dusty road in the evening in August. Better, make it on a beach. With old childhood friends, there is no guard to lower—however many years since you saw them. Our offering was fresh bluefish fillets, interlayered with shrimp stuffing, baked in wine, and a bottle of chardonnay. We'd caught the fish that morning.

Susan's house sits up on a little grass patch above the beach and bay. Marsh stretches out behind, on the other side. The house, built by her father and uncle, had survived the hurricanes of 1938 and 1954 that had plucked at least two other houses off the dune—the end house was pitched into the marsh, but it was hauled out again and set back on its foundation.

I have always liked Susan's family. Her cousins lived a few minutes away in a small house tucked into the scrub of the inner dune. Susan greeted us with a wave, like we'd been over the day before, though it's been thirty years, and said to put the food on the table. She was barefoot. Her children and a dozen other kids were running around the yard. There was an enormous black dog chasing them down the wooden steps to the beach and up and down the sand, but we went inside and felt thirty years younger—the same dark mottled pine planking on the walls, the same salt-stained picture window on the west wall distorting the setting sun—a light that comes into the room and turns every forehead golden.

Now that both her parents are gone—her mother died in this house when we were kids and just a few years ago her father, a big imposing man who had a love for large boats and offshore fishing, passed away—there is a clearing up going on in the house. Things are changing: new white paint, new shingles on the roof, ideas for expanding.

She took me around the house and told me about the work they will do, assuming they can get the local and state permits they'll need. There could be big legal expenses, she said. I can't imagine it will be a problem, I said. Look what they're building all around us—trophy castles and gated fortresses, not beach bungalows anymore. I know, she said, but they'd like to see these houses along the beach roll into the sea, and when they do, they don't want us to be able to rebuild.

Why change it at all, I asked. It's nice the way it is. When it rolls into the sea, haul it out again. Haven't you survived all the hurricanes of the last century? Yes, she said, but we may not survive the next big hurricane or a hundred years beyond that. We went outside. Look, she said, showing me a footing on the southwest corner, we're eight feet above mean high tide here. It's not enough. We've got to get another four feet up—with footings that go much deeper than into six inches of sand.

As we looked into the black under the house, she began to tell me a little of her bout with cancer, the family history, and alluded to cures. Repairing lives. Across thirty years, every life takes repairing again and again and again, she said. Mine was no different.

Her own structures were failing—the invisible winds of internal hurricanes had weakened her immune systems, and chemical poisons, like powder-post beetles, had gnawed into her organs. Poisons from the water we drink, the air we breathe, the food we eat, on top of toxins from all the unexpressed emotional baggage we carry around. I was poisoning myself, she said. So you go on like that until everything has to change. You face your demons. I've heard that's true, I said. I'm a good avoider. Don't avoid, she said.

Soon everyone was eating dinner. The kids had loaded their plates with noodles—they didn't touch what was healthy. Then they were up and gone. The sun hit the bay. We stayed inside and talked about the cars bought when young and the ways we made them run for a summer. How we dealt with the occasional engine fires that burned them up or the wheels that worked their way off axles and bumped down the road. I liked the tenor of this conversation. No one had to dress special for it.

My friend's two half sisters arrived from the Island around 8:00 p.m. Elaine, beautiful, thin as a rail, with closely cropped hair, was my age and had struggled through adult life. I got snippets through my sister from time to time of Elaine's recurring troubles with depression, drugs, and alcohol. The breakup of a family. Living in group homes. Jail. Sometimes we are helpless to change. Those killing forces inside bring us down. Unless something, in spite of all, keeps us going. Some inner land. Some memory of beach and dune, water and fish to keep us going.

Elaine had a lovely silver ring in her eyebrow, and the skin around her face was tight to the contours of her jaw, temples, skull, hawkish nose, and deep-set eyes. It was a look that beauty could still shine through. She had that too-thin translucent skin of a bird. In such a chest, the beating heart is visible.

I talked with her briefly by the doorway to the yard. I do not talk about recovery and the nature of my own pain, so I appreciate the person who does, who makes that gift of their life—of who they are—transparent. It hurts this way, she said, fist to her chest, looking right into me, when they take your children away. When you can't go home. This is the type of pain for that. How when you crave something stronger on the street, almost every other desire disappears.

Do you remember the night we got married? she asked. On the beach? I had forgotten, but remembered as she described it. Someone wore a red blanket for a robe and held up a copy of *Moby Dick* for a bible, or something, wasn't that right? We kissed. There was a bonfire. Boys and girls, long ago—caught in a summer eddy on the riffle of the stream of growing up.

She said, that was all good, those summer evenings on the roads and beaches. I go back there in my mind, she said. And when I get to come home here these days, I know my place is here. It's this beach and I'm with my children again. She began to cry.

I was uncomfortable. I found I was unable to provide any comforting words. There was nothing to say. I might have said that I thought she had many years of good life between now and the burial ahead of her. That we were all of the same predicament. Things ended. That she had a place that would always welcome her and carry her for better and for worse. And then carry her bones. That's what I believed. That the real marriage, years ago, was to this place. And that divorce from it was impossible. That growing old with her children back around her again was entirely in the realm of the possible. That's what home is, even when you can't go there, to carry in your mind and keep you alive. "The star in the pocket of your being," is how she put it once, in writing. But, given her exile, and my current immersion in a marsh home with its clams and eels—its atavistic daily rhythms and its ecological complexity—my perspective seemed superfluous. She was deciding within her biological soul whether to live. Either way, she would arrive home. Nearly cut adrift I thought, but still anchored by a thread to here. A very strong thread I thought—a thread that wouldn't ever break. Even when a life ends. I put down my drink, picked up her words, moved them around and placed them over empty spaces in my mind. I put my arms around her and said nothing but just held her.

— 16 —

sand

To see the world in a grain of sand,
And a heaven in a wild flower,
Hold infinity in the palm of your hand
And eternity in an hour.
   — WILLIAM BLAKE, from *Auguries of Innocence*

WHEREAS IN JUNE and July every member of the marsh community clamors to be productive, and every day something new lifts up its head, in August I walked into the marsh to find life silenced but for a consortium of song sparrows. They seem to have taken over, perched on top of midget junipers on the dunes or on the gray nubbins of bayberry. As stark as the August sand itself with their gray eye stripes and dark breast spot, song sparrows sang from clumps of grass, chunks of driftwood half buried in sand. They wanted to be barely above the lowly sand, enough to be seen and heard, but not enough to be captured and eaten. In August, the white sand of the dunes was crisscrossed by the tracks of sparrows and mice and traced by the tall wands of

CALGARY
PUBLIC
LIBRARY

#000015366-8 May 31, 2017 03:39

90650258761111-90403

040	Overdue materials - Rick Steves' Spain, 2017	$ 0.25
040	Overdue materials - Underground season 1	$ 0.50
000	**SUBTOTAL**	**$ 0.75**
040	**GST** $ 0.00 @ 5%	**$ 0.00**
000	**TOTAL**	**$ 0.75**
103	CASH	$ 0.75
000	CASH AMOUNT PAID	$ 5.00
000	**CHANGE**	**$ 4.25**

Cashier #218 505 - Crowfoot

calgarylibrary.ca
403 260 2600
GST # 10683 1027

Thank you from Calgary Public Library

Cashier #218   Tool/Tool - 808

CHANGE $ 4.52
CASH AMOUNT PAID $ 5.00
CASH $ 0.15
TOTAL $ 0.15
GST   5% @ $ 0.00 $ 0.00
SUBTOTAL $ 0.15

1 lesson $ 0.20
Overdue materials - Juvenile/...

Spea 2011 $ 0.25
Overdue materials - Rick Steves'

t0r08-11181852050900

8-8953J0000   May 31 2011 03 38

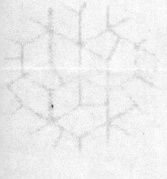

LIBRARY

bright green dune grass *Amophila breviligulata*. Now there's a pair of words, a Linnaean creation: *Amophila breviligulata*. They sound together like the title of an Italian opera. And in form they make such an arousing song, stretched like a green skin drum over the dunes.

How will we lose this place? How will we keep hold of it? What threatens? Is it sea level rise and hurricane floods? Too much privacy or not enough? Is it the loss of the reflective self? Or is it sand? John Teal has written about sand and the sand dunes of this marsh. He bemoaned their loss and asked questions a scientist should ask about the impact of the loss of sand dunes to the life and health of the salt marsh lying in their lee. When dunes disappear, salt marshes become more vulnerable to storms. And as the channels in a marsh fill with sand sweeping in with strong incoming tides, the pattern and depth of the twice daily tidal influx changes. Teal wondered about the fate of Sippewissett and all marshes in an age of global warming and rising sea levels. What happens when the dunes disappear and winter storms and hurricanes intensify?

Thinking back to the tall dunes of my unfettered youth, I wondered if we had brought them down. Here the once tall dunes created an enticing world: mansions full of hidden rooms. As kids we couldn't seem to stay out of them. But marine dunes are delicate, vulnerable to human disturbances as innocent as footprints that displace and crush *Amophyla* roots and provide the merest opening to wind and storm waves. We used these dunes for play, jumping, rolling. At night, more than once, we made driftwood fires here, drank too much beer, and with sand-plugged ears slept under the stars.

Far worse, perhaps, than all our play, was the house once built here. Dunes are designed to move and shift, to drop back and move forward—Taoist warriors—and thus bear up against the full frontal assault of winter storms. Their strength is in their movement and continual rebuilding. Their strength is in time. Houses need stability and are not compatible, generally, with migrating dunes. The man who built a house on the dunes drove pilings down deep into the stony substrate beneath. He dug his well, found water, and lined it with tiles. At first the house lay somewhat hidden, tucked inside the hills of sand and the roves of grass, but then the dunes moved again and opened tunnels to storm winds. Now, thirty years after the house was built, the concrete footings and a twisted rusted pipe that was its water well are all that's left, visible at low tide fifty yards off shore. Fiddler crabs have found a home in the shallow tide pool the old well tile makes, and the pipe's rusted red mouth gapes up out of sand like an eel. It's almost as if the house had never been. The three chunks of concrete tile, half submerged in sand, face east like monuments to the sun. They contain the mysterious runic etchings of the enduring barnacle.

If we are fortunate, sand enters into our consciousnesses at an early age. Toddler children pat it, they pick it up to taste it, and they make funny faces when the grit grinds against new teeth. Then they keep eating. My oldest daughter would sit for an hour with a pained expression on her face as if she were thinking, "Jeez, I can't believe I'm eating this stuff . . . but I can't seem to help it. What is it anyways?" Older ones dig and dig and make cities of sand, knock them down, and fill them in. My son at thirteen is an enthusiastic architect working in sand.

Sand is mostly silica oxide—wind-weathered and water-worn quartz. Silica is the most common element, making up 80 percent of Earth's crust. But even so, in spite of the commonness of sand, every sand has its own unique signature. Black sand and gray sand, sands that have been tumbled smooth in streams for a million years, sands that have been left as massive benches high up on the sides of glacial valleys. With electron microscopy, you can place sand by its shape and chemical content the way a person's accent can identify him or her as an Ohioan.

Sand is a by-product of weathering. It's what's left of rocks when the finer particles or fines—the clays and silts—have washed or blown away. These fines are found in marsh muds and farther out in the bay because they stay suspended in water longer than coarse sand and float in and out with currents and wind. I once took sand from Sippewissett Marsh to my friend Chuck Daughlian who runs the Ripple electron microscopy lab at Dartmouth College. Scanning electron microscopes shoot high-energy beams at things. As the electron beam is moved over the surface of the sample, it scatters back electrons. An image comes from this back-scattered energy. Electron scanning technology is used today for a broad range of activities, from scanning biopsied tissues for cancers and metals for crystalline structural flaws, to computer chip prototypes for impurities, and molar wear in fossil skulls. Daughlian is a master technician. Sitting at his bank of computers, he can look deeply into things in ways that only poets could imagine one hundred fifty years ago.

A typical grain from Sippewissett is rectangular—about 0.5 mm long (500 microns) and 0.15 mm (150 microns) wide. For scale purposes, a large human cell, say a blood cell, is from 10 to 100 microns long and a bacterial cell is fifty times smaller than that. Even in a regular light microscope at 10 power, individual grains jump into resolution so that it becomes obvious that Sippewissett sand is almost entirely quartz derived. There are only a few glints of other mineral elements: the brown clear crystals of garnet and black magnetite. At 10 power, the edges of most grains appear smooth, water worn, having spent time in the bay before pushed by tide and then winds into dunes. At 350 power, what was smooth becomes a rough-coated seed with edges and surfaces. At 1,000 power, a sand grain's entire surface appears feathery with the kind of pattern frost might make on a cold window. At 3,000 power, the surface of a grain of quartz sand has resolved into a planet—the cracks have become estuaries, small canyons with smooth walls. At 5,000 power, the smooth walls of these canyons have deepened and are themselves seen as rough, cracked surfaces—large enough for bacteria to hide inside. With X-ray beams focused on this same small point on another screen, a histogram appears—a graph measuring the spectrum of energy being floresced (emitted like the petals of a flower) by the image: the peaks correspond to elements on the periodic table. There is a spike at oxygen and spikes at sodium, iron, aluminum, and, of course, silicon. Quite beautiful.

Would William Blake have been nonplussed by this technology? What's the point of magnifying sand, he might have said. I've already seen eternity there.

Rob Thieler is an expert on the movement of sand along shorelines. He works for the federal government's Coastal Geological Survey out of Woods Hole. The survey maps shorelines and ocean floor, among other things, and helps plan for the protection of places like harbors, natural shorelines, dunes, and headlands. I met Thieler and David, his two-year-old son, one afternoon at the end of the beach road by the last house. I didn't ask if David liked sand. All children like sand. Once on the ground, David proved my point immediately by throwing some into the sky.

Sand, Thieler explained, is transported by wave action and tides and by wind. An abundance of sand in one place fills up a channel or threatens to close up a salt pond. Somewhere else sand transport is aborted and a beach is lost, or a road is flooded or destroyed by a winter storm. In a classic sediment transport system, sandy headlands provide a constant source of sand that makes it to bays by the erosive force of rain, waves, and wind. Sand moves into bays, and tides and waves move it down the beach. In a high-energy shoreline system that hasn't been too disturbed or manipulated by developers, headlands are constantly shrinking; spits and necks are growing; sediment from inlets and coastal rivers are dumped near shore as the velocity of water slows in broad bays; channels meander. Natural coastal systems like these are characterized by constant movement and change. Stabilizing headlands so that they can be built on—wrapping them in stone—reduces sand inputs at the source, so there's less of it to rebuild beaches. Jetties work as sand traps, so sand piles up on the windward side but is robbed from the leeward side. Houses, or marshes, to the leeward of jetties lose the protection they had against storm waves. Stabilized, channelized inlets—protecting boating and fishing resources—tend to push sediment loads farther offshore and out of the active coastal zone.

We walked down the beach toward the point. This side of Buzzards Bay, Thieler explained, isn't a great example of a classic dynamic sediment transport system. Headlands here tend to be rocky, not sandy, and so sandy beaches are smaller here on the inner bay. While the physics are the same, the scale is smaller. Instead of headlands, the sand source is the vast bay itself combined with wave action. The renewal of sand to these beaches likely comes less from the lateral movement of sand from a headland and more from the horizontal movement of sand from tidal creeks and rivers and from storms in the bay. All the same, beach erosion here is occurring faster than beach renewal—the net effect is the loss of the beach over time.

Once sand gets pushed by tide and wind up onto the beach, it is moved higher by onshore breezes. Grains move so fast the human eye can't see them. But you feel them on a windy day as a steady blast of pinpricks on your ankles. Each sand grain on its way up a dune makes a long low leap downwind, strikes the surface, and rebounds like a little golf ball. Most leaps are only an inch or two, so moving sand can be envisioned as a swirling sheet. This is the process of saltation. Sand moves up and up the dune until it reaches a critical mass of kinetic energy after which, beyond the angle of repose, it tumbles toward the lee of the dune, and the dune creeps farther leeward. Similarly, water moving over sand scallops it into infinitely repeating ridges. Submarinal minidunes.

At the inlet point where the water is beginning to eddy its way back into the marsh, we stopped and surveyed the sand flat at the mouth of the inlet. I pointed out to the east the rusted lolly columns of the old house and the well tile, now far out beyond dry land. It's not clear, or obvious, what's happening here, Thieler said. But you can see across the inlet the formation of new spits. More sand, it seems, is moving up onto the beach there, he said, pointing east, and indeed the dunes on the far side of inlet have grown taller. Behind us, marsh grass has colonized a section of beach well above the high-tide marsh, where a ridge of sand covers seaweed furrows. Thieler points out that *Amophylla* seeds need the structure, nutrition, and moisture provided the seaweed mass.

Did all our jumping and the house bring down these dunes? Well, said Thieler, a house can disrupt a dune system and so can a lot of small feet—killing the roots of dune grass that anchor the dune. And that can open the dune to wind blowouts. But this entire system is decaying, and change here is a function of changes elsewhere in the larger system—changes in the supply and directional movement of sand, for instance, and the wedges of stone jetties farther west, capturing sand and preventing its free movement. Who knows? he said. In another twenty years, things may have reversed themselves, and the tall dunes at the point will begin rebuilding. And a proposal to nourish sections of beach to the west may help build dunes again here.

We move down the edge of the deluge of water sweeping into the marsh. This point, he said, is moving. Look at the energy right here. He pointed to the rush of water through the run closest to shore. It's all being scoured away, and rapidly so, exposing the inner marsh to future storms.

Walking up the inlet, it became obvious that tons and tons of sand from that scoured dune had moved into the marsh over time, settled into the channel and elevated the floor of it. At the second major tributary, we stopped at what had been one of the deepest holes (it scared us to death as kids) now reduced to a sliver of deep water pressed close to the peat bank.

Sand invasion, the loss of the high dunes, sea-level rise, all pose a threat to the marsh, to the community, especially when combined with increasingly violent storms. How real the threat and how distant in the future? Thieler explained that the rate of sea-level rise is well established here at 2.5 mm a year as measured on a seawall in Woods Hole. It doesn't seem like much, Thieler added, and sea levels began rising rapidly eight thousand years ago when the last of the Wisconsin ice sheets started retreating. But there's been an uptick in the rate of sea-level rise again over the past hundred years that correlates closely to rising global temperatures and the heat of the industrial age. So sea-level rise rates could continue to increase due to the lag effect of global warming even if greenhouse gas emissions drop. Many scientists believe global warming will proceed slowly until a tipping point is reached, after which temperatures will rapidly and dramatically increase. There's good evidence to suggest that the strength of storm events is growing with warming atmospheric and oceanic temperatures too. Warmer and longer El Niños appear to be more and more likely, and the probability of a great storm blowing though the marsh and forever altering it and the homes behind it in my lifetime appears to be increasing.

But I still wanted to know about that house in the dunes. It had sprouted up there something like thirty years ago, and now, the blink of an eye later, there was no sign of it and hardly any evidence of the great dunes either. Though it was late afternoon when Thieler, his son, and I parted company, I stopped in to see the woman whose husband, now deceased, had built the dune house. He had fought hard to save the house. Fought wind and water. Fought town and regulators. But the house that had seemed like such an affront, an intrusion thirty years ago, was gone. So was the road we could drive to the end on, sheltered by the dunes. So was the man.

She had grown old, the sand lady. I didn't know how to approach her with the sandy questions that interested me. I wanted to know things she might have long forgotten. There had been a marriage—a house in sand, a place in which all of us might secretly have wanted to live. She invited me in, asking if I might carry some firewood inside for her. Carrying an armload inside, I noticed the chessboard.

Chess? she asked. Do you like to play? So began our first of several chess matches. The chessboard sat between two comfortable wingback chairs directly in front of the fireplace. I'm not much of a chess player, but I had thought chess might be a way to engage her in a discussion of the old dune house and a past life. Instead, mostly we just played chess and drank scotch.

The sand lady (not a particularly useful name—we all live in sand out here) is eighty-something. She has a real name, is slight, white haired, with clear, watery blue eyes, and a very bright smile that trails off just slightly into forgetting. She loves to win at chess. Our first game that afternoon went for over an hour. Losing a pawn was like losing an arm. Between, and sometimes in the middle of a move, she got up and lit lights around the room. A psychological ploy, I thought. With two scotch and waters in me and no food since early morning, I found myself staring at the board with a great intensity even as she took my queen. The game wore on, and her memory wore out. Mine did, too. Through the east window, the last light of the day faded on the marsh. Through the west window, the sun set over the bay. The queen I took from her appeared mysteriously back on her side of the board. I pretended not to notice. The king on her side began to move in a queenly fashion. She stripped me down to the king and a pawn, but I got my queen back—I think. Perfect stalemate, we agreed. Another game? she asked.

Chess turned out to be a poor way to get information, but an excellent way to get to know an aging neighbor. Of the house on the dunes, the one that washed away, the one that by rights should never have been built in the first place, I still know precious little. Of land and community stewardship and its relationship to the proclivities of the human heart, I know still less. As I was leaving, she told me it was her first husband's project. Not hers. She said her first husband was a very private man. Her daughter loved that house, she said. Loved the sound of the waves and the wind through the dunes and over the grass. She said that they had known all along that it was only a temporary affair—that it wouldn't last. What wouldn't last, I wondered, stumbling home? The house? The marriage? Life? The bottle? The game? Water, wind, and sand erase it all.

clam

A HOT AUGUST Saturday at the inlet brings the boats from afar. They anchor offshore at the very end of the beach where the inlet lets out. I counted as many as thirty there. Aldens and Makos, Dyers, and all manner of medium-sized powerboats in the eighteen-to-thirty-foot range strained at their anchors, and farther out a big yawl sat on its chain. Sometimes a truly gigantic yacht will show and grace the flotilla for a little while. With bows bouncing up and down in the afternoon chop and square sterns to shore, they reminded me of troop carriers. Not everyone debarks for the beach though. Sometimes families picnic on the fantails and swim from there. The water in August is clear and warm—the bottom sandy white. Some use their tenders to bring coolers and chairs to the point of sand just inside the inlet. Kids play in the sand. Dogs chase balls, and the men drink beer from insulated cups. The number of bodies is never very great. And I've put out of my mind fretting about impacts to the place because I rationalize that there isn't penetration into the marsh by and large. What brought me to the beach on Sunday was my specialized work in the science of home: place sleuthing. It's the kind of work you need to take your shirt off for. The kind that forces a swim and that wouldn't refuse a beer. Anthropologists call this subjective research. It's why there are so many alcoholic anthropologists (and some drug addicts as well).

Today Barbara was there with her two crew-cut kids. She's the director of the land trust that owns the cabin up in the marsh. The trust owns 40 percent of the marsh too—mostly through bequests and donations. Barbara is a good-looking thirty-something. I know her mostly through e-mails. But we occasionally bump into each other at hearings. She is an entirely delightful person and capable of administering an expanding program that includes ownership and management of landmark buildings, important landscapes including marsh fringes, coastal uplands, trails, a lighthouse, and an organic farm. Barbara, according to the president of her board, has the best job in town. He's an active board president and manages some of the heaviest lifting himself. But having been a land trust director, I can't help but marvel at the perceptions of the volunteer board member toward the work of the chief executive officer who is, undoubtedly, understaffed and underpaid. Psychic income only buys psychic bread, and though it fills the heart, it doesn't fill the belly. Turnover in small nonprofits is high.

Barbara's husband offered me a beer. He's a local guy who grew up in town and stayed on, marrying his high-school girlfriend. He knows my sister because she owns and moors a boat in the harbor and he serves on the board of the boat owner's association. Her Hereshoff, a most handsome wooden boat with lines like beach grass, is moored just beyond the green bridge. He's a powerboat guy though, and knows all about nitrogen pollution because it was his association's lawsuit that ultimately forced the town to deal with the nitrogen problem in the harbor.

This day there was a remarkable amount of penetration going on in the marsh. People were floating deep in, all the way to the first flats at the bend. I could hear the osprey on the first pole keening at the disturbance. There were kids across the marsh on the tracks walking north and several parties up in the channels.

Ralph Waldo Emerson used this word *penetration* too, but not in reference to the physical fact of entering deep into a marsh on a hot summer day. He used it to configure a relationship between the cold and hard facts of science and the moral laws of the universe. Nature was proof of God's—the ultimate artist's—design: the material facts of nature as described by science needed to be *penetrated* by the poetic mind to arrive at truth. Natural facts were reflections of spiritual truth. The mind ordered, but the heart understood.

I asked myself how much metaphysical penetration could be going on around me with the physical. Cold beer on a hot day can lead to self-reflection, I suppose, but the sun, the bright ordering light on a hot Sunday, burns into us a kind of dumb and lovely inattention. We focus on sand and water, on clams.

A middle-aged man was digging clams on the first flat. I watched his progress, wondering if he knew that what he was doing was illegal. Here was a teachable moment, I thought. When he began walking back our way, I walked up the marsh and slowly crossed the channel to intercept him. What I was doing, I realized, smacked both of vigilantism and hypocrisy (may I see your clam license and registration, please?), but really, I was hoping to get some insight. I was curious to know what he knew. How deep the penetration. Hi, I said, and we made small talk. I asked casually, finally, about clams. Did you know the clamming is closed here, I asked. No, he said. The signs are posted everywhere. I pointed to one of them about twenty-five feet away. I came by boat, he said. Hmmm, I said, hoping he'd tell me more, but he didn't. Well, it's too bad, I said, but the marsh has been closed for years. High coliform bacteria counts closed it down. Just so you know. Thanks, he said. By the way, what kind of diseases can you get from clams, he asked. Mostly of the diarrhea family, I said. But also paralytic shellfish poisoning. Look, don't worry about it, there was a red tide this summer, but you'll probably be fine. Cholera's also pretty rare. You're looking good. He narrowed his eyes and looked at me like he thought I was trying to get his clams. Look, I'm sorry I had to be the bearer of ill tidings, I said. Never mind, he said. He tightened his grip on his clams. Later I saw him rowing out to a most ungodly huge motor yacht. God, I thought, what an ass I am.

It is true that we shouldn't eat the clams here, and it is true that most abide by the law. On the other hand, don't I poach the occasional symbolic oyster? That puts me on a moral marshland, sinking into the mud of moral relativism. It's what liberal progressives are constantly being accused of by people like my father. I'm guilty of it, but I live here and can still see my grandfather's generation bent over their clam rakes. I eat the oyster to honor their memory. I don't think Emerson would have cared much for clamming. But he would have loved the metaphor of penetration here, the notion of floating all the way up in to some sort of emancipating enlightenment. The Zen *aha!* He would have quickly and fully grasped the notion of marsh as a microcosm—a gnomon for the whole world. He'd have been somewhat interested in the particular scientific facts researchers like Teal had gleaned over the years about marsh chemistry, but would have been thrilled by the vision of the whole. For Emerson, science didn't merely described mechanical relationships between particular organisms, but was the essential half of a process of relationship building between the ordering mind—that organ with its faculty of divine reason—and the understanding heart that arrived at truth through its own light. He would have quickly grasped the vital need for restoring damaged ecosystems—and the role an enlightened mind and citizenry—would play.

But it's a big job to clean up even the smallest marsh. We're a land-developing nation that probably wants to have its clams and eat them too. I do. It's not such a big job from an engineering perspective. It's a big job of thinking differently. Emerson would have seen it as a big job of self-reordering. A new self-reflective resolve would be called for. He would have written an essay about it called "Reciprocity."

In the morning, I had been up in the tower of the cabin watching ospreys on pole number two. A high tide had flooded up over the banks of the channel, and I watched a family motoring slowly up through the channels in a whaler. A father about my age piloted, while his three young children, all with orange life preservers and sun hats on, sat facing forward in the bow. One held a crab net, like a pike or a banner, straight up. When they came along my section of channel, I could hear the voice of the father over the idling engine talking to them about where to look for the crabs. I liked watching them. This, I could tell, was something he was doing from deep memory. Perhaps initially it had been his grandfather that took him back here. Then his father. Then he came on his own. Few came up now.

Weeks before, I'd done nearly the same thing with my son, and coming back out we'd passed two shirtless kids in a tiny aluminum skiff with an engine that weighed down the stern so that the bow stuck up like the fake shark Jaws. They had a single ratty crab net between them, and who knows where they'd come from. That they had gotten there is all that mattered. Mister, they asked. Is it deep enough to go farther in? Penetration, I thought. Yeah, I said, it's deep enough to go all the way in, but you have to stick to the right bank from here around the corner into the pond. You have to pay close attention. We held up a crab. There are lots more in there, my son said. There we were, my friends and me in a tin boat, I thought, years ago. What had I learned in the ensuing years?

To take care of land first, you have to make it, figuratively speaking, your own. Penetrate it beyond the facts of it. Find its secret light in you. Second, learn what stewardship requires. Third, save those clams. Fourth, pass it on.

— 18 —

naushon

Our best mechanized systems are still very far behind some of the bat's extraordinary achievements. And what does a bat need to function with? An operating system millions of times smaller, a source of power sometimes a billion times less—and a highly adaptive set of mechanisms that seldom need repair!

—FRED WEBSTER, bat scientist

The Circumstance is nature . . . we have two things, the circumstance, and the life. Once we thought positive power was all. Now we learn that negative power, or circumstance, is half. Nature is tyrannous circumstance, the thick skull, the sheathed snakes, the ponderous, rock-like jaw.

— RALPH WALDO EMERSON, from *Fate*

AUGUST IS THE foghorn month; cold nights make mist over warm water. The water is at its warmest, and the false albacore arrive in the bay. In August, we crowd in together—a free-for-all of visiting families—and the matriarch and patriarch hold down the ends of the long dining table. I make off to the cabin in the woods in the early mornings to read and write, taking a break from the technical, which can reveal so much about *where* we live, and resort to Emerson to remember *how* to live. We are biological beings, after all, animals by four billion years of mucky microscopic ancestry, but we are consciousness evolving. Emerson still stands as one of the great American thinkers able to make that synthesis. Nature and magic. Moral and biological. Every night I went fishing on the marsh, I was practicing a little of that synthesis: letting my soul bend back to the starlight swirling in salt water while hoping to hook and kill a large striped bass. Here on the marsh, there was the light both from new houses and the starlight above. The stars brought down to Earth are colder, but better company. Here more than anywhere else, here at home in August, my life seemed to be made by dual circumstances.

Emerson, the radical religious reformer from Concord, thought, at one point in his life, that he might become a scientist. "I will become a naturalist," he wrote in his journal during a trip to Paris. He had spent a day in the great French morphologist Cuvier's museum, Musée Nationale d'Histoire Naturelle, and he was impressed by the organized diversity on display. His first wife Ellen had died of tuberculosis a year earlier. He had recently resigned as minister to the Unitarian Church in Cambridge, having outgrown Christianity earlier and now rejecting all institutional faith in favor of personal revelation. The new facts of science partially replaced his outworn religious doctrine. He probably would have made a terrible scientist, but I do believe he gave birth, unwittingly, to modern stewardship science. For Emerson, the ultimate purpose of science was to glean human meaning.

Stewardship science is, after all, a fundamental part of a synthesis of understanding created when nature and culture are viewed in relationship—within an ethical framework. It isn't too great a leap to see an Emersonian synthesis there. Yet, the world still threatens to fly apart. We haven't embraced either the picture of material wholeness ecology gives or moral truth. What we have today is both too much and too little of each.

Back home in our little white Unitarian Universalist church at the south end of the Woodstock green, every Sunday you can find Fred Webster. At ninety-one, he's one of the eldest of the church elders. He comes down out of the Pomfret Hills, guided by one of his caregiving assistants at near the stroke of ten and sits on a straight-backed bench by the door for the service. Then, as soon as the benediction is spoke and the postlude sung, he's gone.

Fred is the great grandson of Ralph Waldo Emerson. Edith Emerson, Emerson's oldest daughter, married William Forbes. Their daughter, also Edith, married Fred's father. Fred is tall, with deep-set eyes, and a hawkish nose: he looks uncannily like the etching of Waldo that hangs in his hallway, and, in fact, his life took up where his great grandfather's left off in some ways and carried through the unnerving early decades of the twentieth century—from World War I right through to life by computer chip. But now Fred's memory is fading. "He's great in the present," Barbara, one of his home caregivers told me. "But don't ask him to remember what he just said." Fine, I thought, an Emerson *would* be great in the present, the present being the only point where time doesn't exist. Every day, Fred sits at his desk piled high with books. His office doubles as an open dayroom with a woodstove, his black dog, and a slumpy couch. When I came to visit, he greeted me as if I were an old friend, but I suspected there was a mental reset going on, so each day I gave him my coordinates again. He spent his time now like this, entertaining visitors, dozing, walking—nearly two miles up or down his road out in the wooded hills, each day. Until an enormous mansion with a gate was built at the very top of his hill by a wealthy widget maker, his was the last house. Like his great grandfather, he loved being outside in the company of trees and weather, ice and the fire of autumn leaves. And like his great grandfather, he had an amazing capacity for reflection—for making intuitive Emersonian leaps of mind.

Fred made his career in science. First as a physicist and mathematician, he did his undergraduate work at Harvard under famed mathematician Norbert Weiner who coined the term *cybernetics* and developed early thinking around thinking machines. Weiner was intrigued by Fred's right-brained intuitive approach to problem solving. "I started out at the bottom of the class," said Fred with a twinkle in his eye and not a little hint of pride. "But then I adapted my learning approach and ended up at the top."

Fred stayed on as a graduate student doing work in the psycho-accoustics lab at Harvard. His particular interest was the physics of sound waves, the binaural perception of sounds—sound perceived by two ears or two other kinds of hearing sources. His questions revolved around how pure tone is recognized and separated from masking background noise—white noise. Other researchers had discovered that when the pure tone, or signal, has the same phase relationship to noise, then it's difficult to distinguish tone from noise: when out of phase, though, the signal tends to be heard more clearly. Fred presented one of the first general theories to account for this phenomenon. It has been broadly applied to developing signal radar and sonar technologies to identify distant objects in the air and underwater.

Eventually, Fred's "time difference theory" led him to bats and echolocation. Working for the military out of the Lincoln Lab at MIT, he designed a series of complex psychological behavioral and neurophysiological studies using high speed multiflash photography to try to determine how bats perceive and hunt and capture prey; how they detect objects, drink in flight, and land; and how they learn. His aim was to understand the limits and capacities of a genetically designed and driven echolocation system—one the military might learn from as it designed its own. To use his own favorite definition of bionic, Fred's work involved "the art of applying knowledge from living systems to the solving of technical problems." Fred's work and thinking were part of the early scientific enterprise of imagining thinking machines. It was research into adaptive systems. What better animal than the bat, thought Fred, to base your thinking on?

He took his studies north, building a large Quonset hut up in an old field on his property. Here he raised bats and trained them to eat mealworms. His mealworm "guns" fired mealworms up into the dark of the Quonset hut, and he'd photograph bats at all stages of hunting and dining on mealworms, caught with webbed wing or tail and flicked to the mouth in midair trajectories. He'd fire other objects up with mealworms, including disks of various sizes, and record the split-second avoidance behavior of bats, their capacity to "see" with their own returning sound waves the shape of invisible things. He got interested in coevolution, as well, and studied the phenomena of moth/bat, predator/prey interactions. Some types of moths developed the ability to detect the presence of bats and devised behaviors to avoid them. His images are remarkably clear—the most interesting are his "streak photos" where moths and bats show up like looping airplanes in a dog fight—only they appear as streaming smokelike light in intersecting trajectories.

Fred also became somewhat of a circuit preacher—starting first in the Unitarian Universalist church on the Woodstock Green. Four or so times a year, he'd take to the pulpit and deliver long, well-researched treatises on a wide range of topics, all under the general category of science and religion. So popular were his sermons that he often was asked to travel to other churches in northern New England to give them again. Listen to his titles: "Some of What Science Can Contribute to Religion," "Must We Become Bionic?," "Is There a Human Future," "Are We Civilized?" Certainly an Emersonian synthesis going on there. But make no mistake, Fred was a scientist first and foremost. Unitarians today are a particularly rational lot. Though from highly diverse religious backgrounds, they tend to like their religion light and on the side, and dogma is something they'd like to avoid stepping in. Fred's approach bespoke his orientation both to the rational and to *an inspirational energy outside rationality*. But don't ask him to go much further in his definition of God. God is where ideas come from—a thought like an apple fallen not far from the Emersonian tree.

The thing that initially sparked my research interest in Fred's life, aside from his famous great grandfather, was learning of his grandmother Edith Emerson's marriage to William Forbes. William was the son of John Forbes who, with Massachusetts governor John Swain, purchased most of Buzzards Bay's Elizabeth Islands from the estate of William Bowdoin in 1832. They maintained a kind of new Eden there and still do to this day. The biggest island, Naushon, and its collection of smaller islands is still off limits to the general public, and life and landscape have been left alone there over the past one hundred fifty years. Naushon and the Elizabeth Islands are a source of fascination for the entire region—a feast for the imagination for those of us who extol unspoiled places and love most what we can't have.

William and Edith spent their summers on Naushon. Ralph Waldo Emerson was a frequent visitor there. So was Alexander Agassiz (Louis Agassiz's son), Isaac Hedge, and other influential transcendentalist writers. And Fred, three generations later, would spend many of his summers at Naushon. From the deck on the roof of the cabin on the marsh at Sippewissett Marsh, I can see on a clear day those shores and can easily imagine Waldo sailing Buzzards Bay waters on his way to and from New Bedford, or simply on an excursion—and I can imagine Fred Webster droning overhead in his float plane and setting it down in Hadley's Harbor in full view of the stone house, to arrive back into the nineteenth century with a technological flourish. Fred had become so enamored with bats and flying that he had learned to fly himself. He bought a used seaplane for a few thousand dollars, fixed it up, and so began his flying back and forth to Naushon. Naushon was his Walden. During college, he surveyed and mapped it—improving on the work accomplished by his great Aunt Lydia Forbes, who paced around the islands, mapping them, noting plants, and making astronomical observations back in the 1830s.

Fred once loaned me, but just for a careful few days, his precious copy of *An Anthology of Naushon, 1833–1917*, edited by Kathleen Allen Forbes and Fred's sister, Edith. The anthology is a wonder book of journal writings that account for day-to-day activities on the island, providing lists of visitors and noting provisions arriving and farm goods produced. It gives accounts of fishing and sailing adventures and horseback and "bathing" trips to Naushon beaches. The book also gives the history as told by family members over time, including visits by Ralph Waldo Emerson.

Life on Naushon was truly idyllic in a gilded-age sort of way. Nature was the foremost shaper of experience for families on Naushon. There are references to "deer stalking without intent to kill" and a search for rare plants. From Miss Dorr's journal in 1835: "went to the glade, found *Orchis obiculata* and *Artaca alba*, specimens of which I procured." Nature *is* the nature of Naushon. Still. A beautiful vision of partaking of the place comes from Robert Swain's journal, written as a young man at Exeter Academy in the 1840s (he died several years later of tuberculosis):

"Every time I look out our window and see the trees and sky and everything looking so beautiful, it sets quite a train of thought in motion through my brain and something like a steam engine running around in a circle with a long train of cars attached thereto. Naushon being the engine takes the bend, drawing after it a long train of boats, birds, fish, flesh, and fowl."

Ralph Waldo Emerson probably first visited Naushon in 1856. From Alice Hathaway Forbes journal: "Mr. Emerson was very agreeable of course, and seemed as much above common mortals as ever. He stayed till Friday afternoon when both he and Mr. Hale took their departure."

From his son Edward's journal:

"Father enjoyed the voyage in the boat for all his rebellious conversation of the night before. The instant we landed at Naushon (where the steamboat put in) its beauty became apparent. The rains have made it green and fresh and the sea suddenly became bright blue while there was a sky that father called 'mystical.'"

One of my favorite passages from the Naushon book is a story about Emerson as told to Henry Forbes by Henry Cook, who was for many years the boatman at Naushon. Cook had been given the detail of taking Emerson out in a rowboat for a row in the harbor. Two ospreys appeared in the sky overhead directly above them and began "fighting" (mating perhaps?) in midflight. Emerson watched them and presently said, "Henry, someday men will be flying and fighting like that up in the sky."

Of course, I can't help but think of Fred, his bats, and his airplane. Once as a young man, to prove a scientific point about adaptability, Fred began landing his seaplane at around dusk at Hadley's Harbor, Naushon. He kept taking off and landing, over and over again as it got darker and darker around him—until, finally, he couldn't see. His last trip down to the waves, he said, was all ears and all sound and careful timing. Batlike. Too dark to see anything but the faintest glow from an altimeter and a rising mystical moon.

Emerson's last trip to Naushon occurred in 1879 just a few years before his death. On that visit he saw his daughter Ellen's baby in its "nautical nursery." He visited the garden at night with Edith and seemed to be very happy. Though he slept only "one long minute" that night, the next day he read to the children from *Richard II, Brook Farm,* and his poem "The Snow Storm."

I sure would like to meet Emerson out on my marsh. It would be good to know him through, say, clamming. Or sunset watching. But I content myself with looking out from the cabin's platform toward Naushon where years ago he'd turned himself into Fred Webster—scientist, thinker, inventor, circuit preacher. This was morphogenesis in the truest sense—Fred, the new man of the twentieth century, just like his great grandfather, stood the material on its head and kept at it—rearranging the world.

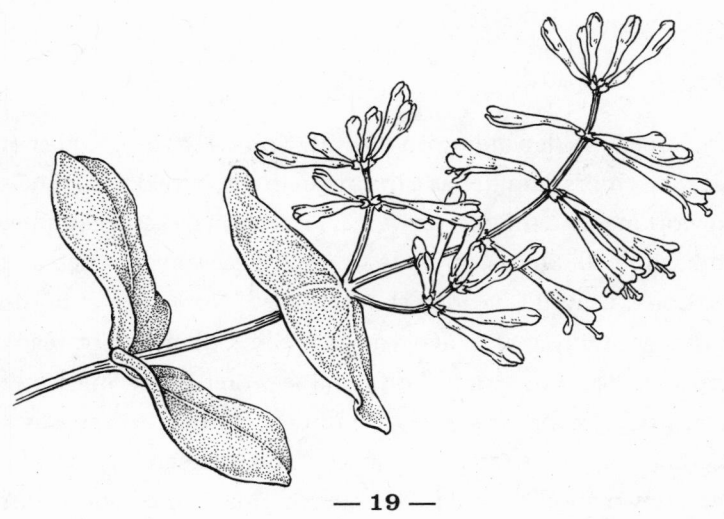

— 19 —

daughters

WE SET OUT from the dock at seven in the morning, my daughters and I, in a trio of kayaks, dawdling our way to the green bridge with the vaguest notion of making it to the breakwater, then coming back in time for breakfast with the lay-a-beds. It was summer's end for the girls. I would soon be giving both away to college.

The older daughter, Kalmia, would return as a senior to the University of Vermont, not too far from our Vermont home. She's a sea sprite, slight with dark curly hair, an easy smile, and an easy way. A free-spirited jazz musician, she paddles down the aisle of sunny water toward the green bridge, the bay, and her liberty. She will soon be unburdened by classes for the first time in sixteen years. She worries about paying the bills. But I tell her to play her music. Live cheap while she can. Practice!

My middle child Mollie, straight brown hair pulled back and tied in a sheaf on her neck, disciplined, thoughtful, goofy in private, but quiet in a group, paddles toward her doom or another kind of freedom, depending on whether you listen to her or listen to me. She enters Stanford as a freshman in a few weeks, and she's been working up a mighty set of fears to conquer—and conquer, I think, she will. She's not ready to go, she says over coffee and tears. Look, I say, it's a candy shop. College. Not much at home will change. Only you, when you're ready. But she's not ready to grow up and live apart, she says. She won't fit in. She won't have any energy for classes. She'd rather stay in her room. But, I think, here she is, attractive, funny, a string of piercings up one ear and down another, and full of deep curiosity and concern for the world. The Ladakhi symbol for mountain tattooed on her ankle. What could be cooler?

The girls are different. While her sister marches to her own beat, playing that sax and twirling that virtual baton down the road, Mollie is apt to have her hands in her pockets. Such may be the legacy of the middle child. When we travel as a family—and we try to do that often—it's Mollie who says, in all seriousness, no irony intended, "I want to live here" (pineapple farm in Mexico, fish shack at the bend in the river, apartment above farmers' market, tiny cabin in Olympic Mountains). Kal, on the other hand, will always be home, carrying music like a snail shell around her. Both are finding their way home. I am proud of them. But I worry. The TV adage, of course, always gets it wrong. It's not, "It's ten o'clock. Do you know where your kids are?" It's do you know *who* they are.

On the cove, the sun comes across low, flashing into our eyes. The water is as still and smooth as blue beach glass. It's ebbing, but still high up on the *Spartina alterniflora* that lines the cove. We go three abreast in silence to the green bridge. It's quiet this morning. Quiet is surprisingly rare in paradise because the owners are always working on improvements, not to mention the steady parade of delivery trucks, gas, water, mowing companies, trash/recycling pickup. Yesterday, a contractor's skid steer ran all day, emitting a multitoned white noise that could have been trance music or an accordion playing an E minor chord. But it's quiet now, and there's a sharp clarity to things. The Stanwood's dock, the whaler and its black engine propped up, all the edges of land where the water meets it are clean and hard, the colors solid. My daughters are strong, good paddlers, at home in these boats. Their bodies disappear into the hulls, and they turn into water fauns, part fish and part human, solid, material, and known.

When the children came, I found myself slowly giving up things I thought had been important, so that I could give time and attention to them. So that I could look after their material well-being. Looking back, I see that material well-being was the easy part. I find myself now pondering their souls. In this well-ordered home place, the beauty of the material world that surrounds, the wonderful perfume to all our senses that life here expresses, pre-occupies us, always reflecting back what we have and what we do but not necessarily revealing who we are. Beyond the chemistry of boat paint and the blue reflecting dust of the sky, beyond a child's genome and the entire collection of living genomes, how we go in the world is the hidden question that matters the most. All else masks and follows: stewardship of the world follows. Science: knowing what we sense, is less than knowing what we can't sense. Material well-being is a sneaky foil, and it's difficult to penetrate through it.

If I were paddling with my son, we would be man-of-wars, alternately seeking the weather gauge and taking every opportunity to ram and even sink each other. I would be dragging a fishing line. But the girls spin around the bridge pilings looking for those places where windows of light open the water to schools of baitfish, the occasional bass that shows illumined against the clear bottom sprinkled with benthic life, waste heaps of calcium carbonate, scallop, oyster, quahog, and clam—ruined minions. Neither is in a hurry to get somewhere.

We drift with the tide into the assemblage of pleasure craft beyond the bridge. Boats are tethered to their moorings like hobbled hoof stock. We like to float among them, admiring lines, choosing favorites, discerning the beauty of a particular hull or name. The names of boats are always a source of amusement and wonder. My sister's Hereshoff is named *Ibis*. Prim and sleek, riding high like a white bone china serving dish, *Ibis* is the prettiest we think, the perfect manifestation of the idea of a day sailing on the bay. Her name fits her well. Her stern, one of her finest points, is raked back and met by the stiff collar of varnished combing around the cockpit. She's birdlike. On the other end of the spectrum is the impressive *Banshee*, a thirty-eight-foot Little Harbor motor yacht, blue with a thin red waterline, owned by the family that built one of the first new generation castles nearby behind a jagged row of junipers. The boat, with its flat bottom, shallow draw, gorgeous slim stern, and its fine upcurved bow, runs on a pair of turbo water jet engines. An apt name would be *Leveraged Buyout,* my daughters think, or *Mr. Big*. It would be hard for the owners to take her unnoticed through the harbor. But that wouldn't be the point, would it? A boat's form is after all a reflection of its function, a question of practical objectives and goals. When you want and can afford access to all the bay on any given day, a large picnic cruiser with wet bar for the islands, for Cutty Hunk, Newport, Block Island, and beyond makes sense. The hardest but best thing to have is the satisfaction of doing without—a voluntary happiness.

Boats, boats. Beware, the temptation to buy one. We certainly have succumbed. In the main harbor, we circle cats, a new-to-the-fleet motor sailor with a curious rounded stern and real port holes. There is the *Seaquester*, a forty-foot beauty fit for circumnavigation, banners atop the mast flapping in the new breeze. Speaking of flags, my daughters see prayer flags. No, I say, those are signal flags or something else. But I'm wrong. We paddle abreast a yawl next to the black *Stone Horse* with its antique-looking cabin lines, and strung along the aluminum main mast and jib halyards are Buddhist prayer flags in bright yellow, blue, and red. The girls love prayer flags. Each daughter has brought them home as gifts. Kal gave them as Christmas presents the year before, and now we have them strung from post to white post on the front porch at home. Mollie spent her winter and spring living with a small group of Vermont students in the desert mountains of Ladakh, in northern India's Tibetan cultural region. There they lived with Ladakhi students at eleven thousand feet, near the headwaters of the Indus River at the SECMOL center, a collection of sand-brown mud-and-concrete buildings, solar greenhouses in the middle of nowhere. Prayer flags and stupas—white stone religious shrines—dot the landscape and are a common sight even in the most remote places—barren mountaintops, lonely passes, stream crossings. For a thousand years, the Ladakhis have lived off the land in a sacred landscape.

Drifting up the channel and into the outer harbor, past the little pier and along the ribbon of white sand and again through the moored boats, past the beautiful white *Jade*, a woman with tan shoulders in a transparent camisole top is sipping her coffee, tips her head around when she notices us, squints and smiles. Beautiful lines, I say, as a morning greeting. Dad, my daughter whispers, you shouldn't have said that. I know her, I say. Then we are next to the black *Aleria*, and then out over the sea of eelgrass, we imagine prayer flags everywhere—flying from the tops of the elegant homes on the island, hanging from the tops of every boat—the holy boats of the holy harbor. They would serve to remind us that we float in the middle of things that have been given—that we are grateful; that we are aware that nothing lasts. Here at the edge of the breakwater, where the harbor gives way to the broad bay, there is plenty of beauty. Water, the sky, the terns dipping for bait. Perhaps the beautiful matter of the world, its form and music, is enough for us to know. The flow of things that pull us out beyond the protection of the breakwater and to the edge of oblivion. I ask, would we be better off with prayer flags, with crosses, or minarets ever in view? A stupa for Cleveland's Ledge? We consider it but come to no conclusion and turn back to home.

Caring for the world takes a kind of shared faith in the magic of it. Otherwise, it's business as usual where facts have to compete with lies and illusion in the marketplace of ideas, and values line up behind the facts in a backward hierarchy. If it mattered to us, we would agree on the facts we know and save this world based on a shared faith in the magic of it. Why don't we?

We are paddling back under the green bridge and hail a woman named Helen who holds the longest pole we have ever seen. But it's not a fishing pole. At one end is a plastic bottle. It has a lid she can open mechanically by pulling a wire at the other end. She can gather water samples at a variety of depths off bridges of varying heights, and she has been doing so, faithfully, for twelve years.

Under the bridge and back in the cove, "That's me," Mollie says. "I want to do that. I'm going to live here and do that." Kalmia nods and says, "you already do."

I forget how much this home already means to them. They are here and they mean to stay, and that may be the best news for this place I've heard in a long time.

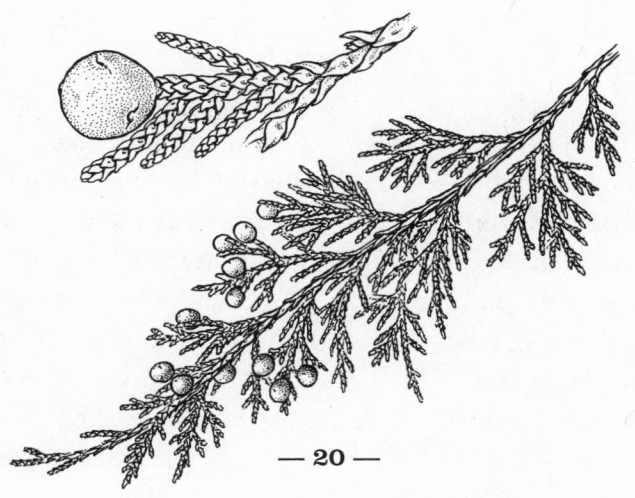

— 20 —

storm

HURRICANE SEASON IS the favorite among East Coast surfers, children, and adult lovers of storms who live on high ground. Surfers pray that hurricanes will track several hundred miles offshore and then stall. A stalled hurricane can send large swells onto eastern beaches for days, causing delight, arm fatigue, and the sought-after near-death experience. Property owners in low-lying coastal areas, especially older ones, who, like old investors that have experienced horrifying stock-market plunges, know what havoc hurricanes can cause. They act accordingly.

I was looking forward to the storm that hit on the first day of September. It was a mere tropical depression with forty-mile-per-hour winds, and it would hit at low tide, so there was no danger of flooding. Forty-eight years ago on nearly this same day, Hurricane Carol arrived unexpectedly. The eye passed just west of the lower Cape. Carol came at dead high tide and at midday with seventy-mile-per-hour winds. But it was a ten-foot storm surge, not the wind, that proved deadly. Two sisters and their three children drowned when they were swept by waves and rip tides from their cottage home and into a Falmouth salt pond.

Around here, the green bridge flooded, and the only exit for cars became the dirt road that went by our house down to the tracks that ran through the marsh. But by 11:30 a.m. water in the marsh had inundated the tracks and lands around the ponds. There was no way out. A man was rescued there by a boy in a small rowboat. Out by the bridge, the fire department rescued an elderly doctor. In all, the fire department evacuated over seventy people. Of course, I don't remember Hurricane Carol. I was seven months old. But my mother remembers. Water came through the back woods from the marsh, and it came up fast into the house. The neighbor came down to help carry the children to higher ground. He remembers water up to his waist and that it was rushing like a river from marsh across this land to the cove. We sat out the storm next door at the neighbor's house. No one was hurt.

Why such a big storm surge? Alfred Redfield published a paper on Carol's storm surge, noting that three factors actually contribute to hurricane destruction: the stage of the astronomical tide; swells and short period waves; and the temporary changes in the general elevation of the sea surface due to transport of water by the storm as a whole (storm surge), the latter being the most important.

Hurricanes are massive low-pressure systems characterized by significant drops in barometric pressure, high winds, and heavy tropical rains. For every millibar drop in mean barometric pressure, water level increases by one centimeter—or one foot per each inch of drop in barometric pressure. Hurricane winds move in anticlockwise fashion. They create a massive spiraling deluge with a coreolis effect that tends to reduce water levels in the center of the storm and elevate them on the edges. Because of the anti-clockwise motion, hurricane winds on the west side of the storm push south and out of the system, whereas winds on the east side of the storm—especially if there is already an easterly wind flow in place before the storm arrives—bring water and energy from the east into the system. To the east of us is the ocean. So water levels on the eastern side of an East Coast hurricane are greater than those to the west. Finally, storm surge is exaggerated in shallow water areas. Within the confines of Narragansett and Buzzards Bay the effects of Hurricane Carol were greatly amplified. Carol passed across the northern tip of Montauk and then just west of Providence, Narragansett Bay, Buzzards Bay, and Cape Cod precisely when the astronomical tide was cresting. In Providence, a twenty-foot storm surge flooded up the Providence River and drowned the downtown area. Woods Hole between 8:00 a.m. and 12:00 noon saw water levels eight feet above normal. It would have ruined the day's fishing in the marsh to be sure.

I'd never actually gone fishing during a hurricane. Or even during a tropical depression. While a fly rod is useless in a strong wind, a stiff surf-casting rod is made for wind. I took mine out of the shed, cleaned the rust off the ferrules, tied on a large white popper, and sharpened her hooks. I pulled on black rubber boots, sweater, raincoat, and ball cap and made my way through the woods, over the stone walls that separate properties, and out onto the marsh. It didn't surprise me to find no one else there. The sky was a gunboat gray, the air full of a horizontal rain that stung like flying iron filings. Except for that, and for the wind that forced me to walk backward holding onto my hat, the marsh was as enjoyable, clean and pure, the way a storm can make things, as I've seen it. And dry. All the water seemed to have been sucked with force out of the marsh. The only water in it was confined to the deepest channels and farther up in the marsh to potholes scoured out of sand at the bends and channel junctions. The northeast wind blew across the channels and seemed to have wrung out the marsh like a sponge. This made fishing all but a useless activity. No water, no fish. But I started casting anyway.

If you take a long surfcasting rod with a heavy plug on the end and have a stiff wind behind you, you can cast exceedingly far. I began aiming at small distant puddles to see if I could hit them dead-on. It was in one of those puddles that my plug received the most violent water-slashing strike I've ever seen in the marsh. I held on and ran up to see this big fish in a bathtub and soon had him, hooks out, half in the puddle. He was well over keeping size and must have weighed close to fifteen pounds. Striped bass, it always seems to me, have that, "OK, what are you going to do now" look on the sand. Except for the storm and the puddle, I would have eaten him. But since I never intended to catch him, for some reason I felt I should let him go. I hadn't worked for him, or even thought much about him. He was a mistake fish unfairly caught in the bathtub. The fish we keep should be ones we intend to catch.

Sun was already peeking through the gray when I knocked on Mrs. Whimbrel's door thinking I could duck in there for a cup of tea. Mrs. Whimbrel lives on the beach side of the marsh in the only camplike structure there—an old place that is a throwback to simpler times. I hadn't ever spoken much to her, but earlier in the summer had been introduced to her daughter—another Vermonter who had told me some stories about the storm in 1954. Mrs. Whimbrel had photos of it: I wanted to see those and also hear the story of her first husband. What had happened to him during Carol?

Mrs. Whimbrel's windows rattle in the wind and light shows

through cracks between boards that make the walls. The house sits low without a barrier dune protecting it from the bay. While the homes around her are wrapped in rock seawalls and even jetties have been built to hoard and hold their sand—sand is a priceless commodity here—her house sits in a gap. She didn't seem overly concerned that someday another big storm could float her away. Yes, it had happened before, but it wouldn't be happening today. She made some wonderful tea on an ancient woodstove. We sat looking at the bay through the salt-stained windows and considered the past.

Her family had been summer people for several generations. Their ownership went back nearly a hundred years. Her grandfather, an archeologist who had made extensive discoveries in Mayan southern Mexico, had owned nearly a hundred acres of beach and marsh.

What was the storm like here? I asked. Hurricane Carol caught us all by surprise, she said. We waited an hour or so, then noticed the water coming up from the marsh side and left the house to go three houses down. We were quite comfortable there. Zelda fixed sandwiches for the twelve of us crammed into that house. Of course, most of the men were gone already—back to work. We could see the roof of our house from the safety of Zelda's. Yes, it was sad and frightening. My children watched the storm wash their home away. Waves came over the top from the bay side, and from the marsh side the flood came up and washed it off its posts. We could see it all happening but there was nothing we could do.

What about your husband? I asked.

He tried to leave just as the water was coming up, to drive back to New Jersey. He got as far as six houses, and the car stalled in three feet of water. He couldn't get back here so climbed up to Ida's porch and weathered the storm from there. We didn't know he was there, so close, really. And then when the storm was over, he left. He didn't come back here. Just left the car and began walking to New Jersey. Hitching a ride out to Route 28 and from there to home.

He might as well have been hitching a ride to oblivion. Did he know his summerhouse had washed away? He must have been traumatized, I thought. Had he even come back down the dirt road again? Or was this marshy place, with its interminable tides and greenhead flies and sulfur smell and heat, something he desperately needed to escape from anyway? A hurricane and sand-filled car was just the tipping point. That was her first husband.

I imagined a man's calling in 1954 had less to do with a housefull of children on a beach, with an unintended storm, and a car flooded by an overbrimming salt marsh, and more to do with work, his postwar role as family provider, and a need to move up in business. But to hitchhike to New Jersey? And no one knew if he'd survived or died? His car full of beach sand? Still, I felt sorry for him. My own father did the opposite. He was in Providence, of all places, itself a federal disaster area after two hours of pounding by Hurricane Carol. He told me he'd left the office at 11:00 a.m. and somehow, eight hours later, made it to Falmouth. What normally would have been a two-and-half-hour drive. The green bridge was out, but the water had dropped by the tracks. He walked the last mile.

Life is full of unintended fish, freedoms and burdens, gifts and losses, comings and goings, isn't it? From her chair by the window, Mrs. Whimbrel swept her hand around the plain room. Well, she said. We're still here. We'd lost part of the house in the thirty-eight hurricane, but found it in the marsh and moved it back in place. I guess we were used to rebuilding. It took a few years but we built again after 1954. Right here, right where it's always been.

Here is a picture of the car, she said, and added, can I get you some more tea?

Yes, please, I said, feeling something like a fish scale deep down in my boot, and for a moment feeling a sense of loss and a grasping desire to have kept that fish I'd pulled onto the sand two hours earlier.

— 21—

saving sippewissett

Science and technology need to be yoked with an attitude of openness to the real transcendent.
— JEREMY STONE, from *A Minimalist Vision of Transcendence: A Naturalist Philosophy of Religion*

A class of experts is invariably so removed from common interests as to become a class with private interests and private knowledge, which in social matters is not knowledge at all.
—JOHN DEWEY, from *The Public and Its Problems*

THINGS QUIET DOWN in October, the golden month here. The summer rush is long over, and bay water is still warm enough for a long swim. I have the house to myself, and I find it too quiet for any real peace of mind, but I have the marsh and the fish to myself. In October, the big fish return to coastal waters, and the marsh is a busy place at night, busy with splashes and stars, and the whole end of things, life closing up shop, wrapping up summer lives. Carpenters bang away in the clan homes around me, replacing old shingles, enlarging, remodeling for the next season. The docks are coming out, leaving piles of pilings, waterlogged floats, and a mess of loose boards in driveways and front yards. It's messy—living in places and sustaining them. Life even in a small and ephemeral summer community is messy and defies simple characterizations. Charles Darwin's life development theory and Adam Smith's economic system have not been particularly helpful when combined and applied to the problems of sustaining good community life, but they are regularly applied anyway in a rough fashion to everything humans do and to a finite set of things deemed to have market value. We fall into the trap of allowing scientists and economists and events seemingly beyond our control to explain to us who we are, what we are, and what life is for. But they miss the mark. Modern human communities with their increasingly transparent links to a scientifically understood landscape nonetheless defy understanding by calculation alone, by the ticking of Wall Street tapes, by the drip of molecular hormones: complex motivations, histories and personalities—spiritual yearning—seem to drive them. The human urge to sustain community—its invisible ecological functions and its web of social and economic relationships—is deeper than biology and material value.

What it will take to save Sippewissett—a landscape that is by and large, by some definitions, saved already—might be best understood by an effort during the middle of the nineties to conserve the oldest place on the marsh—the Saconesset homestead. When her husband died—and he was a longtime protector and advocate for the marsh—the surviving owner thought she might have to sell the property. Local conservationists approached her about conserving it. The larger community was broadly supportive. The property combined many objective values worth saving:

the buildings, including a unique stone barn and an eighteenth-century farmhouse, were historical gems; rich marshlands were included, as were beach and dunes on the southeast side of the mouth of the inlet, an area I never knew well as a kid, since we generally stuck to the west, Black Beach, and the north end.

A promising source of conservation dollars appeared to lie with the U.S. Fish and Wildlife Service. With the support of area politicians, Fish and Wildlife was brought in to consider the feasibility of creating a federal wildlife refuge at the marsh. An earlier inventory of the important marshlands in the region had ranked Sippewissett a high priority for protection. With federal involvement, nearly a million dollars of federal funding might have been available for acquisition of the homestead and the marsh, dunes, and beach included with the property.

Among the U.S. Fish and Wildlife Service's ecological interests was preserving habitat for piping plover, a small, short-billed shorebird, lighter colored than its more common relative, the semipalmated plover, and extremely reduced in numbers across its historical breeding range—the open beaches and dune fringes of the Northeast. Historical accounts had a small colony nesting on the undeveloped beaches on either side of the inlet—not extensive habitat but enough, it was estimated, for five pairs.

The recovery effort for the plover has been a long hard-fought one. And successful. Piping plovers breed on coastal beaches from Newfoundland to North Carolina. During the late nineteeth century, they had all but disappeared due to market hunting for meat and the millinery trade and hobby egg collecting. The Migratory Bird Treaty Act of 1918 provided new protections, and the species had recovered to twentieth-century population peaks by the 1940s. At that time, nearly 90 percent of the nation's coastal barrier real estate was wild and undeveloped. But by 1974, just thirty years later, only 22 percent of Massachusetts coastal barrier lands was left unurbanized. Piping plover numbers dropped precipitously again in direct proportion to the loss of barrier beach lands. By 1986, there were only 139 nesting pairs of piping plover in Massachusetts.

In the early 1980s, the Fish and Wildlife Service listed the piping plover as threatened under the Endangered Species Act and began working on a recovery plan. Recovery planning involves coming to an intimate understanding of an animal's habitat needs, its minimum viable population size, the likelihood of extinction or recovery, and the population's sensitivity to management. Researchers determined what it was that plovers needed and began actions with teams of volunteers and state biologists to remedy human disturbances. Plovers proved responsive to stewardship action. They need, it turns out, sparsely vegetated access routes over dunes and wind-blown corridors through dunes that allow flightless young to move from outer beach areas to inner bays and marsh areas for feeding. Steep dune faces also discouraged nesting. Excavated sand pits, groins, and jetties that trap sand and interrupt the natural long shore drift of spits and bars discouraged nesting, too, so do roadways running along inner dunes. The best potential habitats were identified, and managers went about removing roads and jetties, allowing sand to move again and bars to form. Snow fences and other barriers designed to build dunes were removed and blowouts allowed to occur naturally. One of the most effective tools was education. Volunteer monitors placed signs on beaches and talked to sunbathers and fisherman, explaining the purpose of predator exclosures. These simple wire cages kept marauding raccoons, foxes, dogs, and skunks at bay—animals well adapted to human beach settlements and hungry for plover eggs. Some beaches had to be closed seasonally to four-wheeled vehicles and beach recreation. The payoff in successful plover nesting was slow but sure. By 1995, Massachusetts populations had increased by nearly 300 percent to 441 nesting pairs.

To appreciate the value of a plover and the significance of its recovery does require a certain attitude, a kind of different thinking for most of us, and perhaps a presence of mind bordering on the good-crazy. Piping plovers, after all, are tiny birds that appear to have no bearing on our daily lives; most people have never seen one and wouldn't recognize it if they did. The bird and its pale speckled eggs are designed not be seen—that's part of this cryptic species' genius and a key to its survival for millions of years. They are very hard to notice. And harder to understand. You need a different angle of view.

Why should we care about plovers? There are many forms of care. You can care because you want to acquire one for your birding checklist. Once you've checked it off, it's on to the next box. You can care for the recovery of the bird, the way a vet might tend to the broken leg of a pet dog—a humane kind of care for individual animals. You can care for the bird as a vital piece of an ecological system. This is the kind of care exhibited by agencies of fish and wildlife and private nature conservancies. Or you can care about the bird and its recovery for what caring says about the human community where you live and who you are. We care for our own. There is something about a place that esteems plovers and that goes to great lengths to restore and protect them that makes it vital, more interesting, and more alive. Plover saving grows directly out of the depth and breadth of our humanity, not necessarily out of our ecological literacy and scientific knowhow. The two precede each other, ad infinitum.

Fundamentally, our town is a community of plover savers I suspect, but that doesn't mean we're good at recovering them—

in fact, we hardly remember them. It is so for the whole world, which is full of plovers. We still get our values tangled up by private property boundaries and property values, an irrational fear of the public, old unworkable ideas about government, desire for privilege, and a raging materialism. Finding the right public/private balance is difficult. Our soul appears to have both an individual and collective nature.

Thinking back, I'm asking myself now, why and how we failed to save that land. The Fish and Wildlife Service went about its professional business of assessing the impacts and cost benefits and examining the feasibility of the proposed refuge in a deliberate and systematic way. Environmental Impact Statements (EIS) were invented out of the regulatory cloth of the National Environmental Protection Act (NEPA) in 1974. Since then, EIS has become a familiar and generally accepted practice. But it requires that biologists, who prefer to count things in the field, conduct public "scoping" meetings, officials hearings, and provide public comment periods. At each stage of the EIS process, before and after the issuance of draft and final reports, there are opportunities for public advice, dissent, and support. The process is designed to be a data-rich conversation of sorts, which, if it works well, lets science, economics, human passions and fears, and policy work in concert to develop rational and fair policy. No one really knows what will come out at the other end until something does.

The case for a marsh refuge seemed like a no-brainer to me. The Northeast Coastal Areas Study, conducted by the U.S. Fish and Wildlife Service in 1990, confirmed what many of us had known for a long time: Sippewissett was ecologically significant. There were five coastal habitat types represented here and approximately forty plant and animal species of special concern were supported by the wetland and surrounding upland—all on only a few hundred acres. In addition to piping plover were roseate and least tern, northern diamond-backed terrapin (a small marine turtle that nests in upland sands in New England's inner marshes), and salt pond grass, a rarity that had been found along with sundew (*Drosera* sp.). Rock rose (*Helianthemum dumosum*), a tiny yellow-flowered plant associated with maritime grasslands, Arethusa orchid, and New England blazing star also lived in the maritime upland communities in the sand dunes and small bog communities to the north of the inlet. Even though Sippewissett was tiny and could only support perhaps five breeding pairs of piping plover, these other ecological values came into play and so did the notion that protecting the viability of some threatened species requires an archipelago of tiny places, vital habitats. Think of a necklace made with many small diamonds, each of which makes the others glitter.

Who couldn't love the idea of a refuge? Of living next to one? The word *refuge* is itself dense and reassuring. It's what we all need. Surprising to me, then, that my own neighborhood, with some exceptions, didn't love the word or the idea. My own people fought it tooth and nail. My father was one of the few well-reasoned supporters of the refuge on our road. His letters, I must say, had some additional coaching and encouragement, but few could speak from his position of sixty-five years on the marsh so eloquently and forcefully.

Opposition was based on a commonly held assumption that a government agency like U.S. Fish and Wildlife Service would not and could not serve a small community's interests over time. Refuge status would result in another layer of intrusive and rigid regulatory bureaucracy and a more invasive public to deal with.

"Let us dispose once and for all of the plover complex," wrote the spokesmen for the community. Sadly, plovers were a feathery resource simple to trivialize. The opposition then went to great lengths to refute pro-refuge economic arguments. Dollar value was their first concern. What would happen to property values and to building rights? These were legitimate questions that needed to be asked, but they weren't the only ones.

It's fair for a small community that already feels at odds with local regulatory agencies—besieged, perhaps, is not too strong a word—to seek answers to a number of important questions. What effect would new status as a national refuge have on community life—so connected to an individual's experience of landscape? What freedoms would be lost? Would we lose the right to walk where we pleased? And since walking and thinking are connected, to think as we pleased? Would we lose the right to harvest a fish? To float the marsh the way we always had? Would enforcement put a uniformed officer on the property? What would that feel like? Would something too important to lose be lost? And what gained?

I remember walking once on a headland called Sachuest Point, not far from Paradise Avenue in Middletown, Rhode Island, where my wife and I with our first baby and our first real jobs, that of running a small coastal wildlife refuge on Naragansett Bay, often went to catch the sunset, find interesting birds, and escape the confines of a hot summer kitchen, when a uniformed refuge volunteer blew his whistle at me and told me I couldn't walk off trail anymore. I had walked there for many years long before it became a part of the national wildlife refuge system. Of course, I was no one special and should have been following all the rules. But somehow I had been absorbed by that place and now I needed to adapt to the changes. I didn't know if I could. Can a distant agency working for the public good, most used to establishing boundaries—not fences necessarily—around resources to protect them, accommodate a person or small group's sense of itself and its place? The answer may be yes, it is possible. But a new angle of view is required. And can that small community see that its survival rests on its capacity to invite partnerships? The answer must be yes.

It amazes me what losses to quality of life landowners are willing to sustain for the illusion of individual economic freedom. My view is that living on the edge of a marsh is an exceptional privilege that comes with responsibilities. Some public ownership, zoning bylaws, and special overlay districts are necessary tools designed to sustain the value of the place. They allow us to make good on our own promises to protect the place and thus fulfill our responsibilities. But many of us, it seems, view zoning ordinances as impediments to maximizing the value of our property. When this majority's view prevails, a place can be lost. We need to build a new majority.

If we desire first to protect our investments, then we need to broadly reinterpret the word *investment* too. The loudest naysayers are usually the ones who perceive the word most narrowly and who have the most monetary value at stake in the shortest term: lot owners with a plan on the table to build or homeowners who want to expand. But rational economic thinking ought to tell us to invest for the long term, too, in things outside our narrow self-interest.

The refuge proposal went to hell in a handbasket. Before the Fish and Wildlife Service even issued its final report and recommendations, the historic Saconesett homestead property was sold to a developer. By then, neighbors had offered an alternative to a government purchase. The local land trust, they suggested, could raise the money and buy the property without government help. The notion was that many of the same people who opposed the government's purchase would give money and would work actively to raise money for a local land trust. It certainly could have worked. In fact, our community practically has the capacity to buy whatever it wants to buy. But neither entity, U.S. Fish and Wildlife Service nor land trust, it turned out, would have the opportunity to close the deal.

I met the former owner of the homestead property several years after the property sold. A lively older woman, she'd moved to Vermont after the sale to live part time there and also to travel. She likes to wear lots of silver jewelry and, occasionally, a pair of binoculars, like an optical ornament, around her neck to see the birds of far-off places. When I asked her to tell me why she sold her property to a developer at the eleventh hour, her face and naturally happy demeanor turned dark. There was a lot of pressure, from every side, she said. I was tired. And it was unpleasant. She said she could never go back to the marsh again, though she spent thirty-eight years of her life there. Her husband was a good friend to conservation and over the years their home was open to young researchers, the geographic gateway to science on the marsh. There was an opportunity given. She gave it. But she had limited time. What an odd and unnecessary outcome, I thought, to have become estranged to the place over a dispute essentially of means.

It may be necessary and healthy for a small community, initially, to cast a cold eye on the planners and conservation visionaries. I admire my father's words on that point. He reminded the select board that it was town planners who allowed numerous new subdivisions on the hills above the marsh and the construction of a faulty sewage treatment plant, both of which were impacting water quality. Why should we trust you now? he asked. His words were an implicit challenge to all of us, since in fact we are the government. It will be a measure of our ultimate suc- cess when our agencies of experts at any scale can earn the trust of a small place and a small group of nonprofessional indwellers and when those same indwellers see their own future tied to the community and region beyond them. When we see that a fence cannot save us, that privacy has its costs. That inside and outside need each other to survive.

Saving Sippewissett—the heart of it, its biological richness and diversity, its physical beauty, its human community, the child's world of exploration it embodies—may require reflective thinking over time by the people who believe they own it and by everyone who uses it. It will be truly "saved" when all become saved from our fragmented view, from our excessive and narrow self-centeredness and our obsessive need for privacy. Then we might wake up to a recognition of our true home and begin to shape our politics, our science, and our behavior around the no- tion of caring for the world that supports us, that *is* us. There is a perfect convergence of science and spirit, evolution and creation in this view of home, a merger of the biological and the moral, the stomach, the head and the heart.

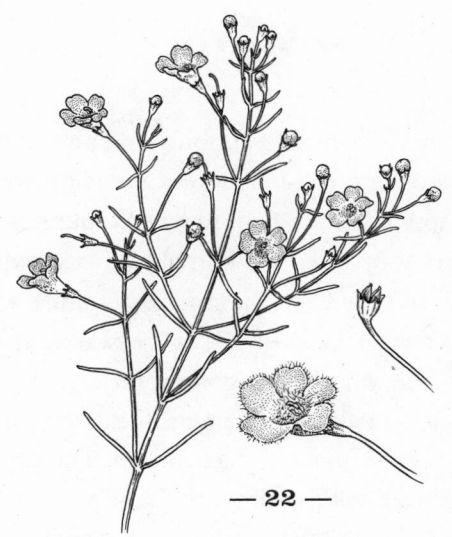

— 22 —

waquoit

IN THE MID-1980s, John Teal's research partner at Sippewissett, Ivan Valiela, abruptly shifted his attention from Sippewissett to a larger ecosystem called Waquoit Bay that, together with a series of elongated salt ponds and bays in East Falmouth, drains an extensive watershed stretching into Sandwich to the north and into Martha's Vineyard Sound to the south. It was Valiela, with a handful of peer scientists, research associates, and their small army of research assistants, graduate students, and volunteers, who designed and began conducting long-term studies of Waquoit Bay that would document and attempt to understand changes to the Waquoit marine ecosystem caused by nitrogen loading, including the loss of eelgrass beds and fish and shellfish populations. While fertilizer plots at Sippewissett continued to yield useful information, Valiela took much of what he'd learned at the smaller system and applied it to Waquoit Bay.

Waquoit means different things to different people. For some, it has become a kind of line in the sand, the front line in a war against nitrogen enrichment in Falmouth. Sippewissett has no eelgrass to lose, but there is a lot more than eelgrass to lose at Waquoit. Thanks to Valiela, the fight to save Waquoit is bolstered by an imposing body of scientific knowledge that promises to grow exponentially as new scientific studies get underway there.

But science can't wage war. People wage war, and there is a certain kind of citizen volunteer a community needs to get the campaign going. David Palmer fits the profile. White haired and no nonsense, Palmer can make things add up. The organization he presides over, called FACES (Falmouth Associations Concerned with Estuaries and Salt Ponds), declared war on the nitrogen-enrichment problem in Falmouth several years ago. Palmer used the scientific knowledge accumulated by Valiela to fuel his campaign strategy. He lined up his people, fired up the presses, grabbed his sword, and waded in. "This is the time," he said. "Here's where we're going. Charge!"

FACES isn't alone on the front lines of the battle against nutrient enrichment in Falmouth. The municipality, its select board, planners, and conservation commission are partners. So are the Pond Watchers—a group of citizen monitors. It's a community militia effort. A town advisory group called the Ashumet Plume Committee works on its own front, addressing the abatement of nitrogen coming specifically from a groundwater plume seeping out of Otis Air Force Base and septic systems in the upper watershed of Waquoit Bay. The state is involved. So is the Cape Cod Commission. In the late 1980s, Waquoit Bay became officially designated as a national estuarine research reserve. The staff of the reserve now coordinate much of the research at Waquoit and are committed to doing battle with the "phantom menace" we created.

I was greeted by Palmer's wife, Stasia, and Digger the dog, a woolly mammoth–like cross between shepherd and husky, at home on Waquoit Bay. Stasia took me up to Palmer's second-floor office—where a 180-degree view of the Waquoit Bay dominates. I waited there surrounded by Palmer's first wife's paintings, large abstract canvasses that used fiery colors and birdlike forms. I learned later she'd died in her prime of a brain tumor. Stasia met David in 1996 when they were both volunteering for the local Waquoit homeowners association. Her house was on his daily bike route. One morning he drew up to the picket fence to ask her how one goes about meeting single people, and she invited him in for a cup of coffee. That's how, she said, with a wink to me.

FACES is an organization of alliances, Palmer told me. When he became its new president in the early 1990s, it was in the middle of a transition in focus and style. The organization had been more confrontational. It had to be. Citizens' groups and landowners had been trying for years to force Otis Air Force Base to clean up a plume of nitrate pollution and toxic chemical waste from stored ordinance that was leaking. Both had fouled wells lower in the watershed, lowering property values and causing financial ruin in at least one case and a human health scare. In the late 1980s, the citizens' groups fighting OTIS won the battle, and the air force initiated a cleanup effort that included $8.5 million of planning money provided to the town of Falmouth for research and plan design. The Ashumet Plume Committee was established and given the charge of developing and overseeing the implementation of the plan to combat nutrient enrichment. With Otis on its way to being behind them, the issues had changed and so had the politics.

Fighting the establishment didn't interest Palmer. He was the establishment, and he wasn't about to get politically radical: picketing, monkey wrenching, putting on political theater—that wasn't his thing. His is a collaborative approach. The nitrogen problems were bigger than Otis and had accelerated with the growing rate of coastal development. Palmer had seen the devastating effects of nitrogen enrichment firsthand. He knew that it was going to be a difficult and expensive problem to solve and that everyone in town would have to be pulling in the same direction to get it done—right and left, town and citizen, builders and environmentalists were all going to have to work together.

FACES was well structured for that kind of effort. To begin with, it was an alliance of organizations, and Palmer thought he could build a big network of collaborators fast. First, he assembled a small management team, just as he'd done at Merrill Lynch. One key member of his team was Jack Barnes, a retired Ford Motor Company marketing executive, who also presided over the local land trust and was chair of the Ashumet Plume Committee. Another was Brad Stumke, a retired navy commander. Palmer tapped into the scientific community and made important connections with local garden clubs, recruiting influential women to his board who knew how to get things done. Within a few years, an all-volunteer FACES, organizing around nitrogen issues, grew from twelve organizational affiliations to forty-two. Of those forty-two, thirty-five were neighborhood associations and seven were important civic or other regional nonprofit organizations, including the Association for the Preservation of Cape Cod. Palmer recruited its director, Maggie Geist, to his board. And he joined the Ashumet Plume Committee. Geist's organization also maintained a Cape-wide business advisory council. Between Geist's network and FACES, Palmer could reach out quickly to thousands of individuals, many of them landowners. Next Palmer focused his attention on building a trusting relationship with the town. He was always looking to find the common ground. And the common ground was money.

"We knew from our surveys," he said, " that two-thirds of the people living in the watershed understood the problem of nutrient enrichment already and believed that nitrogen pollution could erode their property value, increasing property taxes for themselves and everyone else. This problem was hitting people in their pocketbooks. That's what they understood. That's what would motivate them to act."

Meanwhile, Valiela's studies at Waquoit Bay were yielding some surprising results. And the number of scientific collaborators was rapidly expanding. Waquoit, large compared to Sippewissett, is still a small, enclosed ecosystem. Top to bottom, the entire watershed is only twenty-five square miles. It was small enough for researchers to cover the universe of estuarine ecological processes and organisms. Reseach efforts included spatial modeling of the nitrogen cycle and eutrophication studies of all kinds, including aerial imagery–based assessments; studies of contaminant discharge using dense field arrays of seepage meters; and isotopic ^{15}N studies that traced nitrogen loading through the marine systems', multitiered trophic levels. The same kind of intense scrutiny applied to Sippewissett in the 1970s and early 1980s was transferred to the watershed laboratory at Waquoit.

Researchers had already carefully documented how in coastal aquatic systems even slight increases stimulate the growth of floating algae. They knew that eelgrass, *Zostera*, is light limited, dying out in the murky water algae blooms create. Valiela saw the opportunity at Waquoit to go further—to link specific types and rates of land-use change to changing water quality. Waquoit's subwatersheds exhibit different rates of urbanization—from almost none, to very high levels. The land-water data links Valiela made allowed researchers to devise a nitrogen-loading model that could be used to predict with a high degree of accuracy what would happen to shallow saltwater estuaries under different land development scenarios.

The morning I visited, Stasia served us strong coffee, then Palmer took me for a driving tour through the Waquoit watershed. These lands are his battlegrounds: the tidal creeks, estuarine bays, and broad and shallow salt ponds—much longer than they are wide and running north–south. Cranberry bogs, glacial ice-block ponds, and small freshwater rivers draining lands to the north characterize this landscape. There is public land throughout, especially at its south end, protecting several small pristine salt ponds and public beaches, but 75 percent of the land in these watersheds is private. And the land values, especially for property with water views, are enormous.

"Money and value," he said. "Our entire economic infrastructure in Falmouth rests on clean water. The ponds serve as recreational hot spots—harborages for boats, shellfishing areas, and sport fishing. Bass come in and out daily and feed in the channels. All of this is prime real estate. The loss of the ponds is a cost of land development we can't afford. Our job at FACES is to show people that they can't afford not to invest in clean water. But investment must be perceived as having a dollar benefit. It's got to be cost effective."

We stopped at the south end of an old cranberry bog that nearly buries a river channel of the Conamesset River between two bluffs—hardly a river at all, except by Cape standards. The bog is owned by the town and leased to a commercial cranberry grower. The cranberry operation itself contributes to the nitrate problem in Bourne's Pond. "Solutions to nitrogen loading," he said, "will vary depending on where you are in the watershed. For instance, simply by not renewing the lease, the town could stem some nitrate flow."

"But then we erode our declining agricultural base further," I said. "You're right," said Palmer. "It's a trade-off."

At the north end of Bourne's Pond, Palmer talked about the Ashumet plume coming from Otis Air Force Base. "The committee is using the air force money to come up with a plan to abate the nitrogen in the plume, but it's overall contribution is relatively small," he said. "We think a constructed wetland here might be a cost-effective way to get rid of it altogether."

Constructed wetlands are expensive but far less expensive than sewering, and maybe as effective. It means installing dikes and ditches to slow the water down, planting plants that take up nitrate, and seeding microbes that denitrify. This is where the work spins around the science because what's invisible to the naked eye will dictate what gets built.

"The plume committee will spend $300,000 on studies here and hope to have some decisions on whether to go ahead with this by summer," said Palmer. "Thanks to Ivan, we know the science, we know the impacts, we even know the solutions. But getting it done has as much to do with economics and politics as anything else. You can't knock people for resisting spending. If we build a sewage treatment plant here, and we should, it's going to cost everyone probably $600 to $800 per year to pay for it and operate it. We'd like to see that down around the $500 level. We're not overly optimistic that we can do that, but we think it's possible."

The roads in this part of Falmouth run north–south between the long ponds. Between Bourne's Pond and Green Pond, 4,500 homes have been built in the past twenty years. Build-out is 7,500 homes. As we drove through these neighborhoods, Palmer pointed out that they are at 60 percent of build-out and headed to 100 percent. Here's where the bulk of the nitrogen-loading problem lies. These septic systems were not designed to stop nitrate from leaching into groundwater and then into the ponds. They're a prime source of nutrient pollution today.

We stopped for chocolate ice cream and by late afternoon found ourselves sitting in his car watching water sluice out of the cut that connects Waquoit Bay to the sound. It had started to rain.

"Think of it this way," he said. "These ponds are all like toilet bowls. This one is flushing right now. All the ponds open to the sound flush out twice daily. But the flushing isn't enough. Think of these as toilets that won't flush completely, or flush too slowly. Several years ago, Hurricane Bob opened a second entrance to the bay. All that added flushing didn't change nitrate levels. So the solution isn't more flushing, it's to reduce the inputs of nitrogen from above. Why is Falmouth Harbor relatively cleaner now than the rest of the water bodies in the watershed? Because they sewered the neighborhoods around it in the 1960s."

"We have a very serious problem here," said Palmer. "And costly. The most densely developed areas might need a treatment plant. But now you're talking $75 million or so. Politically, it's too early to go to new water treatment. And we haven't exhausted the possibilities."

One big idea Palmer and others are pushing is to establish nutrient management districts. Under this approach, different areas in town that need different solutions can all be accommodated— it's integrative. The costs are integrative, too. You don't pay only for your part of the solution; you pay your percentage—based on property values—of the entire solution. Everyone has to be brought in because there's a total disconnect between what system you have individually, what you pay, and who benefits. Water- front property owners, for instance, may need the least amount of treatment, but they benefit the most. Palmer points out that 30 percent of the overall problem is at the top of the watershed. Land values there are the lowest in town, and those people probably are the least able to pay.

"People have to see the problem as owned by everyone. We're all in this together. One big happy family. If the battle is lost and ponds go and water quality goes, then so goes Falmouth. That's the relationship people need to understand."

"And there isn't a moment to lose," he added. "It might take twenty years, but we will win this war."

Later that evening on a stroll through the marsh I realized that Sippewissett, in some ways, is all but forgotten in the nitrogen wars. So small a place. But even small salt marshes, as Valiela and Teal learned at Sippewissett, buffer shallow coastal bays from nitrogen loading and so are a friend to eelgrass, scallops, fish, and property values. A green rim of salt marsh and land left to grasses, trees, birds, and flowering shrubs, it turns out, is the best management practice of all when it comes to keeping water clean.

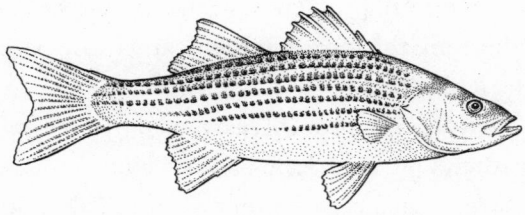

— 23 —

keeper

THERE IS A new house going up on the lot at the end of our dirt road—the last house lot before the railroad tracks is finally getting its home. How happy I am for it. Vierra Construction has been laying up the intricate plywood foundation walls into which concrete will be poured. Two Portugese-speaking men work in the cellar hole in the rain and don't notice me stopping to watch them rake wet concrete. The huge cement truck, completely out of scale with the road, came lumbering down it in the morning and will return again soon to complete the pour.

The marsh is gray in the flat light of a rainy November day, houses around it shut up tight. Last night only a few of the homes on its edges were lit up, but the marsh was full of hungry fish, and I caught them everywhere at the ebbing tide. They seemed less skittish in the off-season, moving and feeding freely, sometimes in only a foot of water. But still, no keepers. The largest fish I caught reached only twenty-two inches. My summer best was a twenty-seven-incher. Today, midday at the height of the push of an incoming tide, I'm going to the farthest creek, which drains a small pond through a culvert at the south end by the oak island on land the Fish and Wildlife Service might have owned.

No one's around. Usually you pass a dog walker or two and maybe a pair of students playing hooky, but never the honest-to-god bum you expect to meet on railroad tracks. Not in this upscale community. Not anymore, at least. When I attended the University of Vermont back in the midseventies and daily jogged up the abandoned rail line along Lake Champlain, through rail yards that twenty-five years earlier were crowded with freight trains, grain elevators, and piles of lumber and coal, I'd run across a red-faced bum or two and got to know a few of them, one in particular, who lived for several weeks in a cardboard crate under a clone of sumac. It was April. With patches of ice still on the lake, I stopped for a cold dip, and he came over from his house and sat down with his bottle and said he was going for a swim, too: cold is no problem for me, he swaggered. And it wasn't. He stripped down to his underwear and swam all the way out to edge of the ice sheet at least a hundred yards offshore. When he got out, his legs were blue and his chest blotchy red. See? he said, menacingly. So I had to swim out to the ice sheet too. Of course, alcohol was his unfair advantage. Mine were testosterone, pride, and youth. By the balls of Goliath I was going to swim out to that ice sheet. And I did. I miss seeing dangerous bums out in broad daylight—it leaves me contemplating my own bum nature. When we've had it all—life, the best of it, handed to us on a silver spoon and freely given—what do we risk finally becoming?

As soon as I make it to that southernmost creek of the three that flow into the marsh and ponds around it, I see the brown dorsal and tail fins of several large bass feeding in the last shallow run before the stream opens into a wide pond in the marsh. I tie on a black feathery fly and move forward to a small cedar. I false cast only ten feet of line and lay the fly onto the water rushing out over algae-covered stones. A bass hits a second later, races sixty feet out into the marsh and breaks my leader and my heart. Had I been a cigarette smoker, I'd have sat down and lit up. Instead, I tie on a second streamer. The second fish hits just as hard and when he runs down the creek, the whole water erupts with the wakes of spooked fish who had been holding there, slurping up whatever baits were coming through. He runs right to the backing and stubbornly resists my pressure to bring him to me. A big fish is worse than a big idea, hard to beach. So several minutes later down on the peat, I bring him in—thirty-six inches! The first keeper I have caught all summer. A striped bass has the most beautiful scales from gills to tail. Fresh out of the water, that hard scaley cover over the gills, the operculum, reflects blue-green like mother of pearl on the neck of a fine guitar.

This time at the cellar hole, the workers were taking a break and notice me cuffing the fish up the road, so I stop again, and we talk about the fish. Fish envy is an ancient cousin to the current and common wealth envy. But with the organic currency of fish, of course, it's a little more visceral than, say, stocks or banknotes. They want to know how and where the fish was caught (I was vague) and what I used to catch it, marveling with new eyes at the technology of the fly rod and line. But, eating the fish—what it might taste like and how many pounds of meat it would give, how I would fix it, that sort of thing—is their preoccupation and mine, too. You can cut a large fish into steaks through the backbone. This one isn't big enough for that. Or you can fillet it, with a sharp knife pulled between skin and flesh to remove the skin. Baked in foil with lemon or broiled, it's exceptionally good. The best recipes involve poaching or steaming: cut into cubes and poached, or placed in a steamer, fresh bass with a drawn butter sauce is better than lobster.

Whether we pour concrete for a living or drive a garbage truck (I've done that), we do view fish and fishing as part of our commonwealth. A wealth that is truly accessible and ultimately satisfying. It's why, in the days of old when fisheries were healthy, fishermen always felt wealthy, even though they had no money to show, they had an ocean to know. It gave them what they needed.

— 24 —

fire

The whole universe together participates in the divine goodness and represents it better than any single being whatsoever.

   —Thomas Aquinas, from *Aquinas*, ST, Q. 47, Art. 1

We have entered a new age. An age where all of us will have to sign a new compact with our environment...and enter into the larger community of all living beings. A new sense of communion with the planet. Earth must enter our minds.

   —Klaus Topfer, UN undersecretary-general and executive director, from an address to the World Council of Churches, Bonn, Germany, October 31, 1999

NOVEMBER IS A good ending time, fitting the season here in New England—and a terrible time to start something new. But ending something always entails the opposite, some new order emerges. Spring bulbs like to go into the ground in November. My plan for the day was to walk the marsh, to say thanks, to say good-bye, to review notes, and to plant bulbs in the front garden. I hadn't planned on the storm. This morning I woke up to a white world covered in ice crystals and slush and a marsh buffeted by wind, a small savannah obscured by mist and cloud. A short walk late in the day might be in order, but what better excuse to stay next to the fire all day than a brutal wind and snow that turns to rain and then to snow again?

But, to have a fire required that I borrow liberally from my absent neighbor's woodpile, just as I've borrowed liberally this year from others' work and ideas to keep an inner fire going. Neighbor, forgive my literal trespasses, but it's freezing in this summerhouse, and I can only warm the front half of me by burning your wood and by bringing this rocking chair to within two feet of the fire, to singe an eyebrow and nearly melt the back of my laptop computer in the process.

To be loyal to a greater vision and an idea—to the home that surrounds—requires some disloyalty to current paradigms and old traditions. I apologize to the family and friends that know me, and who know this place and its people far better than I do, and who have known it longer. If my words seem disloyal to you, I am sorry. Yes, our grandfathers and grandmothers worked hard to build the human dimensions of this idyllic place. And it's our job to carry that work on. But where do our deepest loyalties lie? That's a question worth everyone's asking. Ecologists have given us a new vision of the world and its chemistry of interconnected beauty. With that in mind, our overblown objectivity and materialism—our old focus on the spoils of war and the rewards of successful exploitive enterprise—and our fragmented view call for a new subjectivity. We can't go back. For as surely as I am drinking the last cold drops of this morning's coffee, change is coming and there are things we all must do.

Thomas Berry, a theologian whose ideas take their shape from scholarship across many disciplines including a study of classical thought, history, biology, anthropology, comparative religion, politics, and economics, writes in *The Great Work* that humanity is now faced with the job of moving from the present geological age, the Cenozoic, to the coming age he terms the Ecozoic—an age reflective of the tremendous power of humans to shape the face of the world, to control its chemistry, to upset the order the universe took 10 billion years to produce. Or to restore it. We live in a world dangerously out of balance, and yet tantalizingly abundant in possibility.

The burning question is, What do we do now? The answer lies in the fire, perhaps not next to it.

There are three small creeks that empty into the marsh behind our house. Each represents a discipline brought to bear by ecological science to understand the workings of this marsh. Geology provides a basis for understanding the physical forms of the marsh and surrounding uplands including sand, stones, mud, the glacial moraine, coastal land-forming processes, tides, and the behavior of groundwater. It's this land without relief on the edge of a salt bay that created conditions for twice daily saltwater inundations and evolved life forms that could live successfully on a tableland of peat that grows ever deeper, like a book being forever written over time. Chemistry is the second stream. The outcomes of marsh interactions are ultimately chemical in nature, and chemistry's fluxes and flows are the best way to understand how the system interacts in all its parts, how it changes and yet stays the same. Biology is the third stream—the study of the living elements in air, mud, freshwater, and salt water—a seemingly infinite array of microbial life-forms not even close to being named, let alone functionally understood, and mesocosmic to macrocosmic life we can touch and taste. This stream includes us and our neighbors—fence builders and demolishers all, privacy seekers, savers of plovers, folk who once could clam. The salt marsh gives a picture of a continually interactive system of the living and the nonliving, of complex transactions of systems within systems, each relying on the whole for its continued life.

Of all the inquiries contributing to the understanding of a marsh system, biology is arguably the most interesting, the most dynamic, and the most beautiful. But the creek of biology is really a dozen small strands that converge when you walk up them. All the biological specialties we have today grew out of the now-distant headwater of morphology. Protobiology was the study of life-forms and cataloging the diverse types of created form was the major preoccupation of nineteenth-century field naturalists and continued to be the preoccupation of the first oceanographers and conservers of marine life from Spencer Baird to Henry Bigelow. Morphology branched out into embryology, physiology, genetics, biochemistry, molecular biology, microbiology, and ecology. You can witness that entire progression here in this marsh. The thrusts of biology grew—from the study of the origin of species, particularly the human, to a concentration of how things function from systems of organs, to organs, to organelles, to tissues, to cells, to intracellular bodies, to molecule DNA. But it was the ecological branch of biology that finally took us from a study of the discreet smallest units of life and their interface with the nonliving on up to the grandest global systems level—to an integrated picture of Earth and a new cosmology. Ecology brought us back to the question of preserving the whole. The only piece lost in the development of the biological branch of science from the text of our earliest morphologists was that sense of the sacred.

The marsh is a microcosm of the world. With its peat meadows, meandering tidal creeks, microbes and mud, at the living, breathing edge of continent and ocean, it seems that life must have started here. Every microcomponent contributes to the whole. Discovering how this system works was a biogeochemical pursuit that took years and is ongoing. Hundreds of studies resulted in as many journal papers. Out of the research came a picture of energy and nutrient inputs, chemical transformations and outputs from the marsh. The human factor reduced to chemistry is in these equations—what is flushed down the toilet, pumped into the atmosphere, spread on lawns, and put into drinking water all goes into the marsh, and all is measured. Where, though, is the factor of a family? A sacred community? The human spirit capable of sustaining the world? Where figures consciousness?

Spirit study is not what scientists do and most keep it separate from their work. That's OK—we need them to take apart global process puzzles and put them together again. Others will do the necessary cosmic synthesis. Thomas Berry describes ecology as a "functional cosmology." "Only the whole has resplendent meaning," Berry writes. Knowing what we now know, what, asks Berry, will be our biospiritual response?

The stewardship of home isn't science, after all. At some point, the science of place becomes the spirit of it. Each of us is called to become a steward acting with the spirit of home in mind. Not all our most promising developments in Earth stewardship are coming from scientific circles. The liberal religious traditions are beginning to manifest their rightful Earth stewardship role. And liberal includes the broadest range of Eastern, Western, and indigenous cultural traditions. It includes Islam and the sacred guardian role of khalifa, bestowed on humankind. It includes Judaism's command to preserve all of creation, the Hindu faith that reveres Earth as mother, and Buddhism and the Buddhist compassion for all life, and Jainism's nonviolence to humans and all living things. Christian texts and beliefs are no stranger to Earth stewardship with their transformative Eucharistic rituals—bread from the body of Christ, the Christian God's love for all creation with the constant reminder that humans have a responsibility and duty for the care and well-being of creation. Taoism, Confucianism, Shintoism all grew from the deepest human concepts of order, wholeness, respect and reverence for all of creation. Perhaps it was the indigenous peoples of the Western hemisphere that brought the human idea of sacred relationship to the world to its highest level.

A small but growing constellation of scientists, theologians, environmental and social activists, communitarians, economists, new agriculturalists, and land conservationists are working from a new unity of thinking to address a dire world situation in integrated fashion. *Earth and Faith: A Book of Reflection for Action*, published by the Interfaith Partnership for the Environment and the United Nations Environment Programme, is one book in a growing library of new texts providing a foundation for values-driven, reflectively based action in the world. The voices speaking out of this new synthesis are as diverse as the species of anaerobic bacteria living in the top millimeter of marsh mud. All share a conviction that we need to wake up to new ways of living in the world beginning with a new view of our place in it. Mary Evelyn Tucker from the Forum on Religion and Ecology speaks of the primary challenge as how to experience nature in a numinous way again. Religion is about reordering, she says, reorienting ourselves in the universe and seeing deeply into the pattern of the universe. She's a theologian who speaks of a sacred science that gives us the opportunity to recenter ourselves. Sylvia Earle, a deep oceans explorer and oceanographer, asks us how the health and integrity of natural systems can bear on the moral self. With knowing comes caring, she writes.

Religious thinkers who shift boundaries to consider the wisdom of ecological science offer new ways to imagine the role of religion in our lives. Consider the word itself. *Religion*, points out Ursula Goodenough, a microbiologist from Washington University, comes from the Latin *ligare* which means to bind together. *Science*, from the Greek root *sci*, means to cut up or parse. The greening of faith makes the vital ecological repair, giving passion to the idea rejoining a fragmented view of the world. Calvin Dewitt expands this notion of religion-as-religation to the concept of Earth stewardship growing out of a triad of necessary elements now broken and kept apart. This newly defined trinity, he writes, is science, ethics, and practice. If what we know is separate from what we value, and what we value is separate from how we act, then we can only continue to repeat destructive patterns. He urges a view of nature through the lens of the sacred. The sacred must become as real as the specific weight of calcium, he writes. Thomas Berry, echoing that idea, writes that there should be a carbon component functioning at our highest levels of spiritual practice. Why not a new creationism, they both seem to be asking: an ecological cosmology that integrates the objective and the sacred, the chemical and moral, the known and unknown. A new creationism that recognizes the empirical truths of science but allows that the universe won't be understood solely by what we can measure.

Late in the afternoon, I leave the fire and relative comfort of the house. It's still snowing when I cut across my neighbor's lawn, step over the wall and onto the marsh. I scare up a female marsh

hawk hunkered down in one of the creek beds and keep going up
the marsh, to the path that leads into the clearing where the cabin
sits, to the stairs that lead up to the roof of the cabin. The pond,
the sky, the marsh, the last house on the beach, everything is cold
and gray—except for a gigantic yellow earthmover looming over
the pond. From the roof looking south to the marsh, I remember
how green and lush this view is in summer. I remember summer nights coming in from the black marsh, lighting a candle in
the window and reading for an hour, sometimes sleeping and
dreaming. Sometimes I nearly felt what it was like walking these
sandy roads forty years ago. I can't describe it really, seeing it and
feeling it the original way when I was young on these roads and
paths surrounded by green growing life and embedded within it.
I think that's why I came back here as an investigator of home: I
wanted to see if I could experience the original world that way
again—whistling down the road of life, caught in its splendor and
wonder. I wanted that sense of movement and journey toward
something mysterious that my children still feel.

Why not a new and sophisticated creationism to command
our most loving thoughts and mindful actions toward self, others, the world? Science, then, becomes one way to act out our
deepest values. Standing up on the lookout while the marsh turns
to darker and darker shades of gray and the snow, blowing from
the northeast, fills up my collar, I find it harder and harder to
summon these summer memories. But I work to will them out.
Here are the voices of the dead, who brought us into being and
who made the first small houses on the marsh, and who daily
went out in the channels of the marsh to go clamming. Here lie
our dream fish: here the shiver of first love, the dawn sky. Here,
the first walk over the bridge in a night fog, and here the bed under the eaves, the sound of foghorn, the dreamless sleep.

There is hard good work waiting for each of us in our grown-up selves—a required and difficult retooling that makes us all what we naturally want to be, community builders and workers, dwellers and sustainers of our home places. There is no formula, no recipe, nothing we can buy to find our way. Only the good bread life provides, the oyster plucked from the bank, and the invisible wine of salt air that shows each of us our essential work and moves us along toward a world in balance: mystery and what is calculated, a harmonious antithesis. Only a small flickering flame inside guides us: by means of our reflective focus we hope to grow it into something very bright and scorching.

Meanwhile, the night comes on, and snow crystals melt down my neck. A single prop plane drones far above, the foghorn at the ledge begins its calling out on the dangerous water. And I wait. What warms on a night like this is a vision of standing in the flame, not beside it for a mere random singe or two. We can imagine what that's like by watching certain people who burn with knowledge and energy around us to change the world; or by reading the prophets and poets who made it possible to link head to heart, place to being, and matter to spirit. Those who burn with love. Emerson burned and made all of nature transcendent again. Science, infused with poetic insight, was his transformative agent. The scientists working to unlock the secrets of a salt marsh burned in their own way, too, and deep down hoped to save it all. But the few can't save us. We all need to catch on fire.

And so back through the dark marsh to the fire in my home I went to sit by my hearth that's big enough for both the ashes and light that vision requires. Home is the only place where everything over time can be witnessed, where everything will arrive over time, because it's the place that brought us into being, the place where all things made were first perceived, and the place that takes us back in. Perhaps it's a mistake to think of home as a physical place and better to think of it as where we're going.

However we define home, wherever it is, however we carry it—in clams, or in reasoned analysis in the lab, in mud, in words, in the notion of consciousness we are becoming, or in God—it is our calling to find it. Our home place is the stage for our metamorphosis. That would appear to me, now, here by the fire, to be the only thing that really matters.

selected bibliography

Agassiz, Louis. "On the Origin of Species." *American Journal of Arts and Sciences* 30 (1860): 132–221.

———. "Evolution and the Permanence of Type." *Atlantic Monthly* 33 (1874).

Banus, M., Ivan Valiela and John M. Teal. "Lead, zinc and cadmium budgets in experimentally enriched ecosystems." *Estuarine Coastal Marine Science* 3 (1975): 421–430.

———. "Exports of lead from salt marshes." *Marine Pollution Bulletin* 5 (1974): 6–9.

Bassett, Libby, ed. *Earth and Faith, A Book of Reflection for Action.* New York: United Nations Environmental Programme, 2000.

Behe, Michael, J. *Darwin's Black Box, The Biochemical Challenge to Evolution.* New York: Touchstone, 1996.

Berry, Thomas. *The Great Work. Our Way into the Future.* New York: Bell Tower, 1999.

Bortoft, Henri. "Goethean Science and the Wholeness of Nature." Paper presented at the conference on "Goethean Science in Holistic Perspective: Scientific, Ethical and Educational Implications." Teachers College, Columbia University, New York. May 1999.

Blumer, M. "Oil pollution of the Ocean." *Oil on the Sea.* Edited by D.P. Hoult. New York: Plenum Press, 1969.

Blumer, M., G. Souza and J. Sass. "Hydrocarbon pollution of edible shellfish by an oil spill." *Marine Biology* 5 (1970): 195–202.

Bormann, Herbert F., Diana Balmorie and Gordon Geballe. *Redesigning the American Lawn, A Search for Environmental Harmony.* New Haven and London: Yale University Press, 1962.

Bowen, Jennifer and Ivan Valiela. "The ecological effects of urbanization of coastal watersheds: historical increases in nitrogen loads and eutrophication of Waqoit Bay estuaries." *Canadian Journal of Fisheries and Aquatic Science* 58 (2001): 1–12.

———. "Historical changes in atmospheric nitrogen deposition to Cape Cod, Massachusetts, USA." *Atmospheric Environment* 35 (2001): 1039–1051.

Brooks, Paul. *The House of Life: Rachel Carson at work: With selections from her writings published and unpublished.* Boston: Houghton Mifflin Co., 1972.

Buechner, Frederick. *The Longing for Home: Reflections at Mid-Life.* San Francisco: Harper, 1996.

Burns, K.A. and J.M. Teal. "Hydrocarbon Incorporation into the Salt Marsh Ecosystem from the West Falmouth Oil Spill." *Woods Hole Oceanographic Institute, Technical Report* (1971): WHOI 71–69.

Callaway, D., et al. "Effects of NO_3 loading and salt marsh habitat on gross primary production and chlorophyll a levels in the estuaries of Waquoit Bay." *Biological Bulletin* 189 (1995): 254–255.

Carafiol, Peter C. *Transcendent Reason: James Marsh and the forms of romantic thought.* Tallahassee: University Presses of Florida, 1982.

Carson, Rachel. *Silent Spring.* Boston: Houghton Mifflin Co., 1962.

Coleridge, Samuel T. *Aides to Reflection and the confessions of an inquiring spirit.* London: G. Bell, 1904.

Collette, B. and Grace Klein-MacPhee, eds. *Bigelow and Schroeder's Fishes of the Gulf of Maine.* Washington D.C.: Smithsonian Institute Press, 2002.

Conner, William. "A Small Oil Spill at West Falmouth." Washington: EPA, 1979.

Dall, William Healey. *Spencer Fullerton Baird; a biography, including selections from his correspondence with Audubon, Agassiz, Dana, and others.* Philadelphia and London: Lippincott and Company, 1915.

Darwin, Charles. *The Origin of Species. By means of natural selection or the preservation of favoured races in the struggle for life.* New York: Mentor Edition, The New American Library, 1958.

Driscoll, C.T., et al. "Nitrogen Pollution: From the Sources to the Sea." *A Science Links Publication* 1, no. 2. Hubbard Brook Research Foundation. Science Links Publication, 2003.

Edwards, Vinal. Journals and records 1870–1886. NOAA collections, National Archives and Records Administration, Waltham, Mass.

Eiseley, Loren. *The Firmament of Time.* New York: Atheneum, 1966.

Elder, John. "Stewardship and the Ecology of American Environmental Thought." Paper presented at the dedication of Marsh-Billings Historical Park, Woodstock, Vermont. June 5, 1998.

Emerson, Ralph W. *The Complete Essays and Other Writings of Ralph Waldo Emerson: Edited with a bibliographical introduction by Brooks Atkinson.* New York: Modern, Library, 1940.

Falmouth Enterprise. *Hurricane Extra.* 3 September 1954.

Forbes, Kathleen Allen and Edith Emerson Webster, eds. *An Anthology of Naushon 1833–1917.* Private library of Fred Webster, Pomfret, Vermont.

Ford, T. and E. Mercer. "Population density, size distribution and home range of the American eel (Anguilla rostrata) in the Great Sippewissett Salt Marsh." *Biological Bulletin* 157 no. 368 (1979): 368.

Foreman, K. et al. "The impact of epifaunal predation on the structure of macroinfaunal invertebrate communities of tidal marsh creeks." *Estuarine, Coastal and Shelf Science* 46, no. 5 (1998): 657–669.

Foreman, K., Ivan Valiela and Rafael Sarda. "Controls of benthic marine food webs." *Scientia Marina* 59 (1995): 119–128.

Freeman, Martha. *Always Rachel: the letters of Rachel Carson and Dorothy Freeman, 1952–1964.* Boston: Beacon Press, 1994.

Giblin, A.E. et al. "Uptake and cycling of heavy metals in sewage sludge in a New England salt marsh." *American Journal of Botany* 67 (1980): 1059–1068.

———. "Response of a salt marsh microbial community to inputs of heavy metals: aerobic heterotrophic metabolism." *Environmentally Toxic Chemicals* 2 (1983): 99–102.

Gilbert, Carter R. and Williams, James D. *Field Guide to the Fishes of North America.* New York: Alfred A. Knopf, 2002.

Gross, Paul R. "Laying the ghost: Embryonic development, in plain words." *Biological Bulletin* vol. 168 no. 3 (1985): 62–79.

Hampson, G.R. and H.L. Sanders. "Local Oil Spill." *Oceanus* 15 no.2 (1969): 8–11.

Howarth, R.W. & John M. Teal. "Sulfate Reduction in a New England salt marsh." *Limno. Oceanogr.* 24 (1979): 999–1013.

Howarth, Robert, et al. "Issues in Ecology: Nutrient Pollution of Coastal Rivers, Bays, and Seas." *Ecological Society of America* 7 (2000): 1–12.

Howes, Brian, and Dale Goehringer. "Porewater drainage and dissolved organic carbon and nutrient losses through the intertidal creekbanks of a New England salt marsh." *Marine Ecological Progress Series*, Oldendorf 114 no. 3 (1994): 289–301.

James, Williams. "Louis Agassiz," words spoken by Professor William James at the reception of the American Society of Naturalists by the President and fellows of Harvard College at Cambridge on December 30, 1896. Printed for the University, 1897.

Johnson, Thomas H., ed. *Final Harvest. Emily Dickinson's Poems.* Boston: Little Brown and Company, 1961.

Jordon, David Starr. *With Agassiz at Penikese.* Woods Hole: Marine Biological Laboratory, 1947.

Kaplan, W., Ivan Valiela, and John M. Teal. "Denitrification in a salt marsh ecosystem." *Limnology and Oceanography* 24 (1978): 726–734.

Kronenberger, John. "Lynn Margulis." *Bostonia* 51, no. 1, Autumn, 1977.

Lear, Linda. *Rachel Carson: Witness for nature.* New York: Henry Holt, 1997.

Lillie, Frank R. *The Woods Hole Marine Biological Laboratory.* Chicago: University of Chicago Press, 1944.

Lowenthal, David. *George Perkins Marsh: Prophet of conservation.* Seattle: University of Washington Press, 2000.

Lurie, Edward. *Louis Agassiz: A life in science.* Baltimore: Johns Hopkins University Press, 1988.

Maienschein, Jane. "Agassiz, Hyatt, Whitman, and the birth of the Marine Biological Laboratory." *Biological Bulletin* vol. 168, no.3 (1985): 26–34.

Margulis, Lynn and Dorion Sagan. *Acquiring Genomes, A Theory of the Origins of Life*. New York: Basic Books, 2002.

Marsh, George Perkins and Spencer Baird. Correspondence. Special Collections, University of Vermont.

Marsh, George Perkins. *Man and nature: or Physical geography as modified by human action*. New York: Scribner, 1864.

———. *Report Made Under Authority of the Legislature of Vermont, on the Artificial Propagation of Fish*. Burlington: Free Press Print, 1857.

Martinez, Andrew J. *Marine Life of the North Atlantic, Canada to New England*. Camden: Down East Books, 1994.

Miller, Kenneth R. *Finding Darwin's God, A Scientist's Search for Common Ground Between God and Evolution*. New York: Harper Collins, 1999.

Morrison, Reg. *The Spirit in the Gene, Humanity's Proud Illusion and the Laws of Nature*. Ithaca and London: Cornell University Press, 1999.

Peterson, B. J. and J.M. Melillo. "The potential storage of carbon caused by eutrophication of the biosphere." *Tellus* 37 (1985): 117–127.

Peterson, B.J., et al. "Tidal Export of Reduced Sulfur From a Salt Marsh Ecosystem." *Ecol. Bull.* 35, no. 36 (1982).

Peterson, Bruce J. "Stable isotopes as tracers of organic matter input and transfer in benthic food webs: A review." *Acta Oecologica* 20, no. 4 (1999): 479–487.

———. "Sulfur and Carbon Isotopes as Tracers of Salt-Marsh Organic Matter Flow." *Ecology* 67, no. 4 (1986): 865–874.

Ragotzkie, R.A., L.R. Pomeroy, and J.M. Teal. *Proceedings of the Salt Marsh Conference*, University of Georgia, 1959.

Redfield, Alfred C. "Temperature coefficient of the action of B rays upon the egg of Nereis." *Journal of Gen. Physiology* 1 (1919): 255–259.

———. "The transport of oxygen and carbon dioxide by some bloods containing hemocyanin." *Journal of Biological Chemistry* 69 (1926): 475–509.

———. "The process of determining the concentrations of oxygen, phosphate, and other organic derivatives within the depths of the Atlantic Ocean." *Papers in Physical Oceanography and Meterology* 9 (1942): 1–22.

Richardson, Robert D. Jr. *Emerson: The Mind on Fire*. Berkley: University of California Press, 1969.

Richardson, Wyman. *The House on Nauset Marsh*. Riverside: The Chatham Press, Inc, 1947.

Rockefeller, Steven C. *John Dewey: religious faith and democratic humanism*. New York: Columbia Press, 1991.

Ross, David A. *The Fisherman's Ocean. How marine science can help you find and catch more fish.* Mechanicsburg: Stackpole Books, 2000.

Rouner, Leroy S.,ed. *The Longing for Home.* Notre Dame: University of Notre Dame Press, 1997.

Sanders, Howard. "The West Falmouth Saga, How an Oil Expert Twisted the Facts About a Landmark Oil Spill Study." *New Engineer* May (1974).

Sarda, R, Ivan Valiela and Ken Foreman. "Decadal shifts in a salt marsh macroinfaunal community in response to a sustained long-term experimental nutrient enrichment." *Journal of Experimental Marine Biology* and Ecology 205 no. 1–2 (1996): 63–81.

Shaler, Nathaniel Southgate. *The Autobiography of Nathaniel Southgate Shaler with a Supplementary Memoir by His Wife.* Boston: Houghton Mifflin Co., 1909.

Short, Cathy, ed. "Final Environmental Assessment and Land Protection Plan, Sippewissett Marshes, National Wildlife Refuge, A Proposal." Fish and Wildlife Service, Hadley, Mass., 1994.

Stone, Jerome A. *The Minimalist Vision of Transcendence: A Naturalist Philosophy of Religion.* Albany: Suny Press, 1992.

Tabory, Lou. *Inshore Fly Fishing.* New York: Lyons and Burford, Publishers, 1992.

Teal, J.M. "Energy flow in a salt marsh ecosystem of Georgia." *Ecology* 43 (1962): 614–624.

———. "Energy flow in the salt marsh system of Georgia." *Ecology* 43 (1962): 614–624.

———. "A Local Oil Spill Revisited." *Oceanus* Summer (1993): 65–70.

——— "The role of one salt marsh in coastal productivity." *Proceedings of the International Symposium on Utilization of Coastal Ecosystems: Planning, Pollution, and Productivity* 1 (1985): 241–258.

———. "The West Falmouth Oil Spill After 20 Years: Fate of Fuel Oil Compounds and Effects on Animals." *Marine Pollution Bulletin* 24 no. 12 (1992): 607–614.

Teal, John and Mildred. *Life and Death of the Salt Marsh.* New York: National Audubon Society and Ballantine Books, 1969.

Teal, J.M and Brian Howes. "Interannual variability of a salt-marsh ecosystem." *Limnology and Oceanography* 41 no. 4 (1996): 802–809.

———.Teal, J.M., Ivan Valiela, and D. Berlo. "Nitrogen fixation by rhizosphere and free-living bacteria and salt marsh sediments." *Limnology and Oceanography* 24 (1978): 126–132.

Thoreau, Henry D. *Cape Cod.* New York: W.W. Norton and Company, Inc. edition, 1951.

————. *Walden, or Life in the Woods*. Boston: Ticknor and Fields, 1854.

Tillich, Paul. *The Courage to Be*. New Haven: Yale University Press, 1952.

Valiela, et al. "Macroalgal blooms in shallow estuaries: Controls and ecophysiological and ecosystem consequences." *Limnology and Oceanography* 4 (1997): 1105–1118.

Valiela, I. and John M. Teal. "'The nitrogen budget of a salt marsh ecosystem." *Nature* 280 (1979): 652–656.

Valiela, I., J.M. Teal, and W. Sass. "Nutrient retention in salt marsh plots experimentally fertilized with sewage sludge." *Estuarine Coastal Marine Science* 1 (1973): 261–269.

Valiela, Ivan, et al. "Decomposition in salt marsh ecosystems: the phases and major factors affecting disappearance of above-ground organic matter." *Journal of Experimental Marine Biology and Ecology* 89 (1985): 1–26.

Valiela, Ivan, Kenneth Foreman et al. "Couplings of Watersheds and Coastal Waters: Sources and Consequences of Nutrient Enrichment in Waquoit Bay, Massachuesetts." *Estuaries* 15 no. 4 (1992): 443–457.

Van Raalte, C.D., Ivan Valiela, and John M. Teal. "Productivity of benthic algae in experimentally fertilized salt marsh plots." *Limnology and Oceanography* 21 (1976): 862–872.

Vince, S., Ivan Valiela, N. Backus, and John M. Teal. "Predation by the salt marsh killifish, *Fundulus heteroclitus*, in relation to prey size and habitat structure: Consequences for prey distribution and abundance." *Journal of Experimental Marine Biology and Ecology* 23 (1976): 255–266.

Wahr, Frederick B. *Emerson and Goethe*. Ann Arbor: G. Wahr, 1915.

Walls, Laura Dassow. *Emerson's Life in Science: The culture of truth*. Ithaca: Cornell University Press, 2003.

Weinstein, Michael P., and Daniel A. Kreeger, eds. *Concepts and Controversies in Tidal Marsh Ecology*. Dordrecht/Boston/London: Kluwer Academic Publishers, 2000.

Werme, Christine E. "Resource partitioning in a salt marsh fish community." Dissertation for PhD, Boston University, 1981.

Wertenbaker W. "Anatomy of an Oil Spill." *The New Yorker Magazine* November (1973).

Williams, John B. *White Fire: The influence of Emerson on Melville*. Long Beach: California State University Press, 1991.

Williams, Oscar, ed. *Immortal Poems of the English Language*. New York: Washington Square Press, 1952.

acknowledgments

I wouldn't have made it through the sediments of this marshy manuscript without the help of many people. Thanks to my wife Delia for long-lasting encouragement and good ideas, and to Margo Baldwin and Chelsea Green Publishing for deciding to take a chance on this. Thanks to the Friendship Fund, Lilla McLane-Bradley, Fred Bay and the Bay-Paul Foundation, the Collis Foundation and the Collis family, to Bob Christy and Susan Ritz and the Larsen Fund for funding support, and special thanks to Hal Hamilton and the Sustainability Institute for providing a not-for-profit home for this project. Editor and friend Helen Whybrow gave wonderful advice from the very beginning and professional editing support for an initial rewrite. John F. Austin III, president of Salt Pond Areas Bird Sanctuaries, Inc., the local land trust in Falmouth Massachusetts, gave me the keys to the very special place on the marsh called Marshlands, the old Iddings property, and unlimited use of this refuge (John, I promise that I will someday give the keys back to you). The work of Salt Ponds together with the help of the Three Hundred Committee over the years has been a critical factor to the protection of Falmouth's important marshes, woodlands, and open spaces. May their work continue forever.

Heartfelt thanks also to the librarians at the Marine Biological Laboratories and to Connie Rinaldo, head librarian of Harvard's Ernst Mayr Library at the Museum of Comparative Zoology. Busy MBL scientists, Ken Foreman, Ivan Valiela, Bruce Peterson, John Hobbie, Mitch Sogin, and Linda Deegan were willing to take time to talk when I popped into their offices with questions that were sometimes sophomoric. Emeritus professor at Woods Hole Oceanographic Institute, John M. Teal, was most gracious with his time, and I extend my thanks to his wife Susan for opening up their home and serving great coffee. MBL development officer and science historian Frank Carotenuto introduced me to the entire edifice, people and history of the MBL and then to good fishing, which I was glad to return in-kind. Two very different local environmental activitists, Christiane Collins and David Palmer, generously gave me their time and became friends whom I will always admire and appreciate.

Special thanks to friend and painter extraordinaire Robin W. Koenig for the lasting inspiration of her beautiful work, and to friend and fine botanical illustrator Bobbi Angell who stepped up to create and deliver the illustrations on time and at short notice. Woodstock's finest, Kevin-the-bell-ringer-Dann gave invaluable sources and advice. Robert Finch for his own books that I have always admired, provided key suggestions on the manuscript. Thanks to the excellent editor-in-chief at Chelsea Green, John Barstow, who edited with a deft touch and orchestrated all with the indomitable team at Chelsea Green, including the managing editor, Marcy Brant, the editorial assistant, Jonathan Teller-Elsberg, and project editor, Collette Leonard.

Love and special thanks to my brothers and sisters, Ann, Terry, Sarah, Peter, and Belle, and their spouses, their children and mine, who have all recently entered what I hope will be a long and rewarding experience of home and place stewardship together. On that note, let me extend my thanks to our friends and dear neighbors, new and old, on Little Neck Bars and Black Beach Road. I hope you see this writing effort not as one that exposes us, but rather one that can help show us who we are, and what we have to celebrate and take care of together. That has been my "writer's duty" from the start.

Finally, a bow to the unknown/unknowable friend who fluttered down and inside, and like a red bird, kept wings beating and words flowing until the window was opened and the work was done.

Get Inspired!

Great books to help you change the world

Chelsea Green's celebration of sustainability includes a focus on the natural world and the sustenance it provides to our spirits and bodies. Ranging from the greening of cities to protection of natural areas, these books encourage readers to develop a stronger awareness of connections to the natural world while strengthening the bonds of family and community.

We invite you to learn more at **www.chelseagreen.com.** To place an order or to request a catalog, call toll-free (800) 639-4099, or write to us at P.O. Box 428, White River Junction, Vermont 05001.

Edens Lost & Found: How Ordinary Citizens are Restoring Our Great American Cities
Harry Wiland and Dale Bell
ISBN 1-933392-26-6 | $25

The Man Who Planted Trees
Jean Giono
ISBN 1-931498-72-5 | $17.50

Pinhook: Finding Wholeness in a Fragmented Land
Janisse Ray
ISBN 1-931498-74-1 | $12

Gaviotas: A Village to Reinvent the World
Alan Weisman
ISBN 1-890132-28-4 | $16.95

CHELSEA GREEN
PUBLISHING
the politics and practice of sustainable living

SUSTAINABLE LIVING has many facets. Chelsea Green celebrates the sustainable arts by publishing trendsetting books about innovative building techniques, regenerative forestry, organic gardening and agriculture, renewable energy, whole foods and Slow Food, and grassroots political activism.

For more information about Chelsea Green, visit our website at www.chelseagreen.com, where you will find more than 200 books on the politics and practice of sustainable living.

Shelter

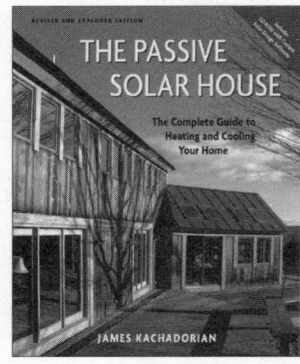

The Passive Solar House:
The Complete Guide to Heating
and Cooling Your Home
Revised Edition with CD-ROM
James Kachadorian
ISBN 1-933392-03-7
$40

Planet

Limits to Growth:
The 30-Year Update
Donella Meadows, Jorgen
Randers, Dennis Meadows
ISBN 1-931498-58-X
$22.50

People

An Unreasonable Woman:
A True Story of Shrimpers,
Politicos, Polluters, and the
Fight for Seadrift, Texas
Diane Wilson
ISBN 1-933392-27-4
$18

Food

Full Moon Feast: Food and
the Hunger for Connection
Jessica Prentice
Foreword by Deborah
Madison
ISBN 1-933392-00-2
$25